Ethics and the Media

This book is a comprehensive introduction to media ethics and an exploration of how it must change to adapt to today's media revolution. Using an ethical framework for the new "mixed media" ethics – taking in the global, interactive media produced by both citizens and professionals – Stephen J. A. Ward discusses the ethical issues which occur in both mainstream and non-mainstream media, from newspapers and broadcast to social media users and bloggers. He redefines traditional conceptions of journalistic truth-seeking, objectivity, and minimizing harm, and examines the responsible use of images in an image-saturated public sphere. He also draws the contours of a future media ethics for the "new mainstream media" and puts forward cosmopolitan principles for a global media ethics. His book will be invaluable for all students of media and for others who are interested in media ethics.

STEPHEN J. A. WARD is the James E. Burgess Professor and Director of the Center for Journalism Ethics at the University of Wisconsin, Madison. He is the author of *The Invention of Journalism Ethics: The Path to Objectivity and Beyond* (2006) and *Global Journalism Ethics* (2010), and the co-editor of *Media Ethics Beyond Borders: A Global Perspective* (2010).

Cambridge Applied Ethics

Titles published in this series:

ETHICS AND BUSINESS *Kevin Gibson*
ETHICS AND THE ENVIRONMENT *Dale Jamieson*
ETHICS AND CRIMINAL JUSTICE *John Kleinig*
ETHICS AND ANIMALS *Lori Gruen*
ETHICS AND THE MEDIA *Stephen J. A. Ward*

Ethics and the Media

An Introduction

STEPHEN J. A. WARD

University of Wisconsin, Madison

CAMBRIDGE
UNIVERSITY PRESS

CAMBRIDGE UNIVERSITY PRESS
Cambridge, New York, Melbourne, Madrid, Cape Town,
Singapore, São Paulo, Delhi, Tokyo, Mexico City

Cambridge University Press
The Edinburgh Building, Cambridge CB2 8RU, UK

Published in the United States of America by Cambridge University Press, New York

www.cambridge.org
Information on this title: www.cambridge.org/9780521889643

First published 2011

Printed in the United Kingdom at the University Press, Cambridge

A catalogue record for this publication is available from the British Library

Library of Congress Cataloguing in Publication data
Ward, Stephen J. A. (Stephen John Anthony), 1951–
    Ethics and the media : an introduction / Stephen J. A. Ward.
        p.   cm. – (Cambridge applied ethics)
    Includes bibliographical references (p.) and index.
    ISBN 978-0-521-88964-3 (hardback) – ISBN 978-0-521-71816-5 (pbk.)
    1. Mass media–Moral and ethical aspects.   I. Title.   II. Series.
    P94.W37 2011
    175–dc23   2011026079

ISBN 978-0-521-88964-3 Hardback
ISBN 978-0-521-71816-5 Paperback

To my students, sources of inspiration and hope

Contents

Introduction: the need for a new ethics   *page* 1
The context of media ethics   2
The structure of the book   3
The meaning of media   5

1 **What is ethics?**   7
The ethical sphere   8
Theorizing about ethics   16

2 **Approaches to media ethics**   52
Understanding media ethics   54
Approaches to media ethics   59
Essentials for ethical reasoning   68
Applying aims and principles   76

3 **Free press and deliberative democracy**   88
Freedom and the turn to ethics   90
The need for ethics   99
Journalism and democracy   103

4 **Reaffirming truth and objectivity**   118
Truth and objectivity in journalism   119
Rise and decline of objectivity   127
Responding to the challenge   134
Pragmatic truth and objectivity   143

5 **Media harm and offense**   161
Harm in ethics   161
Contending principles   164
Restraining principles for media   170
Media harm: cases   185
Media offense   197

6 **The new media ethics**   207
  Ethical revolutions   209
  Where are we today?   212
  Shape of a future ethics   216
  Toward an open ethics   223

7 **Global media ethics**   245
  Going global   245
  Ethical foundations   250
  Application to journalism   257
  Building global media ethics   266

Bibliography   272
Index   285

Introduction: the need for a new ethics

Ethics, as a field of study and as a practice, should confront the deep, normative questions of its time.

Reflection on ethics is carried out by humans embedded in historical eras and in distinct cultures. All societies, no matter how rigid or traditional, face the future. They cannot avoid struggling with new problems and new ethical questions. Ethics, therefore, is not a static set of rules. It is a necessary human activity – the attempt by individuals and societies to respond to quandaries created by changing conditions, unexpected issues, and new ways of thinking.

Ethics at its best is reflective engagement with urgent problems, in light of where we have been and where we hope to be tomorrow. Reflective engagement can occur in any area of society. For example, developments in genetic knowledge call for new ethical thinking in the sciences of life. Is it morally permissible to use genetic knowledge to "design" babies, or to force citizens to be tested for genes linked to debilitating diseases? In recent times our concern about the impact of human activity on nature and on non-human forms of life has prompted the development of environmental ethics and the ethics of animal welfare.

Engagement involves the reinterpretation of norms, the invention of principles, and the development of new and responsible practices. This work of invention and reinterpretation gains urgency when basic principles come under question and when society, in whole or in part, begins a difficult transition to a new era. Today, news media find themselves in the middle of such a transition. New forms of communication are transforming journalism and its ethics. Media ethics requires urgent reflective engagement because basic values are under question and new issues challenge traditional approaches to responsible journalism. Accordingly, this book is structured around how media ethics should address these issues, from disagreement over the definition of journalism and the value of news objectivity to the ethics of digital global media.

The context of media ethics

The context of media ethics is a media revolution of unprecedented proportions. We live at a time when technology is creating an expanding universe of media and communication tools that are available to journalists, citizens, government, and non-governmental organizations. These changes amount to more than a set of new electronic devices for disseminating information. New forms of communication are altering the nature of human society, while making possible the globalization of trade, economics, and culture. Not only is society increasingly linked through networks of media but what humans know of their world is increasingly mediated by global, interactive media. The issues of media ethics are the issues created by a media ecology that shapes how humans think, feel, and communicate on a global scale.

This media ecology is a chaotic landscape evolving at a furious pace. Professional journalists, who once dominated the media sphere, now share the space with tweeters, bloggers, citizen journalists, and social media users around the world. The future of professional journalism in various forms, such as investigative journalism at newspapers, is cast in doubt as audiences migrate online and newsroom budgets shrink. The search is on for new models of journalism, such as "not-for-profit" investigative newsrooms. Meanwhile, much has been written on how new media expands our idea of who is a journalist. This "democratization" of journalism – the spread of publishing technology among citizens – occurs as journalism acquires global reach and impact.

Ultimately, these changes challenge the foundations of media ethics. The intersection of the amateur and the professional in journalism creates both communication possibilities and ethical debates. Time-honored principles such as news objectivity are questioned. Digital media give rise to controversial practices, from using software to effortlessly alter images to using social media to invade the privacy of individuals. Journalists adopt new descriptions of themselves. They refer to themselves as "sherpas" who guide readers through the information maze; as "curators" of information; as "validators" of information; as "aggregators" of information and web sites around the world; and as "facilitators" of online dialogue. All communicators in this global universe work to the demands of a 24-hour news clock.

The expansion of journalism is altering the nature of ethical discourse. Professionals no longer control ethical discussion about proper media practice and responsible journalism. More and more, citizens and non-professional bloggers participate in discussions on media ethics. We are entering a period where citizens and citizen journalists will play a much larger role in articulating the new "rules of the road" for responsible journalism.[1] At a time when citizens use media and engage in normative discussions, it is important that media ethics engage not only professional journalists and journalism students but also all citizens.

In sum, the media revolution is causing a simultaneous revolution in media ethics – the fifth revolution in media ethics since modern journalism began in the seventeenth century.[2] How should we reflectively engage these challenges? Media ethics must do more than point out the tension among traditional and new forms of journalism practice. It must do more than describe media trends. It must evaluate the trends and reconstruct the conceptual basis of media ethics. In the end, nothing less than a philosophical rethinking of media ethics from the ground up will do. As I will argue, we need to construct a multi-media, global media ethics.

The structure of the book

This book is a response to these challenges. It explores the concepts, principles, and questions facing news media in an age of rapid and fundamental change.

In *The Invention of Journalism Ethics*[3] I was preoccupied with the history of journalism and how its ethics had evolved to the present. In

---

[1] Ward and Wasserman, "Towards an Open Ethics."

[2] I describe the five revolutions in "Journalism Ethics" (Ward, "Truth and Objectivity"). The five revolutions are: (1) the invention of journalism ethics by the seventeenth-century periodic press; (2) the fourth-estate ethics of newspapers of the eighteenth-century Enlightenment public sphere; (3) the liberal ethics of the nineteenth-century press, and (4) the professional ethics of the mass commercial press during the late 1800s and early 1900s. Today, the media revolution calls for an ethics of mixed, global media.

[3] Ward, *The Invention of Journalism Ethics*.

this book, I am occupied with helping students, journalists, and citizens think about the future of media ethics. Yet history remains relevant. History helps us to understand how current beliefs and practices were formed; and how changing conditions require a reinvention of media ethics.

Ethics and the Media offers an entry point into the perplexing debate surrounding media. It is intended for anyone who wants to engage in serious thinking about media ethics. The book is neither a textbook of cases nor a book on theory. It is an examination of the leading issues and how media ethics should respond. The examination brings together theory and practice. Principles are explained by examples and examples lead to the formulation – and reformulation – of principles.

The book is shaped by the author's perspective on how media ethics should evolve. I do not provide a neutral account of media ethics, its issues, and its future. On specific issues, I do not balance rival views and leave it to the reader to decide. Instead, I seek to address the issues by putting forward new principles and new interpretations of traditional concepts, while I argue against other interpretations. I attempt to fairly present theories and viewpoints but, in the end, I go further: I present my perspective on the issues and draw conclusions. The upshot is an introductory text that presents my considered view of the future of media ethics. I believe this approach to media ethics is more likely to attract the reflective engagement of readers than studied neutrality. I encourage the reader to critique what I write. By questioning the text, the reader will engage media ethics.

Chapters 1 and 2 explain the nature of ethics and provide a model for reasoning about media practice. The model shows how to think systematically about various difficult situations by applying principles in a holistic manner.

Chapters 3 and 4 explain the relationship between journalism and deliberative democracy, and reaffirm the ideals of truth and objectivity as guides for media practice. Chapter 5 explores the idea of harm and offense in media ethics. It puts forward three major principles for avoiding harm in journalism, and it clarifies the principle of minimizing harm. Chapter 6 discusses a new ethics for mixed news media – a set of norms that guide both traditional and online journalism. Chapter 7 discusses how media ethics must change to deal with a news media that is global in reach and impact.

The meaning of media

Before beginning, we need to clarify the meaning of media for this book. "Media" may refer to any means of communication, from telephone and radio to television and the Internet. Media may refer to almost any sort of "material" or device that facilitates the exchange of messages and meanings. For example, an artist may use ordinary objects as her media to create a pastiche; military commanders may use the media of satellites to coordinate soldiers in the field. Recently, we have begun to refer to web sites that allow us to interact with others as "social media."

Also, people use the phrase "the media" to refer to major news organizations from the BBC to the *New York Times*. However, as mentioned, the boundaries of "the media" today are blurred. In the previous century, it was clear who the (news) media were. They were the professional news organizations that dominated the production of news – newspapers and news broadcasters. Few people were troubled by such questions as "who is a journalist?" and "is this journalism?" Journalists were easily identified. They were the reporters and editors who worked for professional news organizations. They were "the press." Today, advances in media technology, especially the rise of the Internet, allow citizens to publish news and commentary on public affairs. They engage in what might be called "acts of journalism" at least some of the time, whether or not they call themselves journalists. Many of these citizens have no professional training in journalism and are not employed by traditional news media. Hence, notions of "the media" and "journalist" are less precise than in previous decades.

Given this expansion in the world of journalism, I use "journalist" or "news media" to refer liberally to anyone, or any organization, that engages in what once was the sole prerogative of major news organizations – the regular production of news and commentary on public affairs for an audience. Media ethics applies to anyone who engages in journalistic activities, professionals and amateurs. For stylistic variation, I use the pair of terms, "media ethics" and "journalism ethics," and "media" and "journalism," interchangeably in the text. I am aware that media ethics is often used to refer to the ethics of a wider group of media practitioners than what we find in newsrooms. It is used to include the ethics of media advertising, public relations, marketing, and so on. These are important areas of media work but this book will not address their ethical issues directly. For the purposes of this book, media ethics is the ethics of news media, and the journalism of news media.

1 What is ethics?

Suppose that you live with your wife, Ellen, and your mother-in-law, Dorothy, who has been diagnosed with Alzheimer's disease. Dorothy, at 93, is not capable of living alone. Dorothy has become progressively more difficult to live with. Ellen has developed health problems from the pressure of caring for Dorothy. A physician strongly advises Ellen to move Dorothy to a nursing home, a move Dorothy would strongly oppose. It would be easier if you lied – tell Dorothy her move to a nursing home is temporary, while you and Ellen go on holiday.

As you attempt to decide, you experience conflicting emotions and thoughts. How can you do what is best for Dorothy, while respecting her desires and autonomy? Should you simply soldier on, allowing her to remain in your house? Or do you have to take Ellen's physical deterioration as your main concern? What is the right thing to do for Ellen, for Dorothy, and for the three of you?

Most of us recognize this situation as "ethical" because it raises questions about the correct thing to do, apart from self-interest and what is required legally. Ethical situations raise questions about values, responsibilities, and achieving certain goods while not ignoring the rights of others. Deciding on Dorothy's health care exhibits features typical of most ethical problems: pressure to decide under uncertainty; a complex set of facts; conflicting values and options.

We will work with situations of this kind throughout this book only the situations will involve media practice – what responsible news media should do across a range of typical problems. The aim of our study is twofold: (1) to clarify and critique our beliefs about what constitutes ethical media practice; and (2) to develop and improve our ethical reasoning by application to problems. "Improve" here means we act more consistently, think more deeply, reason more acutely, and reach better informed ethical judgments. All of this contributes to the ethical life, the development of ethical citizens, and hopefully to a better world.

This chapter and the next introduce an ethical framework for understanding media ethics and for applying that understanding to major issues and cases. Be forewarned: the framework is *not* a formula for generating absolute answers. The methods of ethics do not prove conclusions as we might deduce theorems from axioms in mathematics. Rather, they provide a systematic analysis of ethical beliefs and problems. The framework has two parts. The first part, the subject of this chapter, is conceptual. It explains the nature of ethics. The second part, the subject of the next chapter, discusses how to use these ideas to analyze the problems of media ethics. We start with general concepts because it is important for our methods to be based on a clear conception of the topic, ethics.

The ethical sphere

What is ethics?

"Ethics" comes from the Greek word "ethos" meaning "character," "nature," or "disposition" – roughly, how someone is disposed to act. This notion is close to the common idea of ethics as an "internal" matter of virtuous character that motivates people to act correctly. "Morals" stems from the Latin "mores," the customs of a group. Morality as "mores" is close to the other common idea of ethics as external conduct according to the rules of a group.

The etymology of "ethics" and "morality" suggests that ethics is both individualistic and social. It is individualistic because individuals are asked to make certain values part of their character and to use certain norms in making decisions. It is social because ethics is not about every person formulating their own rules of behavior apart from others. Correct conduct is honoring rules of fair social interaction – rules that apply to humans in general or to all members of a group. We experience ethics internally as the tug of conscience. We experience ethics externally as the demands placed upon us by codes of ethics, backed by social sanction. Psychologically, one learns ethics as a set of responses shaped by social enculturation and the ethical "climate" of society.[1] My ethical capacities

---

[1] Blackburn, *Being Good*, 1–8.

are nurtured and exercised within groups. Also, ethics requires that I adopt a social perspective that looks to the common good and transcends selfish individualism. Ethically speaking, "how ought I to live?" cannot be asked in isolation from the question, "how ought *we* to live?"

Ethics has wide scope, dealing with the conduct of individuals, groups, institutions, professions, and countries. Ethics is demanding. It demands that we live in goodness and in right relation with each other. Ethics may require us to forego personal benefits, to carry out duties or to endure persecution. Through ethics, we articulate our beliefs about what is of greatest moral value in life. By combining internal and external aspects, we can define ethics as being disposed towards virtuous conduct in society according to certain principles and values.

General principles of ethics, such as "help others in need" and "live a life of non-violence and peace," plus more specific directives and norms, are brought together to form moral systems or codes of conduct, such as utilitarian ethics and Buddhist ethics. The Bible's Ten Commandments is one such general code. In addition, there are codes of increasing specificity for doctors, lawyers, and journalists. As a set of principles, "ethics" can refer to something singular or multiple. We can understand "ethics" as the proper name for a single ethical system. One may believe that there is only one set of correct principles and that is what ethics *is*. Or, we can think of "ethics" as a general term that refers to many ethical systems. "Ethics" as a general term resembles "language" which refers to many language systems. I prefer to use "ethics" in this plural sense, reserving "ethic" for a single set of principles such as a libertarian ethic for a free press. Yet, despite the ubiquity of rules in morals, ethics should not be identified simply with a set of rules, such as "do not steal or lie," "keep one's promises," "treat others as you would have them treat you." A set of rules is too static to capture the dynamic nature of ethics. Ethics is a practical and evolving *activity*. It is something we do. We *do* ethics when we weigh values to make a decision. We *do* ethics when we modify practices in light of new technology.

The idea of ethics as correct conduct according to rules is deficient in failing to emphasize the knowledge and skill required to determine what is correct conduct in a complex, changing world. To do ethics requires three things: (1) analysis: the articulation and justification of principles; (2) practical judgment: the application of principles and rules to issues; (3) virtuous character: a disposition to follow those principles affirmed by (1) and (2). Ethics, therefore, has three concerns: appropriate ethical beliefs, correct application, and the disposition to act ethically.

If ethics is a dynamic, changing form of activity, then ethics is not a set of rules to be followed blindly or defended dogmatically. In many cases, there will be legitimate debate as to *whether* and *how* rules should apply. Even principles we hold dear may have to be reinterpreted in light of new developments. For example, how to apply the principle of respect for life to the issue of how long to keep a dying person alive through new technology. Moreover, the boundaries of ethics shift. As noted, in our time ethics has come to include such issues as animal welfare, protecting the environment and the rights of gay couples. Ethics is not just the disposition to adhere to rules but also the disposition to critique and improve the rules. There is an important difference between living one's ethics, as an activity, and simply following a set of rules. The former rejects the sheer acceptance of rules and conventions. Ethics requires that we follow rules that we have examined critically.

Taken as a whole, ethics is the never-completed human project of inventing, applying, and critiquing the principles that guide interaction, define social roles, and justify institutional structures. Ethical deliberation is *reason in social practice* – the construction of fair ethical frameworks for society.

Ethical experience and reflection

The starting point for ethics is lived experience. We seriously discuss ethics *after* we have had some experience in living well or badly. For anyone who asks "what is ethics?" we can reply: think about your most difficult decisions. Did you break a promise or let others down? Did you have to report improper behavior by a colleague to authorities? Did you promote your career by spreading rumors about a co-worker? Or, think about horrible and dehumanizing actions such as torturing prisoners or child abuse. The heartbeat of ethics is felt wherever people struggle to do good and oppose evil. Reflection within and upon ethics is prompted by doubt and conflict.[2] Faced with uncertainties in our experience, we draw distinctions,

---

[2] The idea of doubt and conflict as the origin of serious thinking was put forward forcefully by John Dewey in *Reconstruction in Philosophy*, 80–83.

generate principles, and clarify goals so as to face the world with a manageable number of clear ideas and guidelines. As experience throws up new situations, we alter our principles. We find ourselves in a circle of experience and reflection.

A variety of experiences stimulate ethical thinking. One experience is the felt inadequacy of our current beliefs, such as when our norms lead to troubling consequences. For instance, we question the value of patriotism when it leads to extreme nationalism. We question our belief in a free press when reporting causes irreparable harm to someone's reputation. We reflect on our values when confronted by people and cultures with different beliefs. We think about ethics when the complexity of experience baffles us. Difficult situations, like the example of Dorothy at the start of this chapter, present us with a "knot" of facts, potential consequences, and options, which swamp our ability to think clearly. Finally, we are moved to take thought by the plurality of value. As complex creatures, humans are torn between their different desires and attachments. We occupy many roles and incur many duties. Inevitably, conflict arises as I try to follow a coherent plan of life. How do my duties as a parent line up with my career ambitions? How can I integrate my desire to help the poor with a desire to retire to my garret to paint my masterpiece? Do I value freedom or security? These considerations force us to rephrase our definition of ethics as the activity of critically constructing and adhering to an *integrated* system of principles and values, prompted by the experience of doubt, conflict, and plurality.

Distinctive features

Yet even this rephrasing is not entirely adequate. It does justice to ethics as activity, but it does not explain how ethical activity is distinct from other activities.

There are many types of agencies that enforce norms, from school boards to the police. Many values and norms are not ethical, such as the value of a good beer or norms for greeting someone on the street. There are the norms of etiquette; the norms of behavior in private clubs; the norms of fashion, aesthetics, law, and ethics. Therefore, when we say we "ought" to do some action we may not mean that we have an ethical duty. We may mean that we ought to be polite, as a matter of etiquette. Or we ought to use seat belts because it is required by law.

Together, these many norms and values comprise society's "normative sphere" – those areas where behavior falls under rules and standards. It is important to distinguish one normative system from another, say law from etiquette, because these systems ask different questions and require different answers. A failure to distinguish these perspectives may cause us to not recognize a situation as raising an ethical issue, or to confuse ethical and non-ethical issues. For example, in a newsroom, consider a debate over whether to publish a sensational and damaging story on the personal life of a well-known public figure. As it stands, the normative question, "should we publish?" is ambiguous. It could mean, "will the publication further the career of the journalist who wrote it," or "will it attract the attention of readers?" It could also mean: "are we legally permitted to publish this story, since it damages the person's reputation?" Or, it could mean: "would it be ethically right to publish it, even if legal?" Ethical reasoning requires the capacity to distinguish these senses.

Why are we persuaded that there *is* a distinction between ethical and non-ethical norms? One reason is our experience. We encounter situations where the question, "what should we do?" goes beyond the law or our self-interest. Our concern for making the correct decision about Dorothy, for example, goes beyond what is convenient for the care giver (what serves his or her interest). In teaching ethics, instructors use examples of exceptional behavior to distinguish between ethics and self-interest. For example, they may note how some white Americans in the nineteenth century participated in the "underground railway," courageously helping black slaves escape to states that had banned slavery. Self-interest dictated that these white people should avoid such risky, illegal assistance. Instead, they acted out of a distinct *ethical* concern for others in distress. Other examples contrast ethics with inclination. I ethically ought to repay a loan to John even if I will never see John again and even if I am inclined to avoid repayment. Further, students are asked to consider examples where ethics and the law differ. Some acts that strike us as ethically wrong, like child slavery, are legally permitted in some societies. Protesting against a country's terrible human rights record is ethically correct but protests may be legally forbidden.

However, using examples to create an intuitive grasp of the difference between ethics and other normative spheres is not fully adequate. Intuitively, we may "get" the contrast between ethical and non-ethical norms but we may still not be able to say what features explain the distinction. Saying how ethics is distinctive is surprisingly difficult. The sociologist Steven Lukes explained it as such: "Moral norms cover matters of importance in people's lives. They are directed at promoting good and avoiding evil, at encouraging virtue and discouraging vice, at avoiding harm to others and promoting their well-being or welfare. They are concerned with the interests of others or the common interest rather than just the individual's self-interest …"[3] Philosopher Thomas Scanlon argues that morality is distinct because of its perceived importance. People feel guilt when they violate these requirements. The victims of unethical actions feel resentment and indignation.[4] Such strong emotions are not caused by a violation of etiquette.

These writers capture essential points. Bringing the points together, we can say that ethics is distinguished by a combination of four features: (1) a specific subject matter defined by a family of concerns and familiar principles, that (2) are approached through an impartial stance. These concerns and principles are (3) serious and (4) justify other norms. Ethics is distinguished by its concerns and how it reasons about them. Let's examine each of these four criteria.

Identifiable concerns: ethics has an identifiable subject matter, even if the boundaries are not precise. So far, this chapter has proceeded by appealing to our implicit understanding of this subject matter. With Dorothy's case, we recognized as a subject matter the responsible treatment of aging people, and the rights of such people to respect and autonomy. Also, we are familiar with ethical rules prohibiting murder and theft, and the virtues of honesty and kindness. In sum, a discussion is ethical when it considers *what is good, what is right, or what is virtuous.* A discussion that did not address any of these three themes would not be "ethics." We will discuss these three areas below.

Seriousness: these three themes make ethics a serious enterprise.[5] Ethics is about the most significant issues in our lives: rights, freedoms and duties,

---

[3] Lukes, *Moral Relativism*, 62–63.

[4] Scanlon, *What We Owe to Each Other*, Chapter 4. See also Lukes, *Moral Relativism*, 63.

[5] Hauser says the moral sphere is characterized by emotion and a "sense of seriousness." Hauser, *Moral Minds*, 238. Adams, in *Finite and Infinite Goods*, 18, talks about "the

respect for others, fairness and justice, and the development of human capacities. What ethical principles people affirm or reject has great impact on others. This is why we think that disagreements over ethics are more important than differences over etiquette or art.

Impartial stance: ethics adopts an impartial stance. A stance is a distinctive approach to something in the world. For example, I can adopt a cynical stance that believes that selfish motives are always behind people's seemingly well-intended actions. An egoistic stance evaluates all actions in terms of what promotes my interests. The ethical stance is an impartial approach to the determination of correct conduct. It requires persons to transcend egoism and give fair consideration to the interests of others. Ethical persons care about how people are treated, and they allow such considerations to restrain their pursuit of goods. The ethical stance can be ignored. Every day, people act unethically from uncaring, partial attitudes. Some people, such as sociopaths, are psychologically unable to adopt the ethical stance.

I "show" my impartiality by being willing to universalize my ethical beliefs. Essentially, I agree that what holds for me holds for others, and what holds for others, holds for me. If I think that John is obligated to do *x* in situation *y*, then I agree that I am obligated to do *x* if I find myself in *y*. I am not thinking ethically if I hold that Mary ought to report someone cheating on a test but I am not obligated to do the same. The rules of ethics are universal in the sense that they apply to all persons in *similar* circumstances. There is no "special pleading" in ethics. There are exceptions to rules. A surgeon is not obligated to keep her promise to take her son to a movie if she must return to her hospital to treat injured people. However, there are no *arbitrary* exceptions. For example, "do not murder, unless you are Stephen Ward or an Irishman," is not a valid rule because it is not impartial. It is partial towards Stephen Ward and the Irish. An exception for murder based on someone's identity is arbitrary.

To be impartial is not to lack feeling. We adopt an impartial stance because we care deeply about being fair. We value impartiality as a means to the goal of correct judgment. Ethical caring is not a hazy, sentimental feeling. It is a tough-minded commitment to living ethically with others.

seriousness of normative discourse." Seriousness is stressed by Kupperman in *Value ... and What Follows*, 113. See also Hare, *The Language of Morals*, 142–144.

Ethical caring may include but does not require that I have an emotional bond to the people with whom I have dealings.

The ethical stance is different from other stances for evaluating conduct. At a formal event, I adopt the stance of etiquette. I make sure to say the appropriate things. My rule-following is neither ethical nor unethical. It is non-ethical. It does not raise ethical concerns. Another stance is that of prudence. Prudence doesn't mean being a prude. It means reasoning about what is best for me. For example, it is prudent to save some of my salary if I desire financial security. Prudential reasoning is not opposed to the ethical stance. In fact, a certain amount of prudence is required by ethics. It is ethically required that I prudently take care of myself. Prudential reasoning need not be egotistic since I may include others, such as my family, as part of my interests. Prudence can motivate ethical behavior. If I operate a neighborhood laundry where everyone knows each other, it may be prudent to deal honestly and ethically with customers. But this coexistence does not erase the difference between ethical and prudential reasoning. Prudential thinking is partial. It is concerned with achieving goods for me or for a particular group. It is not impartial. My ethical duty as a laundry owner to be honest in business dealings is not based on prudence. It is based on an impartial concern for all. The prudential and the ethical are different modes of reasoning and evaluation.

Justification of other norms: the seriousness of ethics means that it is as basic as normative thinking gets, and therefore justifies other types of norms. To be sure, the law deals with serious topics. Laws are more important than rules of etiquette. Laws are justified, ultimately, by appeal to some conception of the good and just life for citizens. Modern constitutions, those fundamental legal frameworks, ground their laws in some ethical vision of the good and just society. Constitutional rights are legal expressions of ethical principles.

Some readers may feel that these four criteria fail to establish a hard line between ethics and other normative domains. They are right. The distinction is a matter of degree, such as ethics being more fundamental than law. We should *not* expect hard and fast boundaries. Etiquette, prudence, law, and ethics all deal with regulating behavior. All speak of what ought to be done, in contrast to what is done. Consequently, there is overlap in language and among the rules. Stealing is both unethical and illegal. Being boorish to a visitor is a matter of etiquette, yet at the extreme it is also unethical since it shows disrespect to other humans. Human society only gradually distinguished these normative domains. Originally, to violate the commands of a tribal chief was socially repugnant, an ethical breach, and against the gods – all at the same time. Law only became a distinct area when societies built legal systems with their own rules, practices, and institutions.

The ethical stance amounts to a distinct and autonomous way to approach life. Ethics is self-justifying. I adopt the stance because I see inherent (and instrumental) purpose in the ethical ordering of our social relations and I see inherent value in the goods, duties, and attitudes that ethics supports. The validity of ethics does not depend on its ability to "prove" to sceptics that it is in their self-interest to adopt the ethical stance. That reduces ethics to prudential reasoning. The answer to "why be moral?" cannot be "because it serves your interests." Ethics may not serve your interests. The answer to "why be moral?" can only be, "because these are the values and forms of life that I deeply care about, and can justify (and recommend) to others." In recognizing the inherent value of ethical concerns, you know why one should be moral. The real issue is not the legitimacy of the ethical stance. The real issue is what principles and actions best express that stance.

Nor is ethics philosophically bankrupt if it cannot persuade the radically unethical person to adopt its stance. If someone can witness pain, suffering, and injustice with indifference; if they care little for goodness or the well-being of others; if, in short, they are unmoved by ethical concerns, there is not much that can be said to persuade them. And not much that *needs* to be said. Ethical insensitivity and radical skepticism are stances that need as much (or more) justification as the ethical stance. The task is to deliberate about principles and norms with people who are *already* disposed to care about such matters.

Theorizing about ethics

We have described what it is to ethically engage the world. Across human history, this engagement has prompted theorizing about ethics. Theorizing develops the ethical impulse "already firmly planted in human experience."[6]

---

[6] Darwall, *Philosophical Ethics*, 8.

Theories explain the activity of ethics, advance certain principles as guides to action, and take positions on ethical questions.

In the rest of this chapter, we describe the major theories. Since the number of theories (and the variations on theories) is vast, we must be selective. We review those theories that have a major influence on media ethics. The aim is not to determine which theory is best or to master their technical aspects. The aim is to obtain an overview of the main theoretical options so we can use them to discuss media ethics. We start by explaining the relation of practice and theory, and by distinguishing between philosophical and applied ethics.

Practice and theory

Ethics is practical in intent, but theoretical in understanding. As noted, we reflect on our experiences, and reflection often leads us into the more abstract realms of theory, as we seek a deeper and more systematic view of the issues. Caught up in an ethical debate, we may ask: what types of statements are ethical statements anyway, and how do we justify them? Given a discussion of what promotes happiness, we may ask: but what is happiness for humans? Faced with conflicting moral views, we stand back and ask: which ethical view provides the best guidance, and why? These questions can have practical import. In many cases, our implicit or explicit theoretical assumptions affect what we judge to be ethical and how we should act.

In the circle of experience and reflection, practice and theory both play an important part, and they inevitably interact. Theory and practice, in ethics or elsewhere, are not separate spheres of life: a sphere of ideas isolated from the world, and a practical world hostile to ideas. There is almost no theoretical reflection where some amount of practical thinking does not intrude; and no sphere of practical thinking devoid of theory. Our thinking is like a rope of tightly compressed theoretical and practical strands that are difficult to untangle. A good deal of our theoretical thinking, such as our view of what constitutes justice or freedom, is influenced by how such views would work in practice. Practical problems, such as how to dig a train tunnel under a river, have theoretical aspects. Many professions, such as medicine, combine intimately the theoretical and the practical. In academia, we study a practical activity theoretically, or study a theory practically by examining its applications.

The theoretical-practical distinction, then, is a matter of degree. Some thinking is more practical or more theoretical than other forms of thinking. The difference is (a) the dominant interest of the thinking and (b) the types of reasons it uses. Practical problems are addressed to us as agents. The dominant interest is what to do. How can we solve a problem or achieve a goal? Theoretical problems are addressed to us as knowers. The dominant interest is what is true, or what to believe, and how to explain some phenomenon. For example, we want to know, theoretically, how sub-atomic forces explain the observable features of ordinary objects, or how certain genes predispose someone to skin cancer. Practical problems are resolved by developing the right practice. Theoretical problems are solved by coming to the right (or true) belief. Theoretical reasons are "reasons for believing" which support a proposition, while practical reasons are "reasons for acting" and support an action.[7]

Ethics is practical because both its dominant interest and its reasons are practical. It seeks reasons for doing action *x*, not theoretical reasons for believing *y*. But ethics is not anti-theory. It is not so practical as to be averse to the careful analysis of ideas, to the raising of technical points, or to questions of principle. The purpose of theorizing is to illuminate our ethical experience, examine its tensions, expose assumptions, construct new principles, and improve our ethical responses. There is no saying, in advance, how theoretical or arcane our thinking must become to sort out an ethical issue. We should follow our thinking wherever it leads. To insist on a practical "anchor" for ethics is not to question the value of theory; it is to remind us that ethical theorizing should be grounded in practical questions.

Theorizing in ethics can be divided into two groups:

Philosophical ethics: includes (a) the nature of ethical statements and the meaning of ethical concepts; (b) how we know, or come to agree on, ethical statements, plus their objectivity; (c) the purpose(s) of ethics given certain theories of society and human nature; and (d) the history of ethics.

Applied ethics: includes (a) criteria of right and wrong; the supreme principle(s) of ethics; (b) lower-level principles that guide how we should act in particular enterprises and professions; (c) how

---

[7] Audi, *Practical Reasoning and Ethical Decision*, 1–2.

principles apply to specific issues; and (d) methods of reasoning.[8] As I will explain, applied ethics is divided into two parts: general normative theories about what principles and values should guide us in life; and a more specific "framework ethics" that focuses on codes of ethics for professions and other significant enterprises in society.

Philosophical ethics (or "meta-ethics") is called "philosophical" because it studies ethics at a high level of generality and detachment. We step outside the daily activity of making ethical judgments and examine (and explain) the activity of making ethical judgments. We adopt the view of an external observer who analyzes ethics as a social, psychological, and linguistic phenomenon. For example, if I stumble upon a wallet on my walk to work, I think to myself, "I ought to return the wallet to the owner." I engage in practical ethical thinking to arrive at a conclusion for action. This is applied ethics, not philosophical ethics. I adopt the view of philosophical ethics to this experience if I step back and ask, for example, what "ought" means in such judgments. What is the source of such feelings of duty to return the wallet? What do I mean when I say returning the wallet is the right thing to do?

In contrast, applied ethics is just that – *applied*. It seeks practical conclusions about the right thing to do and to marshal reasons for doing it. It is interested in identifying duties, rights, and practical principles for guiding action. In applied ethics, we work within ethics. We engage ethical situations and issues, directly. We do not step outside and observe ethics as a human phenomenon. To the contrary, we are actors who do ethics with a dominant practical interest. We argue for the application of certain ethical principles in controversial cases. In applied ethics, we ask such questions as, "did I do the wrong thing when I refused to give money to famine relief?" or "is euthanasia morally justifiable if the dying person is in extreme pain?"

Theories in applied ethics are not abstract theories focused on what "good" or "right" means, or why humans have constructed ethical systems. A "theory" in applied ethics is a general view about what actually *is* good

---

[8] This categorization is close to other schemes, such as the distinction between meta-ethics, normative ethics, and practical ethics, in LaFollette, *Blackwell Guide to Ethical Theory*, 1–3; and the division of ethics into meta-ethics and normative ethics, as in Brink, *Moral Realism and the Foundations of Ethics*, 1–2.

or right or virtuous, in general or in a domain of life. Typically, an applied ethics theory has a distinct view of the three great themes of ethics – what the good life consists of, what is right (or what justice requires), and what the virtues are. Typically, an applied ethics theory advances a view of how these themes are related and which is the most important aspect of ethical life. An applied ethics theory also must explain what its perspective means for leading issues. For instance, where does utilitarianism, communitarian ethics, or Christian ethics stand on such issues as animal rights, our obligations to future generations, or a just immigration policy? The application of theory is crucial for applied ethics. Values such as respect for life, friendship, or happiness, can be so abstract that we need to see how people apply these values to identify where we agree or disagree. After all, both the Quakers and the mafia agree on the value of friendship.[9]

We have already mentioned examples of applied theories, such as utilitarianism, which takes the good as the fundamental aspect of ethics. It declares that the greatest good is the greatest amount of happiness for all. On this basis, utilitarianism takes a wide array of positions on the moral issues of the day. To be sure, any applied theory such as utilitarianism contains philosophical reflections on the meaning of "good" and the objectivity of ethics. But the overwhelming intent of applied theories is practical.

Given this general understanding of the philosophical/applied distinction, we can now be more specific about the area that we are most concerned with in this book – applied ethics. As mentioned, applied ethics has two divisions, general and specific: (1) normative ethics in general, which deals with general theories about what things are valuable, good, and right, what principles should belong to our general morality, and how they apply to our decisions and actions; (2) framework ethics: the development, critique, and application of specific frameworks of principles, such as codes of ethics for the professions. Frameworks are sets of related principles that together govern an entire type of activity, e.g. the code of ethics for physicians or journalists. Framework ethics, of course, does not stand on its own. Applied ethics engages in both normative and framework ethics to study the practice of professions to help nurses, public servants, journalists, and others. Part of the analysis of these frameworks is to examine

---

[9] Lukes, *Moral Relativism*, 123.

whether they are consistent with the more general theories of normative ethics, such as utilitarianism.

Framework ethics asks about the validity, coherence, interpretation, and adequacy of the framework, as well as the validity of specific principles. For example, in journalism we can question whether the existing professional code of ethics is adequate for changes happening in journalism, where citizen journalists become increasingly important. Or we can question a specific principle such as the doctrine of news objectivity. Framework ethics is focused not on the justification of the framework of principles, but on how the principles apply to situations to yield judgments about what to do. For example, if we accept objectivity as a principle of news reporting, what does it entail for the coverage of my country's military actions? The professions use framework ethics to question their principles and to study the dilemmas and tough "judgment-calls" specific to their domains. For example, how much information should a doctor provide a seriously ill patient about their disease? How should a health organization inform female patients that their breast cancer tests were botched by pathologists? What is "informed consent" in a business contract? If a financial adviser owns stock in a company, should he promote that company to clients?[10]

Philosophical ethics

Philosophical ethics asks three large questions. What are we saying when we speak ethically? How do we justify what we say? What is the purpose

---

[10] My term "framework ethics" is non-standard but overall my category scheme captures the essential distinctions made by other schemes. Historically, philosophers have used a variety of terms to capture these differences. For example, the term "philosophical ethics" is used by Darwall, in his *Philosophical Ethics*. Darwall notes that philosophical ethics can be called "meta-ethics" or "critical ethics" or "analytic ethics." See Darwall, "How Should Ethics Relate to Philosophy?" 19. One popular category scheme divides theories into "metaethics," "normative ethics," and "practical ethics." See LaFollette's *Blackwell Guide to Ethical Theory*, and his *Ethics in Practice*. On my scheme, philosophical ethics is meta-ethics. I prefer "philosophical ethics" because it covers a variety of approaches to understanding ethics. My second category, "applied ethics" contains normative ethics, as traditionally understood. I add "framework ethics" to applied ethics to bring out an important area of theorizing for this book – the analysis of professional ethics. Despite this deviance from the usual nomenclature, my scheme captures the main distinctions between philosophizing about ethics, constructing normative theories, and doing ethics in specific areas such as the professions.

of ethics? Theories can be categorized according to which question they ask and how they answer it.

What are we saying?

Philosophical ethics begins with the analysis of ethical language. What are we saying when we assert that something is right, cruel or shameful? What does "ought" mean when we say "you ought to tell her the truth"? What sort of statement is "torture is intolerable"? Are ethical judgments a type of factual statement? Consider this: when we make ethical statements, such as "John has a duty to keep his promise," "reducing harm is the greatest good," and "ethical people are honest, truthful and kind," are we attempting to describe something about John or about people in general? If I say "the hallway door is closed" I describe the door, ascribing an objective feature – being closed – to an object. Is this what we are doing when we say "Mary is good"? Are we describing Mary by ascribing a property to her – being good? If we say "to cause unnecessary pain to anyone is bad" are we stating (or describing) a fact about the world, perhaps a special kind of fact, a moral fact?

This view of ethical judgments as factual descriptions may strike us as improbable. After all, we use many types of statements for purposes other than to describe. The imperative "close the door" is uttered to prompt someone to act, not to describe the door. "I love the sublime music of Mozart" expresses one's love of the composer's work; it is not uttered to describe the music. Perhaps, then, ethical judgments are more like imperatives to do something or subjective expressions of emotion about what I like or dislike. Maybe ethical statements are not meant to describe anything at all.

Theories about the language of ethics can be categorized depending on how they answer these questions. The main rival theories are *descriptivism* and *non-descriptivism*. A theory is descriptive if it contends that ethical statements describe actions or objects in some factual or objective manner, and they are true when their descriptions are true to these moral facts. A theory is non-descriptive if it denies this view and attributes some other function to ethical language.

Our decision to be descriptivist or non-descriptivist will affect whether we believe ethics is factual or non-factual; true or false; objective or subjective. For descriptivists, if ethical statements do *not* describe anything in the world, they cannot be true or false. There must be a moral property or fact corresponding to "good," "right," or "duty" that determines whether the ethical statement is true or false. My ethical statement can only be true if it correctly corresponds to the way the world is, in the same way that my statement about the size of the moon is only true if it corresponds to the way the moon is. Otherwise, ethical statements are false. To deny the factuality of moral statements commits one to the position that they only express subjective feelings or relative opinions. This view is sometimes called "moral realism" because it believes that ethical statements describe what is real, beyond my subjective feelings and emotions. Moral realism takes moral claims literally, as claims that "purport to describe the moral properties of people, actions, and institutions."[11]

Descriptivism can take many forms. One view is naturalism: terms like "good" refer to natural things such as moral emotions, pleasure (or the satisfaction of my preferences), or the maximization of utility. If goodness is pleasure, then to say that an action is good is to say it creates pleasure. It is factual and descriptive. I describe an objective feature of that action. Another view is non-naturalism, which believes that ethical terms such as "morally good" refer to a special moral property of "goodness" that is indefinable and therefore not reducible to natural properties such as pleasure.[12]

Despite their differences, all descriptivists argue that it is clear that ethical judgments describe things. All we have to do is look at how we normally use ethical language. When I say that John is honest, I ascribe the property of "honesty" to him. The statement is true or false depending on whether John has that property or not, apart from how I feel about it. When I say an action is wrong I am saying it has certain properties, such as causing harmful consequences, which make it wrong. When I say Mary is a good person I ground my judgment in objective features of Mary such as her kindness to strangers. To say "Mary is a good person" is to describe her in a way similar to "my Honda is a good car." To say, "x is right" is similar in form to "x is red." Both ethical and empirical judgments are true by virtue of properties in the world. We also say things like, "it is just a *fact* that torturing babies for pleasure is wrong." We say that helping

---

[11] Brink, *Moral Realism and the Foundations of Ethics*, 7.
[12] Moore, *Principia Ethica*, 21.

Mary in distress is *really* good. This suggests that we are describing something. Moreover, if an ethical disagreement is not over a property or fact, then what is it about? If ethics is only about expressing our feelings, then how can we rationally discuss differences in feelings and attitudes? Why debate at all in ethics, why reason and inquire, if we don't think it will get us closer to the truth? There must be something we can be right or wrong about. For realists, there are correct answers in ethics and discussion is to "discover what these objective facts are."[13]

Non-descriptivism rejects this descriptive (or realist) way of understanding ethical language. It holds that ethical statements are not made true by things external to my mind because ethical language is not descriptive, or not primarily descriptive. Descriptivists are mistaken about how ethical language functions. The strongest version of non-descriptivism argues that you are simply in error if you think ethical statements describe anything.[14] You are in the grip of the "descriptive fallacy."[15] Ethical language does not seek to describe or represent the world at all.

What *is* the function of ethical language then? Most non-descriptivists agree that the function of ethical language is to project our values, emotions, and practical attitudes onto actions and objects. There are two main theories. The primary function of ethical language is (1) to express my approval of some action. This is called *expressivism*. Or it is (2) to prescribe some action, not to describe it. This is *prescriptivism*. For (1) and (2) ethical language is not literally true or false, in the realist sense of corresponding to an external fact or property. Instead, the purpose of ethical language is to guide conduct by indicating what we approve of and by commending it to others, so as to influence their behavior. Expressivism holds that ethical judgments such as "*x* is good" express my positive feelings toward and my approval of *x*, while "*x* is bad" expresses my negative feelings and disapproval.[16] Prescriptivism holds that ethical judgments are not descriptions in the indicative form, "*x* is P," but prescriptions in the imperative form, "do *x*." Ethical statements are value judgments that typically take

---

[13] Smith, *The Moral Problem*, 9.

[14] On "error" theory, see Mackie, *Ethics: Inventing Right and Wrong.*

[15] Austin, *How to Do Things with Words*, 3, and Hare, *Moral Thinking*, 67.

[16] Ayer says statements of value are not significant in a literal sense "but are simply expressions of emotion, which can be neither true nor false, Ayer, *Language, Truth and Logic*, 103.

the form of imperatives or commands, such as "do not murder." In making an ethical statement, I am not expressing my attitude toward an action. I am prescribing. I am saying that you ought to do some action, or not do it. R. M. Hare, who developed prescriptivism as a theory, argued that a descriptive sentence such as "the door is shut" tells us something is the case. It differs from the imperative, "shut the door," which is not used to tell someone what is the case. It is used to tell someone "to make something the case."[17] On Hare's view, ethics consists of our most basic and universal prescriptions.

Some forms of non-descriptivism depend on a distinction between the descriptive and the ethical meaning of a statement. It is the latter that makes ethical language distinct. Charles Stevenson was one of the first to forcefully argue for the view that words had an "emotive" sense in addition to a descriptive sense. The emotive power of a word was its causal ability to "evoke or directly express attitudes, as distinct from describing them."[18] This is the ethical meaning of a sentence. For non-descriptivism, ethical statements such as "Mary is good" or "do not kill," have a factual element. When I say "Mary is a good person," I can be describing her on one level. If asked why I think she is good, I can describe several of her features, such as her kindness, her honesty, etc. But, for non-descriptivists, simply naming these features does not make the sentence an ethical assertion. It only becomes an ethical assertion when I *also* implicitly or explicitly commend such features to others. I project my moral attitudes onto the action. This act of valuing and commending, with its public purposes of teaching and influencing others, is the emotive sense. To express these values and emotions is the function of ethical language.

The challenge for non-descriptivists is to show how the expression of feelings or attitudes, or the issuing of prescriptions, can have a rational and objective basis. If I say "I hate x" or "do x" and you reply, "but I love x," or "do not do x," what is left for ethics to discuss?

How do I know what I say?

Asking about the meaning of ethical language leads to epistemological questions about how to justify ethical statements. There are three possible

---

[17] Hare, *The Language of Morals*, 5.   [18] Stevenson, *Ethics and Language*, 33.

justifications: metaphysics, tradition, or rationality. I can ground my beliefs metaphysically by appealing to some source of authority that transcends the world and is beyond natural human faculties. Appeal to religion is one metaphysical approach. To justify my ethical beliefs I may cite the authority of the commands of God. Also, I can ground my beliefs on social customs and traditions. What is right or wrong is what the tradition of my family, ethnic group, or culture says is right or wrong. I may argue that traditional values have served my community for many years and therefore deserve respect. Without traditional values, individuals act in selfish ways against the common good.

Finally, I can ground my beliefs on rationality and experience. This option is sometimes called "naturalism" since it regards ethics to be grounded in natural human experiences, capacities, and needs. It does not ground ethics on a transcendent authority, and it subjects cultural traditions to the test of human experience. An ethical belief is valid or true because one can provide reasons from logic and experience.

It is possible that ethical beliefs could find support from two or all three approaches. My rational belief in the principle of equal respect for all humans may be supported by my community's traditions and by my religion.

Naturalistic theories stress either direct or indirect methods of validating ethical beliefs. Direct theories claim that humans can directly apprehend certain ethical principles and judgments to be correct, by simply and directly examining the ideas contained in the belief. Principles such as "torturing is wrong" do not need a long argument to be shown true. They are not inferences from other things I know.[19] Its "wrongness" is directly evident to me when I consider what is involved in the idea of torture, somewhat in the same way that I know that a triangle's three angles total 180 degrees by reflecting on my idea of a triangle. I may say that I "intuit" that an act of racial discrimination is wrong in the same way that I directly perceive that an object is red, or has a rectangular shape. Intuitions operate in many areas of our lives. On this view, most people hold many ethical beliefs to be obvious or self-evident. Who doesn't intuit that debilitating pain is bad? One knows that one should keep one's promise to Tom by reflecting on what is involved in the act of promising. The philosophical

---

[19] McMahan, "Moral Intuition," 93–94.

formulation of this view is called *intuitionism* and it has been put forward
in different forms by major ethicists such as Henry Sidgwick, G. E. Moore,
and W. D. Ross. Intuition is a form of descriptivism. Ethical judgments
describe what we intuit. Intuitions are "non-inferential cognitions," that
is, they are not inferred from, or justified by reference to, other beliefs
and judgments.[20] Ross thought that, through intuition, we see that we
have a number of basic duties by simply reflecting on the type of action in
question. I intuit duties of fidelity (honesty and promise-keeping), justice,
gratitude, beneficence, self-improvement, and non-injury.[21] Ross did not
think that intuition was a method sufficient for all of ethics. Intuitions
grounded our identification of basic duties, but other methods and considerations had to be used for determining our actual duty in a given case.

Intuitionism is controversial. Critics question the nature of this intuition, and whether it assumes, improbably, that humans have a special
moral "sense." Some argue that to say "I intuit that *x* is wrong" tells us
no more than "*x* is wrong." Intuitions, it is also objected, are just the
product of my upbringing and can be biased. In the seventeenth century, slavery did not strike a good number of people as obviously wrong.
We need to reason about our intuitions.[22] Defenders of intuitions reply
that a principle is intuitively known to be true by those who properly
understand it. Intuitions are not necessarily obvious to all people, or
it may take time. Intuitions compel my belief when we consider them
with a proper understanding. They are self-evident to "an intelligent
and unbiased mind."[23]

Indirect theories deny that there are direct ways of justifying what we
say ethically since everything we know is indirectly apprehended through
a process of interpretation and reasoning. At best, humans know ethical beliefs by using both direct and indirect methods of justification, for
example, some combination of intuitions and forms of reasoning. Some
indirect ethicists are what we could call "holists." They believe that an
ethical conclusion follows from balancing a wide variety of factors such

---

[20] Audi, *The Good in the Right*, 5.   [21] Ross, *The Right and the Good*, 21.

[22] Peter Singer says intuitions are likely derived from "discarded religious systems,
from warped views of sex and bodily functions" or from customs once necessary
for the survival of a group but no longer needed. Singer, "Sidgwick and Reflective
Equilibrium," 516.

[23] Sidgwick, *The Methods of Ethics*, 229.

as intuitions about what is good or right, facts about humans and the situation in question, expected consequences, our basic values and emotions, and the weighing of conflicting general principles. We will explore holistic reasoning in the media in the next chapter. For now, we can note the holistic reasoning that occurred when we imagined ourselves to be deliberating about Dorothy's health care. Our mind sought to balance a range of moral intuitions, facts about Dorothy, consequences for all of the people involved, various options and concern for the rights of Dorothy but also the duties of the health provider. A proper ethical judgment on what to do in this situation cannot simply or directly be intuited. Instead, the judgment is arrived at in an indirect manner, using a variety of forms of reasoning.

Other indirect ethicists are what we might call "monists." To put it roughly, they think the process of justification is simpler and clearer than the holistic process. Monists think that ethical conclusions can be inferred in a fairly direct fashion from one (hence, "monistic") supreme principle. Utilitarianism is monistic in spirit because it uses one supreme principle, the principle of utility, to infer whether an action is good or bad, or which of several possible actions is the best option. To decide what is to be done, we calculate whether the action will produce the greatest amount of utility, or at least as much utility as any other action. Ethical judgments about actions follow as a deduction from the supreme principle of utility. Utilitarianism does not employ a holistic form of reasoning that balances a plurality of values and principles. Instead, it employs one form of reasoning – the calculation of utility. It calculates how various options of action promote utility.

Other philosophers, such as Immanuel Kant, put forward a fairly direct method of ethical justification. Kant uses a method that formalizes the idea, noted above, of being willing to universalize my actions. For Kant, an action is ethically justified if it follows a rule or "maxim" that is consistent with the one great principle of ethics, the "categorical imperative." The imperative tells us to will only those acts that we could recommend to all other rational beings in similar situations.

Another form of indirect theory is found in approaches to ethics that stress agreement among interested parties. One variant of this view is that we come to know what we ought to do by considering whether the act can be justified by principles that all interested parties could fairly and reasonably *agree* to. This is usually a form of non-descriptivism and tends towards holistic reasoning. Ethical judgments do not describe ethical facts. They express those norms that we agree should govern our interactions. One such view is *contract* theory, or *contractualism*, which thinks that what is "right," "obligatory," or "wrong" in any domain of society is determined by principles that define a reasonable co-operative framework. An action is right or wrong "if the act accords with, or violates principles that are, or would be, the object of a suitable agreement between equals."[24] In other words, an ethical principle is justified if it can be derived from an agreement which meets certain conditions such as an equal and fair participation by all participants.

In modern ethical theory, ethics as fair agreement has been developed by major writers such as John Rawls, Thomas Scanlon, and Jurgen Habermas. Impartial reasoning means we are able to justify to *others* our norms, our policies, and our reasons for acting. Justification is an open and fair dialogue among all parties. For Scanlon, I have to argue in terms that people, with similar moral motivations, "could not reasonably reject."[25] On this view, ethics is based not on religion or a common conception of life. We construct our ethics through a process of deliberation. Hence, ethical judgments as agreed-upon rules are better referred to as "reasonable," "fair," and "useful and appropriate," rather than literally true or false.[26]

Objectivity and relativism

Theories of meaning and justification have implications for one of the most difficult and enduring disputes: whether ethics is objective or subjective, absolute or relative. The dispute goes back to the origins of philosophy in ancient Greece where some philosophers, particularly a group called the sophists, argued that the laws of nature were universal but the rules of society, because they were man-made, were not. They were relative to society.

---

[24] Darwall, *Contractarianism/Contractualism*,1.
[25] Scanlon, *What We Owe to Each Other*, 5.
[26] Habermas puts forward a "discourse morality" of equal respect and "solidaristic responsibility for everybody." Habermas argues that, in ethics, we don't project ourselves by imagination into the place of others. Instead, we participate in an actual dialogue with others, where all parties get to give their reasons. Habermas, *The Inclusion of the Other*, 33.

In a famous passage, Herodotus, the ancient Greek historian, describes how Darius the Great, King of Persia, encountered Greeks, who cremated their dead fathers and Callatiae Indians, who were said to eat them. The Greeks were appalled at the practice of eating parents; the Indians were appalled at the burning of their bodies.[27] Plato began Western philosophy by responding to the challenge of relativism. He gave himself the task of showing that objective knowledge about society and human nature was possible and should replace the shifting, relative opinions of most people. Today's ethical relativism is more often described as "cultural relativism," originating in studies of differing cultures by anthropologists and sociologists.

Objectivity has played a large part in the ethics of modern journalism. Here too journalists have disagreed not only on whether news journalism could be objective but also what "objective reporting" means.[28] Two senses of objectivity have dominated the discussion. One sense is "ontological objectivity." To be ontologically objective, a belief must correctly describe or correspond to the way the world is. It must refer to some actually existing object or state of affairs and it must truly describe certain properties of an object or state of affairs, such as size or mass. My belief that there is a flock of pink flamingos in my bedroom is not objective because it is due to my imagination or my dreaming. My belief that there is a yellow tree in my backyard is not objective because the tree is actually dark brown. This is the sense of objectivity in which many moral realists claim that ethical judgments are descriptive and objective.

A second sense is "epistemic objectivity" or "methodological objectivity." On this view, we may struggle to know what is true, or what corresponds to reality; but we can still understand objectivity as good methods and correct norms of inquiry. My beliefs are objective to the extent that they are formed and tested by rigorous methods that detect bias, reduce error, and test for evidence and logic. In science, the hypothesis that a group of genes in the brain is causally related to Parkinson's disease is tested for plausibility and objectivity by studying the methods it used, and by seeing if it meets objective standards of evidence. As we will see, a story in journalism is "epistemically objective" if its claims are based on

---

[27] Herodotus, *The Histories*, Book Three, Chapter 38, Section 3, 185–186.
[28] For journalism objectivity see Ward, *The Invention of Journalism Ethics*.

the best possible journalistic methods for gathering data, collaborating facts, checking a diversity of sources, and so on. Objectivity in this methodological sense does not guarantee truth. In the end, my hypothesis or journalism story may prove to be false.

Descriptivists argue that ethics is either ontologically objective or relative. If "good" means what I or some group think is good, or what I or a group approve, then ethical norms are relative to how we think about them. Also, intuitionism appears to be committed to ontological objectivity because the agent intuits that some action is objectively right or wrong, and that judgment is not relative to culture or individual beliefs. In contrast, Kant thought that ethics was, in our terms, not ontologically objective but epistemically objective, because proper ethical reasoning followed a strict method for testing rules, a method that held for all rational beings. The method was based on principles that were universal and obligatory for all rational beings. Finally, if you think that "good" refers to utility, then ethics is objective because we test our judgments according to an external criterion, utility.

Opposed to objectivity is relativism. Relativism holds that all beliefs are true or valid relative to a background theory or culture. Moreover, there are no impartial criteria to judge that a background theory or culture is better than another. David Wong writes: "Radical relativists hold that any morality is as true or as justified as any other."[29] Moderate relativists deny that there is any single true morality but also hold that some moralities are truer or more justified than others. Ethical relativism says that ethical beliefs are true or valid relative to the ethical values of a group or culture and that there are no objective criteria to decide whether one set of values is better than another.

Since there are many forms of relativism we need to be clear which sense of relativism is being discussed. For Plato and others, the relativism that needs to be opposed is "status" relativism, not "circumstantial" relativism.[30] Circumstantial relativism says that what we ought to do depends on, and must be relativized to, the relevant circumstances of the action. This view is not controversial since it is only common sense to say

---

[29] Wong, "Moral Relativism," 541.
[30] See the distinction between status and circumstantial relativism in Audi, *Moral Value and Human Diversity*, 25–26.

that how we apply principles should take circumstances into account. For example, normally we ought not to slap people vigorously but if someone groggy from sleeping pills must wake up or die, you may be obligated to slap the person, repeatedly. The form of relativism that is controversial is status relativism, which says the justification of the principles themselves are relative to custom or society. The validity of the principle not to slap people unnecessarily (or any other ethical principle) depends on society. There are no universally binding principles. There are no objective principles, where "objective" means justification not relative to society but binding for all societies.[31] For circumstantial relativism, the application of principles is relative to circumstances; for status relativism, their justification is relative to circumstances.

The first assumption of ethical relativism, that cultures in different times and places have different ethical rules and values, seems true. Seventeenth-century England believed slavery was correct; twentieth-century England does not. Today, our culture would question female circumcision in tribal countries; other cultures would not. Our society places more value on individual freedom and egalitarian social structures than cultures that value a caste system, or a strict social hierarchy. Ethical differences also exist among groups within cultures.

However, ethical relativism is not *just* the observation that different groups hold different ethical beliefs. Why not? Because non-relativists can agree that there is a plurality of ethical beliefs and systems. In fact, philosophers have known for centuries that ethical values differed among cultures but most of them did not conclude that relativism was true. One reason was a belief in a God who prescribed ethical norms, absolutely, even if some humans refused to accept them. But there were non-religious reasons. There are ways of explaining the differences in belief that are consistent with objectivity. The fact that you and I disagree whether the world is round doesn't mean there is no correct objective answer. The fact that people differ on the causes of climate change doesn't mean there isn't a correct causal view. The fact that there are different beliefs about any topic proves nothing.

Moreover, non-relativists may argue that differences in practices and ethical beliefs may be variations on underlying objective principles embraced by all cultures. It may be that all cultures agree on general

[31] *Ibid.*, 25.

ethical values such as a respect for life, truth, and non-violence, but they differ on how they practice those values. Therefore the relativist must show that there are substantial ethical differences that can't be reduced to variations of universal principles. The relativist must justify her claim that there are no cross-cultural criteria for evaluating ethical beliefs. The relativist must also explain how relativism is consistent with the engaged stance of applied ethics. Relativism is a thesis of philosophical ethics, not applied ethics. It is the result of adopting the disengaged stance of philosophical ethics. The relativist steps back from ethics and observes the differences among ethical systems. She concludes that ethical rules are relative to different systems. The problem, however, is whether individuals can maintain relativism when they return to applied ethics – when they return to doing ethics and have to argue for the correctness of a judgment or norm, or criticize someone's actions. How can I hold that ethical beliefs are relative yet firmly criticize someone's ethical actions, especially someone who belongs to another group or subscribes to a different moral system? Another problem is whether relativism favors a non-critical form of traditionalism. If I think ethical views are relative and no view is better than any other view, why bother to critically assess and improve ethics? What does "improve" mean if ethics is relative? Why not follow the norms that prevail in my culture?

The objectivist and the relativist portray each other as promoting undesirable and even dangerous doctrines. Relativism is associated with nihilism and extreme skepticism, and a refusal to stand up to unethical practices in other cultures. People fear that relativism will undermine our confidence in cherished values, or leave us with no way to say what is right or wrong. Relativism seems to leave us without the ethical resources to say that Hitler (or some other tyrant) was objectively wrong in their abominable actions. Ethics, it seems, is all a matter of opinion. Relativists reply that objectivism leads to dogmatism and absolutism. Judging other cultures smacks of cultural arrogance or intolerance. Relativism urges tolerance and dialogue, and this is more in line with liberal democratic thought.

Why ethics?

The third question of philosophical ethics is why humans bother with ethics in the first place. Why did societies, over history, not "make do" with law, etiquette, and prudence? One part of this question is a matter of evolutionary history. How and why did humans living in groups agree to co-operate and construct ethical rules? These questions link ethics to biology, history, and the social sciences. Another part of the question is normative, not historical. Assume that ethics can be used in many ways, for good or bad. For example, leaders can use the emotional force of ethical ideals for self-interested purposes. Ethics can be regarded as the rules that hypocritical people espouse publicly but privately ignore, to maintain social status and trust. The normative question is: to what end *should* ethics be used? What is the correct function for ethics, apart from hypocrisy and manipulation?

There are many normative views about the purpose of ethics. All agree that ethics seeks to guide conduct. But after that, views differ. Many of the views are on display at the dramatic opening of Plato's *The Republic*, where Socrates is challenged by his interlocutors to show that the just person is also a happy person. Participants argue that ethics is a sort of social contract. Others argue that "might is right," not love thy neighbor, is the real ethic that governs human relations. Others say ethics promotes social stability and was developed to protect the weak from the strong.[32] Another view, advanced by the seventeenth-century philosopher Thomas Hobbes, is that norms and contracts must be enforced to raise humans from a state of war of "one against all" into a peaceful society, or civilization.[33]

Ethics as agreement, mentioned above, also has a distinct view of the function of ethics. Ethics, at its best, defines agreed-upon principles for fair, social co-operation among citizens, such as the principles of justice. Ethics allows humans to co-operate in society for mutual benefit. On this view, Hobbes was right to see society as a sort of contract among citizens. Humans construct and enforce rules so that society can exist. Rules help society to establish some degree of control, order, and reliability among human interactions. I can act with greater confidence if I know that other people will not steal, lie, murder, or arbitrarily break promises. Ethics is natural and necessary to humans as social creatures, and that is why ethics is an important part of society's normative sphere.

[32] Plato, *The Republic*, Book I and II, 3–52.
[33] Hobbes, *Leviathan*, Part One and Two.

Yet, for ethical contractualists, not just any contract will do. Many societies enforce rules that perpetuate an unjust social order. Ethics seeks to articulate and support norms that promote a fair society for the common good. We want ethics to function as a voice for the good and the right, and to work for the reduction of harm and evil. The most important function of ethics, then, is to help citizens question existing norms and construct better principles.

Applied ethics

We have outlined theories of philosophical ethics concerning what we say, how we know what we say, and why ethics is important in society. We move on to major theories in applied ethics, theories constructed as part of framework ethics. The three themes of ethics – the good, the right, and the virtuous – determine the types of applied theories. Framework theories come in three kinds: consequential (theories of the good), non-consequential (theories of the right), and virtue theories. Consequential theories articulate principles that define goodness and identify actions that promote the good; non-consequential theories articulate principles that say what is just and what is our duty. Such principles are intended to restrain the pursuit of our goods and personal interests. Virtue theories describe moral character and specify the virtues that individuals need to be ethical.

Consequential theories

"Consequentialism" refers to a group of theories that regard the pursuit of what is good in life, or the intrinsically valuable, as the primary ethical concept.[34] Realizing what is good in the world, through actions, is the aim of ethical people. That something is intrinsically good or contributes instrumentally to the good are the criteria for evaluating norms and actions.

---

[34] The term "consequentialism" was first used in Elizabeth Anscombe's article, "Modern Moral Philosophy," which appeared in the *Philosophy* journal in 1958.

Consequential theories define the good in terms of the *consequences* of actions, such as actions that promote a flourishing life for many citizens, or actions that result in an increase in pleasure or a reduction of pain. Consequentialism asks us to look to the expected results of our actions. We look to the "relevant effects" of our actions on the world.[35] As Frey writes, "an act is right if its consequences are at least as good as those of any alternative."[36] On some versions of consequentialism, I am ethically obligated not only to bring about some good consequences but to "maximize" – that is, to bring about the best consequences, or the greatest amount of good. By stressing results, consequential theories come under the broad umbrella of "teleological" ethical theories, because *telos* is Greek for end or goal.

Reasonable forms of consequentialist theories do not exclude other considerations as irrelevant to the evaluation of action. A consequentialist can allow that, in a situation, one should look at other things than the overall good produced. One can consider whether promises have been made, whether any rights will be violated, and whether the action is just. Yet a consequentialist will insist that, in the end, these features are to be valued insofar as they bring about good consequences. In some cases, promises will have to be broken or rights violated to bring about desired consequences. Ultimately, acts are right or wrong by virtue of the goodness or badness of their consequences.

Consequential theories differ according to their different notions of what is good, and how it should be pursued. Consequential theories can be "narrow" or "wide" in what they count as consequences. Narrow consequentialist theories argue that good consequences can be reduced to one type of thing, e.g. pleasure and the avoidance of pain. Other theories think "good" is a composite of different things, such as pleasure, friendship, achievement, wealth, and the development of human capacities.

There are two types of consequential theories depending on whether we evaluate particular acts or types of acts. Act-consequentialism evaluates the consequences of particular acts. Specific acts are good or right if they have the best consequences or bring about the best state of affairs. An act-consequentialist approach asks: what would be the consequences if I did not keep my promise on *this* occasion? What would be the consequences if

---

[35] Pettit, *Consequentialism*, xiii.   [36] Frey, "Act-Utilitarianism," 165.

I spoke truthfully in *this* situation? What are the consequences of my help-ing or not helping *this* person today?

Rule-consequentialism considers the consequences of people following certain types of actions. They follow general rules that say certain types of actions should be done or avoided. We inquire whether an act falls under a general ethical rule, such as to speak the truth or to keep promises. Then we consider the consequences of people following that rule. Specific actions are good and ethically required not because they have good conse-quences. They are good and ethically required because they "spring from a set of rules that have the best consequences."[37]

Why change the topic from particular acts to types of actions? Why move from what is right in this specific circumstance to what is right according to general rules? To take a trivial example, imagine that you walk across your neighbor's newly seeded lawn to save yourself time on a walk to the grocery store. The neighbor sees you and is angry. When you point out that you did very little harm, the neighbor responds: "but what if everyone did that?" For the rule-consequentialist, this response is valid and it tells us something about this approach to ethics. Ethics is about fol-lowing rules for the overall, common good. It is about the consequences of many people acting in certain ways. From traffic laws to ethical principles, we do not usually evaluate actions by calculating the consequences of spe-cific acts. Instead we usually estimate the impact of most people following certain rules. If I carry out a "U-turn" with my car in a "no U-Turn" zone, the maneuver may be convenient for me and cause no problems on this occasion. But it could become dangerous if many people started making U-turns on the highway.

There are more serious examples than U-turns. In ethics, breaking a promise in *this* situation may appear to be ethically allowed. But from a rule-consequentialist perspective, it is wrong because it violates a gen-eral rule against promise-breaking. Rather than ask, "what if everyone made a U-Turn as they pleased?" we ask, "what if everyone broke the general rule to keep promises whenever it was convenient to them?" To take another example, a student may use act-utilitarian reasons to jus-tify cheating on a test. Cheating promoted his utility, it had good con-sequences. No one noticed his cheating, so what harm was done? In this

---

[37] LaFollette, "Introduction," in *The Blackwell Guide to Ethical Theory*, 7.

case, there are more good consequences than bad consequences. Rule-utilitarians would ask, "What if everyone did that?" They would argue that we evaluate not specific acts of cheating but the consequences of many people keeping or breaking rules. Systematic violation of the rule of not cheating undermines not only the long-term integrity of the persons involved but also the academic system of testing. Because the consequences of many people breaking the rule are bad, the individual act of cheating is bad.

Also, take for example the well-known ethical problem of the "free-loader" who cheats on social programs. For instance, Frank avoids, by cheating and other means, paying his proper share of taxes, or he obtains money from a social program to which he is not entitled. He can enjoy these benefits because other people follow the rules and contribute their fair share of taxes. Frank can argue, on act-utilitarian grounds, that his avoiding taxes increases his utility, and his cheating has no great effect on the sustainability of social programs. He is only one person. Rule-utilitarianism was constructed in part to try to meet such arguments. One can always argue for exceptions to any rule at any time by arguing that, in *this* case, no significant harm is done.

Another reason for rule-utilitarianism is that people do not have the time to stop and estimate the consequences of every action, and even if one has the time, it is difficult to predict the results of specific acts. So we rely on rules that past experience has shown have positive, long-term consequences.

Theories of consequentialism also differ according to *how much good* we are supposed to bring about. Some consequential theories require us to "maximize" the good for all in any situation. Other kinds of consequentialism are more modest. One kind is called "satisficing" consequentialism. "Satisficing" refers to aiming at a satisfactory result, which may not be optimum. Consider a simple example. A hotel manager discovers, late one evening, that a car has broken down outside his premises. The occupants of the car are a poor family who cannot afford a room or a meal in his hotel. The manager doesn't take the time to check all the available rooms. He does not give the family the best available room. Rather, he gives them a room for free, even though it may not be the best room. According to satisficing consequentialism, the manager has done the right thing and he is not required to take time to search for the best possible room.[38] Why settle for "satisficing"? Because it is felt that the obligation to maximize is often too demanding. It may require people to act like saints and make great sacrifices. For example, if I am obligated to help others in developing countries so as to bring about the best possible results, doesn't that require an onerous effort on my part? Do I have to provide assistance to the point where I am damaged financially and cannot send my children to university? Isn't it more plausible to "satisfice" and provide a more modest amount of assistance?

The best-known form of consequentialism is utilitarianism. Jeremy Bentham and John Stuart Mill provided its classical formulation in England during the eighteenth and nineteenth centuries. As noted above, utilitarianism defines good consequences as an increase in utility. For Bentham and Mill, "utility" referred to the pleasure or happiness produced by actions. More recently, utility has been defined as the satisfaction of desires or preferences. No matter what the definition of utility is, utilitarians agree that the right action is what increases utility more than if one didn't act, and increases utility at least as well as any other alternate action. In Mill's formulation, the principle upon which all of morality stands is "utility, or the greatest happiness principle," which "holds that actions are right in proportion as they tend to promote happiness, wrong as they tend to produce the reverse of happiness." Ethically, we are obligated to do whatever promotes the greatest happiness of the greatest number. By happiness, Mill says he means pleasure, and the absence of pain, since pleasure and freedom from pain are "the only things desirable as ends."[39] However, Mill's use of "pleasure" is complex and contested. Mill does not define utility as the sheer quantity of bodily and sexual pleasures. He includes pleasures of a higher "quality" such as engaging in intellectual inquiry. For Mill, happiness includes a wide range of goods that make up a full and dignified life for humans.

Classical utilitarianism is a maximizing form of consequentialism. As Mill states, utilitarians aim to produce the greatest amount or "aggregate" of happiness. They aim to be fair and objective in calculating the expected utility. The utility of any group is no more important than the utility of any other group. Utilitarians impartially calculate the sum of expected utility

---

[38] Slote, "Satisficing Consequentialism," 361.
[39] Mill, "Utilitarianism,"68.

across all interested parties. Yet, despite these general instructions, how one calculates utility across individuals and groups is a notoriously difficult problem for utilitarianism. This is ironic since the utilitarian in the nineteenth century appealed to the calculus of pleasure to make ethics more empirical, more measureable, and more objective. Rather than appeal to subjective feelings, utilitarianism proposed a "scientific" approach of deciding what actions and social policies should be pursued by using (apparently) measurable phenomena such as pleasures and pains.

Was Mill an act- or rule-utilitarian? There is evidence for both views. Mill tells us to judge *actions* by their utility, which appears to be act-utilitarianism. But, Mill criticizes the "free-loader" who avoids paying taxes on rule-utilitarian grounds. On free speech, Mill employs rule-utilitarian thinking. The argument is broadly utilitarian. Individuals and society fair better when there is a significant degree of freedom of speech. The argument is also rule-utilitarian because Mills warns that we should not argue for restrictions of free speech on a case-by-case basis, as an act-utilitarian might do. It is always possible to say that, in this or that case, good consequences (or no significant harm) would come from restricting someone's free speech. But he says this undermines the principle. The only way to protect free speech is to protect the rule.

Mill, like other consequentialists, finds value in duties, rights, and justice. They encourage people to follow the rules of justice and to respect other people's interests. But rights and the principles of justice are not ethically fundamental. Utility is fundamental. Utility is the only thing that has non-instrumental value. Other ethical values are valuable because they promote utility.

Non-consequential theories

Consequentialism seems an obvious viewpoint for ethics, since we are accustomed to considering consequences when we make decisions. However, it does not take much thought to realize that a stress on consequences, especially the maximization of the overall good, may lead us to unethical actions, or require us to ignore other values. Non-consequential theories hold that what makes an act right is not its consequences. An act is right because it honors an obligation or fulfils a duty, even if fulfilling the duty has negative consequences, or sets back our interests.

Non-consequentialist theories are called "deontological theories" because "deon" is Greek for duty or what must be done.

We incur obligations in many ways. We incur a duty when we make promises, sign contracts, take on professional responsibilities, or occupy social roles like that of a parent. We saw that deontologists, such as W. D. Ross, argue that we can intuit basic moral obligations. Ross calls these obligations "prima facie" duties to indicate they have a moral force that needs to be considered before one acts. However, these duties can be overridden by other duties, given the circumstances. As noted, the doctor's duty to treat the injured overrides a promise to take a son to the movies.

Non-consequentialism responds to a worrisome tendency in consequential thinking. Whenever we set out to maximize good consequences or results, such as the good or the pleasure for ourselves or for all, there is a danger that arguments for the greater good will justify doing harm to some people. Similarly, to achieve certain consequences, we may justify breaking promises or overlooking the rights of minorities. All may be swept away in the desire to maximize the good of the greatest number.

For example, we may deny rights to homosexuals or place bans on certain types of marriage because those forms of life offend or repulse many people. Discrimination is justified consequentially. It creates the greatest amount of pleasure or happiness among the majority of people. In this manner, consequential thinking can support a "tyranny of the majority." Also, utopian thinking, which is often strongly consequentialist, can justify unethical actions and government programs. In Aldous Huxley's *Brave New World*, the creation of a "happy" and perfectly ordered society justified whatever means were necessary. Our experience with fascism in the past century shows how unspeakable actions can be "justified" to create a totalitarian state.

In ethics classes, students are given examples that purport to test whether they are consequentialists or deontologists, including the famous trolley problem first introduced by Philippa Foot.[40] Here are three examples:

> *A runaway trolley is careering down the mainline track where it will soon hit and kill five people trapped on the track. A bystander can flip a switch that would divert the trolley onto a branch line track before it reaches the five. However, the trolley*

---

[40] See Foot, "The Problem of Abortion and the Doctrine of the Double Effect."

would then hit and kill one person who is on the branch line track. Should the bystander flip the switch?

Five people in a hospital need organ transplants to survive. It would be possible to save them by killing a healthy patient and dividing his organs among them. Would it be right to do so?

You are a Jew during the Second World War. You and a large group of friends and family are hiding in a basement in Munich. Nazi soldiers are searching the neighborhood for Jews to send to death camps. An infant is ill and will not stop crying out loudly. If the infant continues to make such a noise, the soldiers will find your group. Would you be justified in suffocating the infant to death to prevent being discovered?

Overlook the hypothetical and simplistic nature of these examples. Consult your ethical intuitions. What is the right thing to do in each example? Some people think that if you would flip the switch, you are a consequentialist. If you think it is permissible to kill one person to save five on the trolley line but it is not permissible to kill a person to save five hospital patients, you have changed your ethical thinking. You have adopted a deontological mode that stresses the rights of the healthy patient.[41] The duty to do no harm to the ill patient overrides the possibility of doing good to other patients. If you think it is permissible to smother the infant, you have moved back to consequential thinking. These examples show how complex our reasoning can be, and how it contains both consequential and deontological elements which may conflict.

There is another way to compare consequential and deontological thinking. We can think of consequential ethics as stressing goals and deontological ethics as stressing fair processes and restrictions on how we seek our goals. Suppose that a controversial far-right speaker is invited to speak on a university campus. He will speak against free speech, especially for those who would speak out for gay rights, abortion rights, and so on. The invitation sparks heated debate on whether the person should be allowed to speak. Deontologist Marcia Baron has analyzed this situation as such: if free speech is a goal, then one could construct a consequential argument for denying the advocate the freedom to speak. The speaker may have a detrimental effect on some people's beliefs about the value of free speech. Bad results could occur. A deontologist would approach the question as a

---

[41] McMahan, "Moral Intuition," 107.

matter of fair process and rights. Free speech is a right which means that all shall be allowed to speak, even those who deny the free speech principle. What is important is not some goal, or the results, but protecting the process – the right to free speech. Free speech in this case operates as a "side constraint" on our desire to achieve certain goals and results. It is a value not to be violated even if good is not maximized.[42] Another example: should you be truthful to your wife and tell her that you have had an affair with another woman? What should you say if she asks you? Consequentially, you can think about goals. At least one goal is maintaining trust and good relations with your wife. On these grounds, you might conclude that, considering the damage that the truth will do to that goal, it is permissible to lie and deny the affair. But if you think of telling the truth as not a goal but as a duty, as part of an ethical "contract" between you and your wife – a principle that can be honored and not weakened by the consideration of consequences – then lying to your wife is wrong.[43]

Ultimately, the primary difference between consequential and non-consequential theories is not that the former takes the consequences of actions into account, and the latter does not. Non-consequentialist theories are not "anti" consequences. As Rawls states: "All ethical doctrines worth our attention take consequences into account in judging rightness. One which did not would simply be irrational, crazy."[44]

Non-consequential theories respond to these concerns by arguing that pursuing the good is important, but the pursuit should not violate commitments to duty and justice. What is fundamental to ethics and the guidance of conduct is right relations among people. Duties to tell the truth, to help others in distress, to respect other humans as "ends in themselves," and to keep promises are not justified solely by appeal to consequences or utility but also by the more primary intention to act justly. Consequential thinking is not inherently wrong but it needs the restraint of deontological thinking to prevent abuses.

Another way to see the debate between consequentialists and non-consequentialists is as a debate over what is primary in constructing a moral system: basic rights (and obligations) or consequences. The deontologist says the former, the consequentialist the latter. For John Rawls, deontological

---

[42] Baron, "Kantian Ethics," 7.
[43] *Ibid.*, 7.   [44] Rawls, *A Theory of Justice*, 30.

theories are best described in a negative manner. They are non-teleological. They do *not* make the maximization of good prior to the satisfaction of the principles of right and justice.[45] A deontological theory, according to Rawls, does not start with the priority of the good and then try to find a place for considerations of justice. Instead, it starts with the priority of right and then finds as much room as possible for the pursuit of goodness. This is the proper relationship between the good and the right.

Modern deontological theories derive from Kant.[46] His ethical theory argues for the priority of fulfilling our duties. Reason shows that certain duties are necessary and trump other considerations. How do I recognize what ethics requires? I should not begin by looking at what desires I want to satisfy or goods I would like to achieve. I do not consider what might bring me and others happiness. Instead I consider what is the right and dutiful thing to do – what follows the categorical imperative – and I pursue my good and aim at certain consequences insofar as it does not violate my prior commitment to do my duty.

I put aside partial thoughts about my advantage or happiness and start with an impartial, rational procedure. I ask what practical rule or "maxim" I propose to follow in a situation, such as "keep my promises unless they cause hardship to me." Then I ask whether I rationally and consistently can agree that such a rule should hold for all rational beings in similar circumstances. In other words, I try to make my maxim a universal ethical principle, as described earlier. This is a Kantian version of "what if everyone did that?" Kant believes that it is through this universalizing process that we see what our duty is and how that duty takes precedence over other considerations. For Kant, by following this rational procedure, I eliminate bias and partiality. I recognize the "supreme principle of morality" as the categorical imperative: "I ought to act in such a way that I could also will that my maxim should become a universal law."[47]

---

[45] *Ibid.*, 30.

[46] See Kant, *The Critique of Practical Reason*, Part I, Chapter II, Book I, 17–52; *The Metaphysics of Morals*, Part I on the doctrine of right, 9–42; and *Groundwork of the Metaphysics of Morals*, Preface and Chapters 1 and 2, 55–113. Ironically, the term "deontology" in ethics derives from the title of an article by Bentham, the arch-utilitarian, entitled "Deontology together with a Table of the Springs of Action and Article on Utilitarianism," which addressed matters of private, interpersonal morality. See Postema, "Bentham's Utilitarianism," 28.

[47] Kant, *Groundwork*, 15.

Imagine that I am hard pressed for money and I need a loan from Mary. I consider lying to her about my ability to repay the loan quickly. So my maxim is "when hard-pressed for money or other benefits, it is permissible to lie to those who might help me." For Kant, I cannot make this maxim a universal moral law. Therefore the maxim violates the categorical imperative. Such actions are wrong. Kant thinks that the categorical imperative can be formulated in various ways. Reflecting on the respect owed to human beings, he provides a second formulation: "So act that you use humanity, whether in your own person or in the person of another, always at the same time as an end, never merely as a means."[48] Kant's imperative to respect humans as "ends in themselves" is an important deontological restraint on the pursuit of the good.

There are many difficulties with Kantian ethics, such as how to interpret the categorical imperative and how to universalize maxims. Putting that aside, Kant's notion of unconditional duties and of not using humans as only a "means," combined with the impartial evaluation of rules, has made his ethics a cornerstone of modern deontological theories. One misunderstanding of Kant is so pervasive that it needs to be noted. Kant does not say that humans should act without any regard for consequences or for one's happiness. Like Rawls, his argument is for the *primacy* of honoring one's duties and principles of justice. If I have satisfied my duties, I am "entitled to look round for happiness." Man is not expected to "renounce his natural aim of attaining happiness" but he must "abstract from such considerations as soon as the imperative of duty supervenes" and to make sure his motive is not influenced by a desire for his happiness.[49] Your first ethical concern is to do your duty, to act virtuously, and then see about your happiness. Ethics evaluates how the pursuit of good should be restrained by principles of justice.

Virtue theories

Virtue theories are interested in the third theme of ethics. Virtue theories take as their fundamental concern the development of moral character, the nature of the virtues, and how a virtuous person would make

---

[48] *Ibid.*, 38.
[49] Kant, "On the Common Saying," 64–65.

practical decisions. Actions are correct or appropriate insofar as they flow from and are determined by someone of virtuous character. Virtues are strong and persistent dispositions, or character traits, to act in certain ways under certain conditions. The virtues include honesty, truthfulness, fairness, loyalty, benevolence, and compassion. Michael Slote says virtue ethics is about "what is noble or ignoble, admirable or deplorable, good or bad, rather than in terms of what is obligatory, permissible, or wrong." What is right or good is to be determined relative to the pursuit of virtue and excellence in life. Virtue ethics is "agent focused," not rule-focused. Combined with a focus on the inner life of agents, it is a distinct form of ethics.[50]

Virtue ethics is distinguished by its attitude towards consequential and deontological ethics. It is skeptical about deontological theories because it over-emphasizes rules. Rules have impact only if people are motivated to follow them. In addition, the model of ethical reasoning, as applying a principle to cases, is too formal. Practical reasoning is an informal matter of adjusting principles and maxims to complex situations for which there is no formula. One has to weigh and balance norms in a flexible manner, according to changing or uncertain conditions. Without a formula for decision-making, ethics needs the judgment of a virtuous person who has the right personality to discern the appropriate response to situations. It requires a virtuous person who is able to identify the wise, measured response that avoids extremes, and who has the character to carry out the measured response. On this view, wise discernment of the best course of action is not a matter of aggregating utility or of universalizing maxims. It is the all-too-human matter of making a judgment that flows from a person of reason and virtue.

Virtue theory, like deontological theory, worries about consequential thinking, since the pursuit of goods can compromise virtuous character. Yet virtue theory, unlike deontological theory, can be teleological. But it is a different form of teleological theory. Much of consequential theory aims at the promotion of different consequences that are only loosely related. One pursues certain goods as they become available. Or, consequentialists aim at one supreme but narrow good such as pleasure. Teleological virtue theory, drawing on ancient influences, seeks the good life as a

---

[50] Baron, Pettit, and Slote: *Three Methods of Ethics*, 177.

holistic ideal – the overall perfection of the human being through the development of key capacities and excellences. The goal is an ideal human life as a whole, not just the pursuit of good consequences. Virtues are not only instrumental. They are not just qualities of character that a person needs to flourish. A life of virtue is itself intrinsically good. Flourishing *is* a life devoted to excellence and virtue.

Ethical thought in this tradition derives from the virtue ethics of Plato and Aristotle. For Aristotle, the highest good for humans is a life of *eua-monia* (or "happiness") which consists of flourishing in many areas of life. Flourishing is achieved by developing and living according to virtues, especially those virtues that have to do with the use of man's distinctive rational capacities. To have a well-developed soul, one needs to acquire virtues such as courage, temperance in desires, proper ambition, patience, truthfulness, friendliness, modesty, and righteousness.[51] The virtues are "excellences," or the perfection of various attitudes, skills, and capacities. Happiness is not pleasure, honor, or wealth. Humans achieve happiness in the act of developing capacities proper to a rational, social being like man. Happiness is the virtuous activity of soul.[52] For Aristotle, people must not only possess these virtues of character but exercise them so as to act correctly. The ideal is the development of a wise and integrated virtuous character. Practical reason integrates and brings a unity to the virtues. The good life is the life of a person who has rationally ordered his soul so that the virtues of justice and wisdom are not overruled by unruly desires.

In many cases, to have a virtue is to have a disposition to act that lies between two extreme dispositions that are non-virtues. For example, the virtue (or disposition) of courage lies between rashness and cowardice; the virtue of modesty lies between shyness and shamelessness. This is Aristotle's famous "doctrine of the mean" as a way to determine how to act. Aiming at the mean is part of a virtuous human.

Aristotle's mean is misunderstood as saying that to act ethically one must in any situation pick a mid-way point between two extremes of action. A sort of lukewarm compromise. This is an over-simplification of Aristotle. First, the virtues of Aristotle are traits of character, not types of actions. Second, virtue is not always a matter of finding a "mid-point" between extremes. Some dispositions, actions, and feelings don't have a

---

[51] Aristotle, *Nicomachean Ethics*, 104.   [52] *Ibid.*, 75.

mean because they refer to "depravities," such as malice or envy. Some actions such as adultery or murder are evil in themselves. They do not have a mean.[53]

A formalistic view of the doctrine of the mean distorts Aristotle's view of practical reason. Aristotle viewed practical reasoning as a non-formal process of weighing factors under conditions of uncertainty. As we will see in Chapter 2, reasoning in media ethics has this Aristotelian character. Practical reasoning is a process that needs to be guided by a wise, knowledgeable, and virtuous person. The virtuous person is able to discern the proper response, whether it be by finding the mean or by reasoning about the wisest course of action. Aristotle warned that, in ethics, we cannot expect the type of precision or certainty that we find in scientific reasoning. No principle can anticipate every situation. No formal procedure for determining the right judgment exists. Therefore, ethical thinking is more an art or skill than a science. It requires people to develop a context-bound sensitivity to moral distinctions and nuances.

We come to the end of our review of applied theories. Before we end this chapter, we need to note a possibility that may have occurred to the reader. Perhaps the debate as to which theme in ethics is primary is based on a misunderstanding. Some philosophers, for example, have drawn a hard line between a wide "ethics" of the good life, and a narrow and abstract "morality" of rules about what to do. The legal theorist, Ronald Dworkin, expressed this distinction as such: "Ethics includes convictions about which kinds of lives are good or bad for a person to lead, and morality includes principles about how a person should treat other people."[54]

However, perhaps we shouldn't regard ethics as a battleground for theories about the good, the right, and the virtuous. Maybe we shouldn't divide the topic into ethics and morality, as Dworkin does. Instead, perhaps we should regard these theories as identifying three equally important aspects of ethical experience. Therefore, we should evaluate actions by combining criteria from the three themes. Emile Durkheim, for example, thought that ethics always presents us with a dual aspect of duties and ends desired. "Moral reality always presents simultaneously these two aspects which cannot be isolated empirically," he wrote. "No act has ever been informed out of duty alone; it has always been necessary for it to

---

[53] *Ibid.*, 102.   [54] Dworkin, *Sovereign Virtue*, 485n1.

appear in some respect as good."[55] To this duality, we might add virtue, to form a triadic relationship.

In the next chapter, I argue for a holistic approach to ethical reasoning that seeks to integrate our ethical life by weighing and balancing criteria from all three themes of ethics. No one concept or standard of the good, right, or virtuous can be the sole guide. Audi calls this view "pluralistic universalism," where the broadest moral principle would "require optimizing happiness so far as possible without producing injustice or curtailing freedom."[56] I prefer to speak, like Rawls, of pursuing the good within the bounds of the right (or justice), and where the good and the right conflict, the latter takes priority. This view also includes virtue: this fundamental principle of the good in the right is to be internalized so that it becomes part of our ethical character. We exhibit ethical character by being disposed to act in accord with this principle.

Conclusion

This chapter has explained the basic idea of ethics, why ethics is distinct, the role of theorizing, and the types of theories. Ethics was portrayed as a natural and necessary human activity of constructing, critiquing, and enforcing norms to guide conduct. Ethics was not identified with a static code of absolute principles defended dogmatically. Ethics is practical. It starts from the lived experience of ethical doubt and plurality and then seeks integration and theoretical understanding. Ethics is the evolving and dynamic activity by which humans attempt to live an ethically good life. Ethics is a distinct area of society because of its impartial approach to its serious and distinctive subject matter.

The chapter then examined why people theorize about their ethical experience, and argued that theorizing should make sense of our ethical experience. Ethical theorizing was divided into two types, philosophical and applied. Applied ethics was divided, in turn, into framework and

---

[55] Durkheim, *Moral Education*, 45.

[56] Audi, *Moral Value and Human Diversity*, 17. Prior to reading Audi, I had separately come to an ethical position that is close to what he calls pluralistic universalism. I had published my ideas in works such as "Philosophical Foundations for Global Journalism Ethics" before Audi's *Moral Value and Human Diversity*. Also, Audi has elaborated on the Kantian-Rawls idea of the good in right in his earlier books.

pragmatic forms. The chapter reviewed theories in philosophical ethics according to the three questions of what we say, how to know what we say, and why we speak ethically in the first place. Among the theories we inspected were descriptivism, intuitionism, and relativism. In applied ethics we examined consequential, deontological, and virtue ethics.

I spent considerable time on ethical theories because it is essential preparation for media ethics. For example, many journalists use utilitarian arguments to justify the violation of privacy of story subjects. Critics use deontological notions of rights and obligations to argue for journalistic restraint. Even intuitionism, relativism, and objectivity play a part in practical discussions of media ethics.

We have acquired the first half of our ethical framework, the basic concepts of ethics. We are ready to acquire the second part. In the next chapter, we learn how to apply these ideas to understanding media ethics. We will develop a model of reasoning for complex problems in media ethics.

Questions for discussion

1. Before reading this chapter, what was your idea of ethics? Was it similar to or different from the definition of ethics in this chapter? Has reading the chapter altered your views of ethics, or not?
2. If ethics is an "activity" and is not a set of unchanging principles, then what is the value of principles in ethics?
3. Do ethical principles change, and can they be "invented"? If not, why not? If so, give some examples of change. How much have your own ethical values changed over recent years, and why?
4. In any major book store, there are "self-help" books that tell people how to live, how to be happy, how to be successful, how to achieve peace of mind, and so on. Do you agree with the view in this chapter that many of these books are *not* books on ethics?
5. How do you distinguish ethics from custom, or law, or prudential reasoning?
6. Do you agree that ethics is more basic than law? Are there aspects of ethics that make it different but are not mentioned in this chapter?

7. What do you think people mean when they say something is good or right? Using the definitions provided, are most people that you know descriptivists or non-descriptivists? What are *you* doing when you make ethical judgments?

8. How valid is relativism in ethics? If you accepted ethical relativism, would it make any difference in your life or your ethics? Would it mean that you shouldn't criticize people with different ethical beliefs?

9. Both relativism and absolutism are attacked as being dangerous to society, or praised as essential to a good society. Which is the correct view?

10. How do you answer the "trolley" example? Would you flip the switch? If you would, does that make you a consequentialist?

2 Approaches to media ethics

Suppose you are a reporter in London, England. You are covering a hotly contested general election for Parliament. Someone tells you at a social event that there are allegations that John Jones, the Conservative Party leader, has sexually harassed women on his office staff. That "someone" is Jason, a senior election worker for the Labour Party. Jason mentions that a woman in Jones's office, Martha, has told fellow staffers about his actions. You contact Martha by telephone. She confirms she was sexually harassed by Jones. She hints there may be other victims, but refuses to go into detail. Martha says she is considering laying a complaint with the police. "Please don't use my name," she asks.

Sitting at your newsroom desk, you feel uncertain about your next step. Should you report this allegation immediately, using the information that you have? How would that affect the woman, the politician, the election? Should you use the woman's name? Why are you feeling uncomfortable when this is a *great* news story?

This case is an example of the difficult ethical situations that confront news media on a daily basis. To learn how to address these situations in a responsible manner, we need to show how our understanding of ethics applies to the domain of news media.

In Chapter 1, we discussed the nature of ethics and how we theorize about ethics, philosophically and practically. Chapter 1 provided the first part of our ethical framework – the basic concepts of ethics. We now apply this general orientation to media ethics. We develop the second part of our conceptual framework: how to approach media ethics and how to reason about issues. We will be working in the area of applied ethics, combining normative and framework ethics. The framework in question will be the general principles that appear in major codes of media ethics.

Let us summarize how Chapter 1 applies to the topic of this chapter, media ethics. First, we regard media ethics, like all of ethics, as a natural human activity. It is the construction and evaluation of norms to guide conduct in journalism, an important part of our society's public communication system. Media ethics is not identified with a static code of principles defended dogmatically. Media ethics is a form of normative reasoning that uses an evolving set of principles that seeks to adjust to the changing conditions and social roles of media. Media ethics is the dynamic activity by which journalists seek to develop the best possible ethical framework for their place and time. Media ethics is practical. Its dominant interest is in determining what journalists ought to do.

Second, the practice of media ethics should exhibit many of the distinctive features as ethics in general. Practitioners should adopt the impartial ethical stance toward issues and situations. They should deal with identifiable and serious ethical concerns – issues of what is good, right, and virtuous when communicating in the public interest. Like ethics in general, media ethics has three areas of concern: principles appropriate to journalism, their critical application to problems, and virtuous character so journalists are disposed to follow the principles.

Third, the origin of media ethics is the same as for all ethics – the lived experience of journalists and anyone who publicly communicates. Doubts about how to communicate arise in myriad situations, and values conflict. This gives rise to an attempt to integrate the plurality of journalism values, to fashion them into a coherent framework of principles. Integration leads, as elsewhere, to theorizing about media ethics, and the development of forms of reasoning appropriate to its domain.

We now need to go beyond these general ideas about ethics. We need to develop a more specific conception of how to analyze issues and problems specific to news media. This chapter provides a set of analytical tools over three sections: the first section explains the nature of media ethics and major approaches to media ethics. The second section puts forward a specific approach – the democratic approach and its framework of principles – that will guide discussions in this book. The third section provides a four-step model for applying this democratic framework to cases. The result is a comprehensive method for reasoning about media ethics.

Understanding media ethics

What is media ethics?

Where is media ethics on the "map" of ethics? Media ethics is a type of applied ethics. Media ethics is the analysis and application of ethical principles of relevance to a particular domain of society – the practice of news media. It studies the principles that should guide responsible conduct among journalists and regulate their interactions with other citizens.

Responsibility

Media ethics is concerned both with advancing free and independent media while stressing responsible use of that freedom. The idea of media responsibility derives from notions of responsibility that we use to evaluate people and their actions in everyday life. To be responsible means to be concerned with the consequences of one's actions on others. For instance, John the dentist acts responsibly when he makes sure his patients are informed about their dental procedures, makes sure his dental equipment is clean and in good working order, and when he shows up for work sober and able to perform his functions. If things go wrong, he is accountable. He is willing to admit errors, explain mistakes, make reparations, and improve his procedures. John takes his duties to others seriously. He is acutely aware of the potential impact of his actions.

In contrast, Frank is an irresponsible parent if he ignores the health and everyday needs of his wife and children so as to enjoy himself at the pub, to gamble at the casino, and to live a life of pleasure seeking. Frank does not act with due care. He ignores his duties. He dismisses friends' attempts to make him consider the consequences of his actions.

To summarize, persons are responsible when they are willing to guide and restrain their freedom to act according to the impact of their actions on others. What those responsibilities are depends on a person's place in society, such as being a parent, teacher, or airline pilot. Responsible persons are neither reckless nor selfish. They worry about the consequences of their actions and they attempt to minimize or avoid harm to others. Responsible persons balance their rights and freedoms with their responsibilities. They are accountable for their actions, and seek to repair damages. To act responsibly is to restrain one's freedom by ethical considerations about the rights, duties, and freedoms of others. The impulse to be responsible is an expression of the desire to act ethically – to live in right relations with others.

Affirming responsibility does not eliminate ethical perplexities. Reasonable people can disagree on what responsibility means for a given profession or for a person in a specific situation. How much information should John the dentist provide to ensure that patients give their informed consent to his procedures? How much fog must shroud an airport before we call a pilot's decision to land "irresponsible"? Is a journalist irresponsible if she publishes secret military documents on how her country is carrying out a war? Despite these difficulties, the idea of responsible action remains valid as an ideal for evaluating actions and articulating duties.

When we describe responsible media, we apply the same idea of responsible action. The media is responsible to the degree that journalists and news outlets are willing to restrain their freedom according to the impact of their actions on others. Responsible media are neither reckless nor egotistical. They foresee the consequences of their actions and attempt to minimize harm. Responsible journalists do not simply insist on their freedom to publish. They balance their right to publish with their responsibilities. Like responsible persons, responsible journalists are accountable for their actions. They admit errors, explain mistakes, improve editorial procedures and seek to repair damages. To act responsibly in media is to restrain one's freedom by ethical considerations about the rights, duties, and freedoms of others.

The first step towards responsible media is for journalists to explicitly acknowledge that they have responsibilities. This may sound like a truism. But the reality is that some journalists think talk of responsible reporting is diametrically at odds with a free press, and they place greater value on the latter. Therefore, responsible media is impossible if journalists sarcastically dismiss media ethics as an oxymoron. For a journalist to deny that they have ethical responsibilities is as reckless as a dentist denying that he has ethical responsibilities to his patient. Also, responsible media are impossible if journalists regard media ethics as entirely subjective. On this view, each journalist follows their own idiosyncratic set of norms. On this view, there is no higher ground by which to evaluate the actions of journalists. To deny that journalism has an ethics or to declare it entirely subjective amounts to the same thing, practically: both views dodge the demands of ethics. If media ethics is entirely subjective then there is no professional ethics. There is no set of principles that apply across a group of practitioners. "To each his own" is the attitude. If this is so, why bother with serious discussions about what the news media should do? When members of the public are outraged by the irresponsible actions of a journalist, the latter can simply reply: "but I am only following my own ethics." Imagine a dentist who, when criticized for irresponsible practices, replies that while he has responsibilities, his ethics is entirely subjective and up to him. He is only following his own norms. If this response is implausible for dentists, why is it not implausible for news media?

If journalists routinely cause harm, and if journalists have identifiable social roles, then the ethics of journalism cannot be left to each individual journalist or newsroom. The public can reasonably expect that journalists as a group follow basic principles and acknowledge certain responsibilities.

How is media ethics different?

So far, we have stressed the continuities between ethics in general and media ethics. What is different about media ethics? One difference is that media ethics applies ethical thinking to a set of issues and concerns distinctive of the practice of news media, such as protecting the anonymity of a source for a news story, or covering hostage situations "live" without provoking the hostage takers. Also, media ethics pays special attention to journalists' relationships with sources, the conflict between reporting the truth and causing harm to story subjects, and what objectivity means in a news report. These specific problems, raised by the nature of news reporting, give rise to distinctive practices, rules, and interpretations of ethical principles.

In addition, media ethics may interpret general moral principles differently than other professionals. Media ethics shares with ethics such general principles as truth-telling and promise-keeping. Yet journalists may apply these ethical principles differently. For example, investigative reporters argue that there are situations where a journalist may deceive someone or tell a lie to verify a story, such as the abuse of elderly people in a nursing home. The journalistic tolerance for deception is greater than we find in many other professions. Take another example. We don't usually demand that people go to jail to keep their promises. Yet many journalists believe they have a duty to protect the identity of a source that has been promised anonymity, even if it means time in jail.

Media ethics also differs from ethics in general with respect to moral foundations. In Chapter 1, we said that ethics is the ground for values and principles in other normative areas of society, such as law. The ultimate principles of ethics are just that – ultimate. They are not justified by more basic principles. The same does not hold of basic values in media ethics, such as news objectivity, earning the trust of sources, reporting independently. While these journalistic principles are important they are ultimately justified by more fundamental principles that are to be found in normative ethics and other areas, such as political philosophy. For example, the justification of a free press often depends on an appeal to the democratic (and political) ideal of a self-governing citizenship. Or, to take another example, journalistic arguments that justify deceiving a source or publishing confidential government documents are often based on some normative theory, such as some version of utilitarianism. In Chapter 3, we will show in detail how a major normative theory about journalism – the ideal of democratic journalism – is based on more basic social and political principles. In Chapter 5, the principle of harm in media ethics will be traced back to the fundamental principle of normative ethics of avoiding unjustifiable harm in any walk of life. Ultimately, our philosophy of journalism – including our ethical approach to journalism – will appeal to some broader social and political conception of the good life and the good society.

This justificatory relationship between media ethics and ethics means that we can expect appeals to general ethical values, from liberty and equality to social justice, to appear as premises in our ethical reasoning in media ethics. In media ethics, we are always doing two things, simultaneously – checking our use of a framework for media ethics, say our code of journalism ethics, while also checking on how that framework is supported by our more basic ethical commitments about life in general. In this way, the ideas of ethical writers, from Plato and Kant to Habermas, may appear in our discussion.

Another consequence of this justificatory relationship is that what one regards as a question of journalism ethics is influenced by one's ethical and political philosophy. It is commonly said that a question about journalism is an *ethical* question, as opposed to a question of prudence, custom, or law, if it evaluates conduct in light of the fundamental public purposes and social responsibilities of journalism. But journalists in different cultures may ascribe different "fundamental public purposes" to news media.

Problem areas

Media ethics addresses issues at two levels, the micro and the macro. It considers micro problems of what individual journalists should do in specific situations, and macro problems of what news media should do, given their role in society. The issues of media ethics include: the limits of free speech; accuracy and bias; fairness; respect for privacy; the use of graphic images; avoiding conflicts of interest; the use of anonymous sources; and the representation of minorities and other cultures. Some typical questions of media ethics are: how far should journalists go to protect the anonymity of a source from the courts or police? How graphic should images of a brutal civil war in Africa be? When should I report damaging facts about the personal life of a religious or political leader? Can journalists ever break the law to get a story? What are the social and ethical purposes of journalism?

Typical issues

A major task of journalism ethics is to determine how existing norms apply to the main ethical issues of the day. Some current problem areas are:

- *Accuracy and verification*: how much verification and context is required to publish a story? How much editing and "gate-keeping" is necessary?
- *Independence and allegiances*: how can journalists be independent but maintain ethical relations with their employers, editors, advertisers, sources, the police, and the public? When is a journalist too close to a source, or in a conflict of interest?
- *Deception and fabrication*: should journalists misrepresent themselves or use recording technology, such as hidden cameras, to get a story? Should literary journalists invent dialogue or create composite "characters"?

- *Graphic images and image manipulation*: when should journalists publish graphic or gruesome images? When do published images constitute sensationalism or exploitation? When and how should images be altered?
- *Sources and confidentiality*: should journalists promise confidentiality to sources? How far does that protection extend? Should journalists go "off the record"?
- *Special situations*: how should journalists report hostage-takings, major breaking news, suicide attempts, and other events where coverage could exacerbate the problem? When should journalists violate privacy?
- *Ethics across media types*: do the norms of mainstream print and broadcast journalism apply to journalism on the Internet? To citizen journalists?

Approaches to media ethics

Five historical stages

Approaches to media ethics have developed over the history of modern journalism. Therefore, before we identify the major approaches, we need to gain an overview of the major milestones of media ethics. The history of media ethics can be divided into five stages (or revolutions).

Media ethics can be traced back to the beginning of modern journalism in Europe during the seventeenth century. The first stage was the invention of an ethical discourse for journalism as it emerged in Western Europe during the sixteenth and seventeenth centuries. Gutenberg's press in the mid-fifteenth century gave birth to printer-editors who created a periodic news press of "newssheets" and "newsbooks." Despite the primitive nature of their newsgathering, and the partisan nature of their times, editors assured readers that they printed the impartial truth based on "matters of fact." The approach to journalism at this time was decidedly authoritarian, and reflected the hierarchical and undemocratic nature of early modern society. The news press operated under strict state control, through censorship and state licensing of the press, and harsh measures against illegal presses or offending content. Monarchs believed that the decision as to who printed news and what was printed was a royal prerogative. All publications had to serve the state, not question it.

The second stage of media ethics arrived in the eighteenth century, particularly in England as press controls weakened. Journalists espoused a "public ethic" which served as a creed for the growing newspaper press of the Enlightenment public sphere. This ethic anticipated the liberal approach. Journalists claimed to be tribunes of the public, protecting their liberty against the government. They advocated reform in the public's name and eventually the press played major roles in the American and French Revolutions. By the end of the eighteenth century, the press was a socially recognized institution, a power to be praised or feared, with guarantees of freedom in the post-revolution constitutions of the USA and France. This public ethic was the basis for the idea of a fourth estate – the press as one of the governing institutions of society.[1]

The third stage was the evolution of the public ethic, and its idea of a fourth estate, into an explicit liberal theory of the press, during the nineteenth century. Liberal theory began with the premise that a free and independent press was necessary for the protection of the liberties of the public and the promotion of liberal reform. The fourth stage was the simultaneous development *and* criticism of this liberal doctrine across the twentieth century. Both the development and the criticism were responses to deficiencies in the liberal model. The "developers" were journalists and ethicists who constructed a professional ethics of objective journalism, bolstered by social responsibility theory. Objectivism sought to use adherence to fact and impartiality towards political parties to restrain a free press that was increasingly sensational (or "yellow") and dominated by business interests.[2] The "critics" were journalists who rejected the restraints of objective professional reporting and practiced more interpretive, partial forms of journalism such as investigative reporting and activist (or advocacy) journalism.

By the late 1900s, the liberal and objective professional model was under attack from many sources as journalism entered its fifth stage, a stage of "mixed media." Not only were increasing numbers of non-professional citizen journalists and bloggers engaging in journalism, but these communicators used interactive multi-media that challenged the ethical norms of

---

[1] Ward, *Invention of Journalism Ethics*, 89–173.
[2] See Baldasty, *The Commercialization of the News in the Nineteenth Century*, and Campbell, *Yellow Journalism*.

cautious verification and gate-keeping. As a result, journalism ethics was (and continues to be) fraught with disagreement on the most basic notions of what journalism is and what journalists are for.

Main approaches

With these stages in mind, we can better appreciate the main ethical approaches that developed across history and remain a force in media ethics today. They were constructed as journalism passed from one era to another, and as journalism came to be embedded in new forms of societies organized around different political principles. These approaches remain influential today in the practice of media, in disputes over regulation of media, and in influencing people's approaches to media issues. The main ideas of these approaches are embedded in theories about the role of the press in different countries.[3]

Authoritarian-utopian

The first "theory" of the press and its duties was the authoritarian view. On this view, the press's social duty is to serve existing authority, be it a king, political regime, or party. Today, this approach continues to exist in many countries in various forms. The authoritarian approach is popular with military dictators and repressive regimes. But the authoritarian premise – that the press serves the state and its programs – is also prominent in utopian attempts to engineer the perfect society. Reaching that future society is so important that the press must be enlisted as a tool for moving society towards that goal. This is the approach that was used by fascist regimes in the previous century and still exists in communist states such as China, and theocracies such as Iran. The purpose of the press in a communist society is to support the communist party as the agent that, ideally, moves society toward a perfect classless society and protects society from counter-revolutionary forces. For all of these varieties of authoritarianism, the freedom of the press can be legitimately limited and controlled to a significant degree.

---

[3] See Siebert *et al.*, *Four Theories of the Press.*

Classical liberalism

The liberal approach refers to a number of liberal-minded approaches to understanding media, in contrast to non-liberal tendencies. Classical liberalism is distinguished by the emphasis that it places on the value of a free and critical press.

Classical liberal press ideas, as espoused from John Milton and David Hume to J. S. Mill and Thomas Paine, were part of liberalism as a political reform movement for the surging middle classes. Liberalism sought the expansion of individual liberties and an end to the privileges of birth and religion that marked non-liberal, hierarchical society. In economics, liberalism supported laissez-faire attitudes; in press theory it supported a free marketplace of ideas. Mill's *On Liberty* appealed to the individual *and* social benefits of freedom, within specified limits. This ascendant liberalism supplied the ethical ideology for both the elite liberal papers, such as *The Times* of London, and the egalitarian popular press, from the penny press to the mass commercial press of the late 1800s. For liberal theory, journalists should constitute an independent press that informs citizens and acts as a watchdog on government and abuses of power. Today, the liberal approach continues to be used to justify arguments for a free press against media restrictions, such as censorship of offensive views, and the abuse of libel laws to curtail publication.

An extreme form of liberalism is a *libertarian* approach, an approach that gained strength in the second half of the nineteenth century. The *libertarian* approach makes free expression and an unfettered press the primary value, trumping at every turn other values that attempt to restrain free expression, such as a concern for fairness or careful representation. This was not the view of Mill in *On Liberty*, although his position is often mistakenly thought to be libertarian. For the libertarian view, the value of a maximally free press, over the long run, for individual liberty and a free society, outweigh any attempts, legal or ethical, to restrict the exercise of that freedom. Hence, the libertarian view is not especially interested in talk of a code of ethics that specifies restraining duties and norms that a free press must honor. In fact, some libertarians may be hostile to the whole concept of media ethics as imposing responsibilities on journalists.

Classical liberal theory, although it originated in the nineteenth century, continues to underpin current discussions about media ethics, if only to act as a theory to be revised or criticized.

Responses to liberalism

A number of major approaches can be characterized as attempts to respond to liberalism. These alternate approaches are liberal in spirit. They support a free press, but they also believe classical liberalism is not an adequate philosophy of responsible journalism. Therefore, the approaches respond to perceived weaknesses in liberalism through (a) criticism and reform of liberal theory, and (b) elaborating upon values not stressed by liberalism. In particular, these approaches respond to what they see as an excessive individualism in liberal press theory and a lack of emphasis on the responsible use of the freedom to publish. They are especially critical of the libertarian version of liberal press theory.

These approaches include (1) a professional objective approach, or "objectivism," (2) social responsibility theory, (3) interpretationism, (4) advocational journalism, and (5) an ethics of community and care applied to media.[4]

Let's begin with (1) and (2). Historically, objectivism and social responsibility theory were twentieth-century responses to a wide-spread disillusionment with the liberal hope of the nineteenth century that an unregulated press would be a responsible educator of citizens on matters of public interest – a hope still nurtured by libertarian views. That hope flagged in the late 1800s and early 1900s as a mass commercial press turned into a business of news directed by press barons. One response was to develop the ideal of an objective news press, with codes of ethics and other professional features. The liberal idea of a social contract was used to argue that society allowed professional journalists to report freely in return for responsible coverage of essential public issues.

From the early 1900s to the middle of the twentieth century, objectivity was a dominant ethical ideal (and approach) for most mainstream newspapers in the United States, Canada, and beyond. Objectivity was less popular in Europe. By the 1920s, major journalism associations in the United States had adopted formal codes that called for objectivity in reporting, independence from government and business influence, and a strict distinction between news and opinion. The result was an

---

[4] There are many ways to divide the field of normative journalism ethics. I divide the field into liberal, socially responsible, interpretative, advocational, and "care" approaches because they identify fundamental ideas present in all major forms of contemporary journalism.

elaborate set of newsroom rules to ensure that journalists reported "just the facts."[5]

Another liberal response was social responsibility theory developed by scholars and journalists in the United States.[6] While liberal theory recognized the idea of press responsibility, social responsibility theory (SR theory) argued that the press was neglecting its duties to inform the public in a responsible manner. In the United States, the Hutchins Commission into the Freedom of the Press in the late 1940s gave SR theory a clear and popular formulation.[7] In its report, *A Free and Responsible Press*, the commission stressed that the main functions of the press was to provide "a truthful, comprehensive, and intelligent account" of news and events and "a forum for the exchange of comment and criticism." The press should provide a "representative picture of the constituent groups in society," assist in the "presentation and clarification of the goals and values of society," and "provide full access to the day's intelligence." If journalistic self-regulation failed, social responsibility proponents warned that government regulators might intervene. Today, SR theory has "won global recognition over the last 50 years," such as in European public broadcasting and as far afield as Japan.[8] Moreover, the theory continues to provide a basic vocabulary for new ethical approaches, such as feminist and communitarian theories, while providing standards by which press councils and the public can evaluate media performance.

While objectivity and SR theory oppose libertarian views, another two approaches are distinct in rejecting objectivity as a guiding principle of a liberal press. These two approaches are *interpretationism* and *advocational journalism*. Both views embrace the liberal ideal of a free press but they do not stress the value of a neutral or objective journalism reporting only the facts. Journalists should be interpreters of complex events and advocates of important causes. Interpretationism believes that the primary role of the liberal journalist is to explain the significance of events

---

[5] See Mindich, *Just the Facts*.

[6] Peterson, "The Social Responsibility Theory of the Press".

[7] The core ideas of social responsibility theory were discussed years in advance of the Hutchins Commission. See Cronin & McPherson, "Reaching for Professionalism and Respectability."

[8] Christians and Nordenstreng, "Social Responsibility Theory Worldwide", 4. See also Tsukamoto, "Social responsibility theory."

while the tradition of activist journalism seeks the primary role as one of reforming society. Both interpretive and activist traditions believe that journalists have a duty to be more than stenographers of fact and official comment.

Journalists have long interpreted events. But it was only at the start of the 1900s that the importance of interpretation in journalism was elaborated into an explicit approach to reporting that justified going beyond the facts. Interpretive journalism was put forward as an alternative to the ideal of objective reporting. One motivation for developing interpretationism was the emergence in the early 1900s of an interpretive journalism that was not strongly ideological. Interpretive reporters were not mouthpieces for political parties. Their task was to rationally and independently explain an increasingly complex world. For instance, Henry Luce's interpretive journalism was the model for *Time* magazine in the 1920s. In the 1930s and beyond, scholars, foreign reporters, and journalism associations acknowledged the need to supplement objective reporting with an informed interpretation of world events, wars, and economic disasters like the Great Depression. Newspapers in the 1930s and 1940s introduced weekend interpretations of the past week's events, beat reporters and interpretive columnists with by-lines. This tradition of interpretive journalism would gather strength in the second half of the twentieth century in the hands of broadcast journalists, literary journalists and, then, online journalists.

Meanwhile, from the 1960s onward, advocational theories of journalism gained ascendency. Advocational journalists served the public by challenging the status quo, opposing wars, and promoting social causes. Advocational journalists sought to organize public opinion against government and private sector misconduct and unjust policies. Advocational journalists were anticipated by the reform journalists of the late eighteenth century in England, and by the revolutionary journalists in the USA and France. Advocational journalists also share many values with the muckraking magazine journalists in the USA during the first two decades of the 1900s. A more moderate form of advocational journalism entered the public sphere in the 1990s. American journalists, fearing that democracy was being ill-served by a cynical but "objective" press, called for a moderate reform journalism that they named "civic journalism." Civic journalism called on journalists to abandon neutrality. They should act as a catalyst for civic engagement and reform, and create a more participatory democracy.[9]

Today, many Western journalists see themselves as some combination of informer and interpreter. A smaller number also see themselves as an advocate – not so much an advocate for rich lobby interests but for causes such as social justice, or giving a voice to the powerless. Traditional values, such as factual accuracy, are not completely jettisoned. Even the most vocal muckraker or activist journalist insists that their reports are factually accurate, although they reject neutrality.[10] Facts are embedded in interpretive narratives that draw conclusions.

The fifth approach was the application of communitarian ethics[11] and a feminist ethics of care to the practices of journalism.[12] Both approaches provide criticism of, and an alternative to, liberal theory. Both approaches emphasize the restraining principles of minimizing harm and being accountable while de-emphasizing the proactive principles. The liberal perspective stresses individual freedoms and rights; the communitarian and care perspectives stresses the impact of journalism on communal values and caring relationships.

Communitarianism in journalism ethics reflects a revival in communitarian ethical, legal, and political theory over several decades.[13] Communitarians stress the communal good and the social nature of humans. They argue that no ethical theory can be neutral among different views of the good. Journalists should join other citizens in supporting their community's commitment to substantive values and conceptions of the good life. Communitarian media ethicists, such as Clifford Christians, use the primacy of "humans-in-relation" to argue that the main function of the press is not a "thin" liberal informing of citizens about facts and events. The main function is the provision of a rich, interpretive dialogue with and among citizens that aims at "civic transformation."[14]

[9] See Rosen, *Getting the Connections Right.*
[10] See Miraldi, *Muckraking and Objectivity.*
[11] See Christians, *et al., Good News.*
[12] See Koehn, *Rethinking Feminist Ethics.*
[13] See Seters, *Communitarianism in Law and Society.*
[14] Christians, "The Case for Communitarian Ethics," 65–66.

The communitarian approach is close in spirit to theories of care, developed by feminists and other scholars.[15] The promotion of caring human relationships as an essential part of human flourishing is a primary principle. Feminists promoted an ethics of care "founded on notions of community rather than in the rights-based tradition."[16] An ethics of care attempts to restrain a news media that is often insensitive to story subjects and sources. As Jay Black has written, feminist scholars have argued that by paying attention to the tenets of an ethics of care, "a fuller, richer media system may emerge, that can and will consider such concepts as compassion, subjectivity, and need."[17]

Let's summarize the ethical view embedded in each of these approaches:

Authoritarianism-utopian: the ethical aim of journalism is to support and promote the authorities in power and their programs, whether the aim of authority is utopian or more modest. A maximally free press playing a watchdog role for open democracy is not as primary as social solidarity, political stability, restricted dissent, and the people's belief in their leaders.

Liberal: the ethical aim of journalism is to provide the information and views necessary for a free and self-governing liberal society. Freedom of speech is more important than not embarrassing authority.

Objectivity-social responsibility: the ethical aim of journalism is the same as liberal theory – to be free so that journalists can inform citizens and act as a watchdog on government. However, in carrying out this role, the freedom to publish should be restrained by norms of objectivity and the social responsibilities of responsible journalism.

Interpretive and *advocational*: the ethical aim of journalism is not simply to inform or to report facts but also to interpret the world for citizens

---

[15] Interest in theories of care is shown by the fact that in 2000, a group of ethicists, philosophers, and others gathered for a colloquium at the University of Oregon on "Caring and the Media." The papers formed a special edition of the *Journal of Mass Media Ethics* (Black, "Foreword").

[16] Patterson and Wilkins, *Media Ethics: Issues and Cases*, 292.

[17] Black, "Foreword," 99.

and/or to advocate for reforms and social causes. The interpretive and advocacy approach is skeptical about impartiality, neutrality, and objectivity.

Care-communitarian: like social responsibility theory, the care-communitarian approach wants journalists to be free but to use that freedom responsibly. Here, "responsibly" refers to specific aims such as helping to develop caring human relations and communities and fairly representing minorities and other disadvantaged groups.

Essentials for ethical reasoning

Developing the approaches to media ethics examined in the previous section is part of framework ethics. The approaches seek to articulate the aims and basic values of good journalism. These approaches can then be developed in two ways. We can explore how these basic values are related to more general normative theories of ethics such as utilitarianism, deontic theories, virtue theories, and so on. Also, we can use an approach both to develop codes of media ethics and to critique existing codes. At this point, we enter the sphere of framework ethics. We explicitly study and apply frameworks of principles for media practice. The rest of this chapter examines these frameworks and puts forward one specific framework, the framework of democratic journalism. In addition, it provides a four-step model to apply the framework to situations. In short, we are going to "do" media ethics.

Three elements needed

To do media ethics systematically, we need to be clear on three things: the aims and functions of journalism; a framework of basic principles whose observance supports those aims; and a method (or "model") for applying these aims and principles to concrete situations and issues. Together, the three elements amount to a framework.

This three-element framework won't provide automatic answers to practical questions and it is always possible to mis-apply one's own principles. One's framework may be flawed. Nevertheless, a framework is a necessary condition for solid reasoning.

Kinds of premises

The goal of ethical reasoning is to arrive at a practical normative conclusion such as "ethically, I (or a journalist, or newsroom) ought to do *x* or *y* in situation *z*," or "I should inform my readers that I was paid by an advertiser to write a review of their product." More generally, we may conclude that "journalists should always do *x* or *y*, as a matter of good ethical conduct." In the latter statement, "*x*" and "*y*" refer to kinds of actions, such as "journalists should always disclose to their readers any money they receive from advertisers," or "journalists should never accept money from advertisers when reviewing their products."

But how do we get to such conclusions?

We argue from a variety of premises. First, there are empirical premises: we argue from the facts. Not all of the facts of a case. We use the most important and relevant facts from the perspective of ethics. Despite a widespread mistaken view that ethics is just about opinion, a good ethical argument depends on a careful grasp of the central facts. Consider the case where a female TV reporter does an extremely positive review of a city's police chief. Later, a newspaper reports that the reporter had a sexual relationship with the chief and the article suggests that this amounted to improper journalistic behavior – promoting a person with whom one has a close relationship. It is vital to drawing any reliable ethical conclusions that it *is* a fact that the sexual relationship occurred. Other facts are important also, such as when the relationship occurred – before or after her story was broadcast?

Reasoning in media ethics also contains ethical premises that identify the ethical issues at stake and what principles may be violated. To return to the police chief example, suppose we conclude that the reporter should not have written her glowing story; or, more generally, she should not have reported on the police chief at all, if she was becoming involved with him. What reasons can we give for these conclusions? We may use as a premise the ethical principle of editorial independence. This means that reporters should not report on people with whom they have close relations since this creates a conflict of interest. Such conflicts may impair a reporter's ability to report independently and objectively. A sexual relationship is one such conflict of interest. We might also add as a premise the principle of transparency. Journalists have a duty to be transparent to the public whether or not they have a close relationship – sexual, financial, or otherwise – with the subjects of their stories.

Someone could ask us why independence and transparency are so important that we call them principles. The reply might be: independence and transparency are necessary to ensure that reporters provide the public with objective and unbiased reports, and such reports are crucial for a well-informed citizenry in a democracy. Here, we add to our premises an even more general principle concerning the role of journalism in society; or, to put it another way, we make this assumption explicit. Finally, reasoning in media ethics usually contains some implicit (or explicit) premises about which principles are most important when values conflict. Therefore, our reasoning will usually be based on premises which hold that principle x trumps principle y in general or in certain types of situations. For example, the freedom of the reporter to have a sexual affair with the chief is trumped by the professional principle that such conflicts will be avoided so long as the reporter wishes to report on the area in question.

Or consider a case where my investigations unearth damaging facts about corruption among leaders of a native tribe. One could argue that the principle (and duty) to expose wrong-doing to the public trumps the harm such reporting will do to the public image of the tribe and its leaders.

To do media ethics we need, at the least, the identification of and evaluation of the facts of the case and their relevance to the ethical debate, plus the ability to identify the main ethical issues. Also, we need to be able to construct arguments for certain conclusions that bring together a number of premises – empirical and ethical premises of varying levels of generality. Among the ethical premises, we can identify at least four kinds: concrete rules about journalistic procedures such as don't report on groups of which you are a member; general principles such as independence; principles that tell you how to balance values when they conflict; and premises about the functions of journalism in society. Two skills are involved: the ability to identify and analyze the basic facts and basic ethical issues of situations; and an ability to then construct an argument, combining these facts and principles, that ends in a conclusion about correct conduct.

Importance of aims

This is the general structure of ethical arguments and reasoning. Now, let us look at an essential component: a clear conception of the ethical aims of journalism. Then we can move on to consider the two other components, principles and a method of application.

"Aim" includes the ultimate social purposes, goals, and functions of journalism, according to one's philosophy of journalism. We need a clear conception of journalism's aims so that the actions of responsible journalists have a target to shoot at; we can evaluate actions insofar as they bring us closer to our aims. Aims are also useful in evaluating our principles, methods, and even entire codes of ethics.

When engaged in ethical reasoning about media, we should ask: does the reasoning promote our overall ethical goals for news media and journalism? What are those goals? We should also ask: do our principles and standards, which operate as premises in our arguments, promote our aims, in general and in specific circumstances? For example, much of the current debate over the value of objectivity as a method in journalism is an argument over whether adopting objectivity promotes the aims of democratic journalism.

We draw the aims of journalism from within and without the practice of journalism. Some of our aims may be relatively narrow and contained within the profession of journalism. For example, a news broadcaster may aim to produce an accurate set of reports for the nightly news as part of a commitment to competent professional practice. Often, the aims are supplemented by aims from ethics, political philosophy, and almost any domain of life. Recall that earlier we said media ethics was based on principles of ethical and political philosophy. This also applies to aims. Journalists may take the ultimate aims of journalism to be the promotion of democracy worldwide, the flourishing of their country and its citizens, and so on. Philosophy and ethics provide many possible aims for journalists. The candidates include the perfection of human nature, human flourishing, freedom, happiness, a just society, and various forms of utopian society.

If we review our overview of the approaches to media ethics, we see that the history of journalism has put forward many types of aims. They can be summarized in one sentence: to report and disseminate; to interpret; to act as watchdog; to advocate for reform or revolution; to be an activist for certain causes; to educate the public and guide public opinion; to serve the public, the party, or the state. These ends form a continuum from factual reporting and interpretive writing to social activism.

If people disagree on journalism's primary aims and roles, they will likely differ on the value of certain types of journalism. For example, if journalism's primary role is thought to be supporting the existing social order, government policies, and public authorities, as is often the case in non-democratic countries, then little emphasis will be placed on a critical press that embarrasses authority, questions policies, and generates dissent and debate. However, if journalism's role is thought to be that of helping citizens govern themselves and hold authorities to account, there will be strong emphasis on an independent press that facilitates debate, that challenges, that embarrasses.

Principles: a sample code

We have described the structure of ethical reasoning in media ethics by considering the kinds of premises used, and the important role of aims. But what about the second element of doing media ethics – the principles? What sorts of principles should make up the framework of media ethics? Answering this question is made difficult by the fact that the content of our ethical system depends on our varying approaches to journalism. So one cannot put forward one set of principles that all journalists and citizens agree upon. However we can put forward the sorts of principles that regularly appear in major codes of ethics in Western news media. These are the principles of journalism found in developed liberal democracies, although the principles also occur in codes beyond the West.

The framework for Western codes consists of two types of principle – what I call "proactive" and "restraining" principles. To use the code in a situation requires that we balance the proactive and restraining principles. Proactive principles assert that journalists do not simply have freedom to publish. They also have a *duty* to publish the most accurate and comprehensive truth on matters of public interest, and to report independently without fear or favor. Principles of free and independent news-gathering urge the journalist to be proactive and courageous in collecting news and investigating stories. Such reporting supports the role of journalists to act in the public interest and as a watchdog on abuse of power.

Meanwhile, restraining principles call on journalists to use this freedom to publish, and to seek truth independently, in a responsible manner. Restraining principles include the duty to minimize harm to vulnerable subjects of stories, such as children or traumatized persons, and the duty to be accountable to the public for editorial decisions.

A good example of such a code is the influential code of the Society of Professional Journalists (SPJ) in the United States (www.spj.org). The SPJ Code of Ethics is voluntarily embraced by thousands of journalists, regardless of place or media platform. It is widely used in newsrooms and classrooms as a guide for ethical behavior. The code is intended not as a set of absolute rules to be applied in exactly the same way in every situation. It is intended as a resource to be consulted when one attempts to make an ethical decision on how to act. The present version of the code was adopted by the 1996 SPJ National Convention, after months of study and debate among the Society's members.

The SPJ code has two proactive principles, "seek truth and report it" and "act independently." There are two restraining principles: "minimize harm" and "be accountable." These are the most general principles possible, and they will have to be interpreted and applied to cases, under the objective stance.

The code then places specific standards and norms under four principles seek truth and report it, act independently, minimize harm, and be accountable.

Since we will be referring to these principles and norms throughout the rest of the book, the code is reproduced below:

Code of Ethics: Society of Professional Journalists

Preamble
Members of the Society of Professional Journalists believe that public enlightenment is the forerunner of justice and the foundation of democracy. The duty of the journalist is to further those ends by seeking truth and providing a fair and comprehensive account of events and issues. Conscientious journalists from all media and specialties strive to serve the public with thoroughness and honesty. Professional integrity is the cornerstone of a journalist's credibility.

Members of the Society share a dedication to ethical behavior and adopt this code to declare the Society's principles and standards of practice.

Seek Truth and Report It
Journalists should be honest, fair and courageous in gathering, reporting and interpreting information. Journalists should:

- Test the accuracy of information from all sources and exercise care to avoid inadvertent error. Deliberate distortion is never permissible.
- Diligently seek out subjects of news stories to give them the opportunity to respond to allegations of wrongdoing.
- Identify sources whenever feasible. The public is entitled to as much information as possible on sources' reliability.
- Always question sources' motives before promising anonymity. Clarify conditions attached to any promise made in exchange for information.
- Keep promises.
- Make certain that headlines, news teases and promotional material, photos, video, audio, graphics, sound bites and quotations do not misrepresent. They should not oversimplify or highlight incidents out of context.
- Never distort the content of news photos or video. Image enhancement for technical clarity is always permissible. Label montages and photo illustrations.
- Avoid misleading re-enactments or staged news events. If re-enactment is necessary to tell a story, label it.
- Avoid undercover or other surreptitious methods of gathering information except when traditional open methods will not yield information vital to the public.
- Use of such methods should be explained as part of the story.
- Never plagiarize.
- Tell the story of the diversity and magnitude of the human experience boldly, even when it is unpopular to do so.
- Examine their own cultural values and avoid imposing those values on others.
- Avoid stereotyping by race, gender, age, religion, ethnicity, geography, sexual orientation, disability, physical appearance or social status.
- Support the open exchange of views, even views they find repugnant.
- Give voice to the voiceless; official and unofficial sources of information can be equally valid.
- Distinguish between advocacy and news reporting. Analysis and commentary should be labeled and not misrepresent fact or context.
- Distinguish news from advertising and shun hybrids that blur the lines between the two.
- Recognize a special obligation to ensure that the public's business is conducted in the open and that government records are open to inspection.

Minimize Harm

Ethical journalists treat sources, subjects and colleagues as human beings deserving of respect. Journalists should:

- Show compassion for those who may be affected adversely by news coverage. Use special sensitivity when dealing with children and inexperienced sources or subjects.
- Be sensitive when seeking or using interviews or photographs of those affected by tragedy or grief.
- Recognize that gathering and reporting information may cause harm or discomfort. Pursuit of the news is not a license for arrogance.
- Recognize that private people have a greater right to control information about themselves than do public officials and others who seek power, influence or attention.
- Only an overriding public need can justify intrusion into anyone's privacy.
- Show good taste. Avoid pandering to lurid curiosity.
- Be cautious about identifying juvenile suspects or victims of sex crimes.
- Be judicious about naming criminal suspects before the formal filing of charges.
- Balance a criminal suspect's fair trial rights with the public's right to be informed.

Act Independently

Journalists should be free of obligation to any interest other than the public's right to know. Journalists should:

- Avoid conflicts of interest, real or perceived.
- Remain free of associations and activities that may compromise integrity or damage credibility.
- Refuse gifts, favors, fees, free travel and special treatment, and shun secondary employment, political involvement, public office and service in community organizations if they compromise journalistic integrity.
- Disclose unavoidable conflicts.
- Be vigilant and courageous about holding those with power accountable.
- Deny favored treatment to advertisers and special interests and resist their pressure to influence news coverage.
- Be wary of sources offering information for favors or money; avoid bidding for news.

Be Accountable

Journalists are accountable to their readers, listeners, viewers and each other. Journalists should:

- Clarify and explain news coverage and invite dialogue with the public over journalistic conduct.
- Encourage the public to voice grievances against the news media.
- Admit mistakes and correct them promptly.
- Expose unethical practices of journalists and the news media.
- Abide by the same high standards to which they hold others.

Applying aims and principles

The chapter has explained the idea of media ethics, reviewed the history of approaches, and explained two of the three elements in analyzing media ethics – aims and principles. Now we provide the third element: a model for applying the aims and principles to cases. First, we need to note one further feature of reasoning in media ethics: its holistic nature. The holistic nature of ethical reasoning was implied by our earlier discussions – the idea that we must use many kinds of premises in our reasoning and balance rival principles. We need to describe this holistic process more carefully so we better understand what we are doing – or should be doing – when we reason in media ethics.

Holism

As noted in Chapter 1, some forms of normative ethics apply a "top-down" approach to deciding what is right or wrong by, for example, judging actions according to one (or perhaps several) supreme rules, such as the principle of utility or the categorical imperative. Chapter 1 also mentioned a less hierarchical and holistic form of reasoning that requires the weighing and balancing of different principles at different levels of generality. Holistic reasoning is eclectic. It draws upon many types of facts and values. The model to be presented in the rest of this chapter is an example of this holistic method.

This complex form of analysis is required for reasons already stated: principles, no matter how important, need to be interpreted as to their application in any context; principles and values are many, and so we need to introduce a priority ranking among our commitments, and then we have to see how that priority ranking works in cases; finally, our principles can conflict. This is the reason why we talk of ethical "issues" or "dilemmas."

The holistic approach makes sense for journalism.[18] Reasoning in journalism ethics challenges journalists to reach a "reflective equilibrium" among their intuitions and principles.[19]

In journalism, there is a constant tension between proactive and restraining principles. To report the truth independently may harm an individual's or an institution's reputation, or endanger a military mission. Yet, not to report essential facts about an event so as to minimize harm or avoid offending a minority may violate journalism's duty to report fully and truthfully. In such cases, journalists will have to decide which principles have priority. The principles of seeking the truth and of independence reflect a liberal idea of the press, while those of minimizing harm and accountability reflect the deontological and compassionate side of ethics.

The SPJ code assumes that journalists will work in a holistic and eclectic manner. In their textbook, *Doing Ethics in Journalism*, authors Jay Black, Bob Steele, and Ralph Barney explain that the four principles of the Society of Professional Journalists are "intended to work in tandem, and not alone," and ethical dilemmas entail "a balancing act between or among two or more of the principles." Also, there is a ranking of principles: "All things being equal, journalism's first objective is to seek out and report the truth."[20]

To see why a holistic form of reasoning is necessary for media ethics let's return to the example at the beginning of this chapter, a rumor that a politician seeking election is sexually harassing women on his staff. Anyone who carefully analyzes the example should come to see the value and necessity of holistic and eclectic reasoning. One needs to bring together separate and independent considerations. From a consequential perspective, there is the impact of such a story on the election campaign. From a

---

[18] For an example of a holistic approach to practical reasoning in media ethics textbooks see the "point-of-decision" model in Land and Hornaday, *Contemporary Media Ethics*.

[19] Rawls, *Political Liberalism*, 8.

[20] Black, Steele and Barney, *Doing Ethics in Journalism*, 29–30.

duty perspective, the journalist should act as watchdog on abuse of power. From a rights perspective, Jones has the right not to be falsely accused. The principle of minimizing harm urges us to protect the confidentiality of alleged victims of sexual harassment. A utilitarian calculus might conclude that the politician's good reputation is secondary to the greater good of publishing the allegations. Moreover, there is the journalist's right to publish. It is not plausible to maintain that such decisions can or should be made by consulting only one principle, such as utility. Within and without journalism, we confront a diversity of goods and duties that cannot be evaluated according to one moral criterion.

Applying the SPJ code holistically, we can clarify the evaluative task at hand. The ethical decision amounts to whether the principle of freedom to publish independently, and to act as watchdog on abuse of power is, in *this* case at this *time*, trumped (or limited) by the duty to substantially verify serious claims, to minimize harm and negative consequences, and the right of the politician not to have a career destroyed by allegations. Whatever decision is taken, the journalist in the end must be accountable to the public, by being able to explain and justify the decision to publish or not to publish. The code provides a framework for addressing the tension between the proactive and restraining principles.

How frameworks apply to cases in journalism can be understood by considering a real-life example. In 2008, Melissa Fung, a reporter with the Canadian Broadcasting Corporation (CBC), was kidnapped by militants while reporting outside Kabul, Afghanistan. The CBC feared that media coverage of her kidnapping might damage efforts to obtain her release. Media coverage might encourage escalating demands for ransom or the release of terrorists from prison. Also, media coverage might prolong her time in captivity or threaten her life. The CBC decided not to report the kidnapping and asked the same of other major news organizations. Assume that the CBC's concern about the consequences of coverage is plausible. How would one use the principles of journalism to evaluate the CBC's request to refrain from reporting?

A top-down or non-holistic approach would stress the overriding force of one principle, such as freedom to publish. One might argue, journalists have a duty to seek truth and report it and that always trumps the duty of journalists to consider the negative consequences of publishing. In fact, just such a view was advanced by journalists and media commentators in Canada after Fung was released by her captives and the news "blackout" was revealed.

The holistic approach offers a better method of evaluation. We start by recognizing that any journalism case worth discussing will require the balancing of conflicting values. Slogans and intuitions won't cut it. Instead, we stand back and take all the major principles of media ethics into account and seek to balance them with respect to the facts of this case. For example, journalists may argue that the news blackout is ethically valid because it honors the restraining principle of avoiding (or minimizing) harm. In Fung's case, avoiding harm trumps the proactive principles of reporting freely and independently her kidnapping. To fully justify this judgment, of course, would take a complex argument. But my point is not about the detail of the argument. My point is about its general structure. The argument accepts the burden of balancing various principles and facts. It assumes that simply emphasizing one principle won't be persuasive. Instead, one must construct a more careful argument that weighs many considerations.

The value of a framework, such as the SPJ code, is not that it provides "instant" answers on which we can all agree. The value is that it encourages a nuanced form of holistic reasoning that balances values, rights, and duties given the facts of the case. In the Fung case, the framework shows that responsible journalists must construct an ethical argument that incorporates into their practice both a love of freedom and a concern for others.

A model

We are now prepared to propose a method or model for applying the SPJ code (or other codes) to cases in a holistic manner.

The application consists of four stages to be carried out by individual journalists, or by a group of journalists in a newsroom: (1) awareness, (2) analysis, (3) evaluation, and (4) judgment. The first step requires that we sharpen our awareness of ethical aspects of actions, routines, and general practices. The second step requires a careful analysis of the main components of the situation in terms of basic facts and conflicting values. The third step involves using the analysis to identify a range of possible courses of actions, and their ethical evaluation in terms of our framework of principles. The fourth step involves coming to a judgment about what the best course of action is, and a later evaluation of that course of action, and a readjustment of our ethical norms given this experience. We now describe each step in more detail.

Step one: awareness

The application of the model begins with the recognition of an ethical problem surrounding a situation. Becoming aware that an ethical problem exists is equivalent to raising an ethical red flag in the newsroom. It is a sign that a discussion is necessary. This awareness may begin as a question in one's mind about the appropriateness of a report, or being uncomfortable with how a story is being approached. It may be a tug on one's conscience.

Recognizing an ethical problem is not as obvious a step as it may appear to be. Often, editors fail to recognize ethical issues amid the deadlines of daily journalism, or recognize them only after the questionable story has been published. Also, journalists may fail to distinguish an ethical problem from a problem of law, or may be lulled into ethical complacency by following the usual editorial rules and routines.

To identity the existence of an ethical issue, we use what was established in our discussions so far. We know that ethical issues are identifiable, serious concerns. They ask about rights, duties, and the consequences for ourselves and others. They ask whether we are acting from an impartial frame of mind. Such questions are asked independently of legal considerations. Also, we ask whether the action honors or violates the public role of journalism as a critical, independent public informer. If there is any doubt about the answer to these questions, we should raise an ethical red flag and probe deeper. That is, move to the next stage, analysis.

Step two: analysis

Analysis is the process by which we determine more exactly what ethical issues are in question, what values are in conflict, and what facts are most relevant to the ethical discussion. The goal of ethical analysis is to set out these "materials" clearly before us for evaluation.

The analysis consists of three steps. The first step in analysis is to identify the ethical issues and separate them from matters of law, prudence, and the usual routine. We state in specific terms how the issue is ethical, e.g. it violates an ethical aim, principle, or standard; and we state how the issue is *not* reducible to other forms of normative reasoning. For example, imagine that I live in a country where the public health records of leading politicians are not public documents. They are protected by privacy laws. I learn from sources that the health minister has become an alcoholic and his addiction is affecting his work. Through a source, I gain access to the minister's health records that show that alcoholism may indeed be a problem. Should I publish this fact? Remember: the point of analysis is not to directly answer this question. The point is to identify the main issues, values, and facts for evaluation.

Our analysis, using the SPJ code or some other code, may state the ethical issues as such: there is an ethical issue over the aims of journalism. Is the ethical aim of journalism to reveal failures of government ministers, or to respect their personal privacy? Is the aim to act as a watchdog on the public performance of government officials, or is it to avoid publishing embarrassing personal details about their lives? The analysis should note that the question, "should we publish this story?" is being asked ethically, not legally. Whether or not the publication would be legal or illegal, we want to consider whether the story should be published. At this point, the analysis may identify tensions between several ethical principles found in the code. For example, not reporting the story would seemingly violate the principle to seek and publish the truth, while publishing would appear to violate the principle of avoiding or minimizing harm (as well as the norm of respecting privacy).

Factually, the analysis does not list all the facts of the case, which is potentially a very long list. We pay attention to those facts that could affect our ethical judgment about the case. To change the example, consider a case where a reporter violated the privacy of Mary, a member of parliament, to investigate whether she was accepting bribes. Whether the bribes are in American dollars or British pounds is not of great relevance, ethically. The fact that the reporter was a woman or a man is also not relevant. What is relevant is that the fact that the reporter used a hidden camera to obtain information on Mary in her home. The use of hidden cameras is relevant because it affects our ethical judgment about the case. Returning to the case of the alcoholic minister, a factual analysis needs to consider whether the evidence strongly shows that the minister is an alcoholic and that his drinking problem is actually affecting his public performance.

In addition to identifying the key facts, an analysis should question the overall reliability and scope of the facts. Are any important facts unknown or uncertain? If the information is provided by sources, how trustworthy are the sources and what are their motivations? In the minister's case, there may be good evidence that the minister is a heavy drinker but weak evidence that it is damaging his public work. Or the information may be supplied by political enemies of the minister, whose motivations are suspect.

At the end of the analysis, we should be able to produce a list of clearly stated ethical issues and relevant facts. Analyzing the issue is not to pre-judge it. It is to prepare us for evaluation.

Step three: evaluation of options

Evaluation begins by identifying what appears to be a range of ethically permissible actions, given the facts of the case. Typically, the ethical choice is not between dozens of possible actions. Many possible actions will be clearly unethical, such as recklessly publishing a libelous story. The decision often comes down to a choice among two or three actions, each of which has some ethical weight.

In determining the options, journalists need to consider two possibilities that arise for almost every controversial case in media ethics: first, journalists have to decide whether it would be ethical to publish the story or image in the first place. This is a major hurdle to get over. The decision whether to publish arises, for example, in cases where editors grapple with the decision to publish a graphic photo that shows a raped and murdered woman lying on a street in a pool of blood; or whether to publish war stories that might reveal a weakness of one's country's army and give the opposing forces an advantage. Second, if the decision is to publish the story or image, the range of options have to do with *how* and *when* to publish the story.

If we are uncertain about central facts or allegations in a story, one option is to publish *after* reporters have done more research and verified key claims. Even if we feel confident in the facts, there are other options to consider. How should the story be written or displayed on the page (or shown on the broadcast)? For example, should we publish a less graphic version of the photo of the woman, perhaps an image taken from a long-lens camera? Should we obscure her face or parts of her body? Should we publish a story on a victim of a physical or sexual assault but not name the victim? Also, how should we display the story? What will our head-line be and how much prominence should we give to the story? Should this story or image appear on the front page or should it appear inside the paper?

To return to the example at the start of this chapter, one option may counsel publishing the sexual harassment allegations because that is what a free press does, or it is information that the public need to know. Another option counsels not reporting the allegation because that would cause real harm to the subject of the story. Another option may steer a middle course. It agrees that the story should be published but argues about *how* and *when* it should be published. One option is to wait until more facts are verified; or one publishes the article without revealing the name of the complainant.

Once we have identified several options concerning whether to pub-lish and how to publish, the serious work of comparing the options vis-à-vis our ethics code begins. In this stage, the focus is not on analysis but rational evaluation and justification. The journalist assesses each option in light of the main principles of media ethics. She balances reporting truthfully and independently with minimizing harm and being account-able to the public.

Step four: considered judgment and review

Eventually the journalist using this model arrives at a judgment about the best course of action, all things considered. "Best" means that the pro-posed action comes closest to fulfilling the ethical principles and aims of journalism, duly weighed and balanced in a holistic manner.

The journalist then acts accordingly. But the ethical task is not yet com-plete. After the action has been carried out, journalists should review the wisdom of the decision based on outcomes. The outcomes may be so nega-tive that they prompt a revision of practices in this area of journalism, or cause us to rethink some principle. At this stage, the principle of account-ability plays a large role. Journalists should ask themselves whether they can ethically justify to the public their editorial decisions and their actions. Some people will be angered by their editorial decisions and disagree with their judgments. However, the task is not to please or appease all people. The task is to be able, in the face of public outcry, to justify decisions on a principled basis.

These are the four stages of analyzing any situation in media ethics. The stages may seem cumbersome but the more one uses the model, the more efficient one becomes at identifying the key issues and evaluating the options. If we follow the model, we will increase our chances that we will be consciously and consistently following our principles and aims.

Before we end the chapter, let's consider one more example of how to apply the model. Consider a difficult decision regarding a sensitive photo. Imagine that John is one of your newspaper's best photographers. He has just returned from an area of town frequented by drug dealers and heroin addicts.[21] John has a compelling photo to go with a story on the effects of drugs on children. The photo shows two children, Maria, age 5, and her 3-year-old brother, Jorge, whose parents are addicts. The parents think their children don't see what they do, but the photo shows differently. The picture shows the children playing "junkie" in a gritty public alley outside their home. They pretend to stick needles in their arms. Maria and Jorge's parents gave your photographer permission to take pictures of the children for publication. Since then, however, the children's grandmother has heard about the photo and called our newsroom to ask that you not run the photo. There are mixed opinions in the newsroom. Should the photo be published?

Applying the model, step one is easy. It is clear that ethical issues are involved. A responsible editor would feel at least some doubt or uncertainty about publishing such a dramatic picture of children. Step two, analysis, should identify the ethical issues to include the role of journalism to publish the unvarnished truth, independently (regardless of the grandmother's views) versus the duty to not exploit or harm the subjects of stories through reporting, especially if the subjects are of a vulnerable age. Yet many facts are unknown. Under what circumstances did the parents agree to this photo? Why did they agree? Were they in a condition to provide informed consent? Is consent needed in this case?

---

[21] The example is taken from Wilkins and Coleman, *The Moral Media*, 143.

The evaluation phase begins by identifying the options, which appear to be: publish the photo as is, don't publish the photo, or publish the photo under certain conditions, such as not naming the children or family, or their address, or obscuring the faces of the children. The evaluation of these options requires the balancing of two major principles: the principle of journalistic truth-telling in the public interest – drawing public attention to a serious social problem (parental addiction) – versus minimizing the harm of publishing the faces of these children. Proponents of publishing the photo may argue that reporting the unvarnished truth in this case is not only consistent with the journalistic role of reporting the truth but it also fits with journalism's duty to promote the social good and to draw public attention to serious social problems. Proponents of using the photo may appeal to one of the apparent aims of journalistic truth-telling – the alleviation of social ills. Perhaps the story will prompt officials and child protection agencies to do more to protect children in such situations. The reply might be that the photo exploits the children for a dramatic story and to sell the news. It violates the rights of the children to privacy and the photo will stigmatize these children for the rest of their lives. Moreover, it is not journalism's role to fix social problems or to call in child protection agencies.

The model shows what the ethical options are, the uncertainties involved, and how one might construct a full ethical argument for or against publishing the photo. The model doesn't provide "the answer" but it makes sure, through a step-by-step process, that an ethical framework is applied, relevant questions asked, and rival values identified. The model shows how one should practice the general skill of ethical reasoning through eclectic "weighing and balancing."

For easy reference, here are the four stages of the model in bullet form.

Step one: awareness
- If one's intuitions suggest a problem, throw an ethical red flag that calls for discussion.
- Use the approach and code provided above to detect and articulate ethical problems.

Step two: analysis
- State how the issue is ethical, rather than a matter of law, prudence, or etiquette.
- Determine the primary ethical issues and conflicting principles.

- Determine the primary facts, their reliability, their ability to be verified, and the strength of one's evidence in total.

Step three: evaluation of options
- Identify the full range of possible actions.
- Identity a smaller set of what appear to be ethically permissible actions.
- Evaluate ethically the main contending options, using our approach and code. Compare the case with previous actions in similar cases in the past.
- Choose the action that best honors our ethical aims and principles.

Step four: act and review
- Act upon the best ethical course of action.
- Review the outcomes. Where needed, revise one's practices and principles.
- Be accountable for one's decision. Be prepared to justify and explain.

Finally, here are some questions that journalists can ask to prompt ethical reflection.

1. Why am I doing this story? What are my motivations?
2. How does this story fit my overall ethical values and my journalistic values? Am I acting in a consistent manner?
3. How would I feel if this story was written about me? Would I consider it accurate, fair, and responsible? What if I pretended that this story was published by some other reporter? Would I consider it a good piece of journalism?
4. With whom should I consult, before acting?
5. How will I feel about doing this story when I wake up tomorrow? Can I live with this decision? How do these actions affect my integrity and my profession?

Conclusion

We have come to the end of our introduction to media ethics. We have developed a framework for understanding and analyzing issues. In the chapters ahead, we will study the main issues of today's news media in light of this understanding of media ethics. We start with the debate over what sort of free press a liberal democracy needs.

Questions for discussion

1. What is the place of media ethics in ethics? How is media ethics one type of applied ethics?
2. What are the main problem areas for media ethics?
3. What are the five historical stages of media ethics?
4. A communications revolution has created new forms of journalism that use many types of media, and allow citizens to publish globally. How have these developments created new challenges for media ethics?
5. What is the difference between proactive and restraining principles in media ethics?
6. Do you think that codes of ethics contribute to responsible journalism? Or are they only "nice words" that journalists ignore?
7. What do you think are the main aims of media, and do they differ from the aims listed in this chapter?
8. What is a "model for reasoning" in media ethics? Using an example from media, show how the four-step model presented in this chapter can be used to ethically evaluate a case.

3   Free press and deliberative democracy

In late 2010, the web site WikiLeaks provided online access to hundreds of confidential cables sent by American diplomats abroad to the US government, obtained from an unnamed source. They contained candid observations about world leaders and an analysis of the political motivations of countries from North Korea to Iran. Major news organizations used the cables as the basis of news stories.

The web site's actions caused a worldwide debate on whether journalists, news media, and web sites should publish secret documents. Julian Assange, the director of the web site, argued that the release of the embarrassing and sensitive documents was the proper work of a free press. Journalists, he noted, have long exercised their freedom to publish confidential documents so that they can fulfil their obligation to inform the public about what their governments are doing in secret.

We will examine the WikiLeaks case in greater detail in Chapter 5. I introduce the controversy over the web site to make the following point: many journalists hold the freedom to publish as the primary value in journalism. Yesterday and today, journalists and citizens defend the freedom to publish without undue restraint or legal restrictions. Media freedom falls under freedom of expression, which is regarded as a condition of democracy.

Since democratic societies evolve, the link between a free press and democracy requires constant scrutiny, clarification, and reformulation. This is a task for media ethics.

Since the press is a central channel for public information and debate, issues of press freedom appear in many guises in numerous areas of society. Questions about the value and limits of a free press arise when citizens use web sites to deny the Holocaust or spread pornography; when the public considers the regulation of advertising or violent video games.

The same questions arise when negative press reports damage institutions; when investigative journalists reveal secret government papers; when journalists oppose a war. In each country, the culture, form of government, and laws determine how these issues are understood and addressed.

This chapter does not attempt to cover these many issues. Instead, it will examine how the principle of press freedom fits with contemporary society and contemporary media ethics. One issue, noted in the previous chapter, is whether we are inconsistent if we insist that the press should be both free and responsible. Is the idea of press freedom antithetical to the idea of a press restrained by ethical duties? This question has special import for today's media environment. In a media-connected world, the growth of Internet communication means that the public sphere has a greater number and greater diversity of voices than before. Many online writers, bloggers, and citizen journalists argue that online communication constitutes a new and better marketplace of ideas for democracy. They argue that, in the online world, freedom to express oneself is a primary value that should not be abridged by either press laws or press ethics, such as the restraining norms of balance, fairness, and objectivity. Some think that the freedom to publish online is sufficient for a robust democratic public sphere. Talk of a restraining ethics is passé.

However, it can be questioned whether a public sphere, enlarged by online communication, constitutes a new and adequate marketplace of ideas and whether simply adding more voices via the Internet is a sufficient condition for healthy democracy. Also, it is possible to question the view that online news media does not entail ethical responsibilities, especially where online communication is incorrect and causes harm. The extension of the freedom to publish to citizens, beyond the sphere of professional journalists, is to be welcomed in principle. Yet we should not ignore the fact that it raises new questions about the value and limits of freedom. The place of freedom among our communication values has become a central issue for contemporary media ethics.

This chapter examines how freedom can be, and should be, incorporated into today's media ethics. The conclusion is that freedom is a necessary but not sufficient condition for ethical journalism or a democratic public sphere. What else is needed, beyond freedom, are other values such as accuracy, objectivity, and a commitment to deliberation via the media.

These values are needed to circumscribe and limit journalistic freedom. Put more positively, they are needed to guide the responsible use of the freedom to publish. The challenge for media ethics is to say how to balance press freedom with other values such as equality, fairness, and reliable information in a rapidly changing media environment.

The chapter casts doubt on the view that there is a necessary link between a free press and a democratic press. A marketplace of ideas, even if realized in ideal form, is not sufficient for a democratic press. If a free press wants to be democratic it needs to construct an ethics that promotes a clear conception of democratic society. To promote democracy, the press has to use its freedom in certain ways. As this chapter will argue, it needs to use its freedom to support deliberative democracy.

The chapter starts by outlining the relationship of freedom to publish with other values such as editorial independence and the aim of truth-telling. It charts the history of the battle to establish a free press and it shows how media ethics was created to guide that freedom.

Freedom and the turn to ethics

Why value a free press?

Before we analyze the place of freedom in media ethics, let us remind ourselves of why freedom for news media is important in the first place. The great value of freedom is that it directs journalists to seek to report and comment in ways that are free of domination, manipulation, and distortion by government and powerful groups. It allows dissent and alternate ideas. It encourages journalists to oppose forces that threaten the freedom to publish and other liberties.

There are three types of reasons why we should support a free press:

1. *Individual and social development*: as liberal philosophers have stressed, freedom of expression (and freedom in its many forms) is essential to the creation of a society which allows individuals to pursue their plans of life and to develop their rational, moral, and social capacities. Freedom is a condition of the flourishing of individuals. Freedom is also essential to creating a society where citizens can experiment with new and better ways of living. J. S. Mill's classic work, *On Liberty*, is an extended argument about the need for liberty if society is to develop

creative, self-actualizing individuals. Without liberty, individuals struggle to resist the conforming pressures of majorities and society in general.[1] Isaiah Berlin argued that Western traditions rightly emphasize the value of negative liberty – the right not to be interfered with by others.[2] John Rawls viewed freedom of expression as one member of a family of basic liberties that define liberal society and together are of great value.[3] Journalists both enjoy and contribute to the strength of those freedoms as citizens and public communicators.

2. *Epistemological value*: freedom of expression and its corollary, freedom to publish, is a condition of open and fruitful inquiry. Freedom of expression allows inquirers to think and defend new thoughts and to encounter other views, thereby improving existing knowledge. Freedom of expression decreases the ability of others to manipulate us by not allowing other perspectives and other facts to be heard. It demands that others provide the basis for their assertions. Freedom of expression helps us get closer to the truth by allowing inquirers to freely collect evidence and evaluate arguments without fear or favor.

   By extension, freedom of the press is a condition for good journalistic investigation into, and public discussion of, major events and social problems. No journalist can inquire in a credible manner without having the freedom to ask questions that need asking, to speak candidly to people who hold power, and to freely obtain evidence and evaluate arguments. To be restricted by others, or to be influenced by one's biases, are ways of not being free. They signal that a journalist is not independently pursuing the truth.

   To be sure, freedom to investigate is not enough for good inquiry. One also needs rigorous methods and intellectual virtues, such as the disposition to question one's assumptions. But without freedom to inquire and publish, these virtues and methods are limited in their effect. In journalism and elsewhere, freedom to inquire and publish is tied to other values such as impartiality. Impartiality is freedom from the distorting influence of partialities and partisan perspectives. The debate over whether journalists can be independent from

---

[1] Mill, *On Liberty and the Subjection of Women*.
[2] Berlin, "Two Concepts of Liberty."
[3] Rawls, *Political Liberalism*, 291–292.

their funders, advertisers, or public pressure is a debate about how journalists can be free in their daily practice.

3. *Political value*: freedom of the press is valued politically as a mark of a democratic society, a society where the press is free to perform the watchdog and forum functions of journalism. Freedom of the press also encourages political participation among citizens by giving them a means to express their views and to take part in decision-making. Participation in public discussion helps citizens to inform themselves, learn about issues, and become engaged in decision-making. When conducted properly, such engagement encourages citizens to argue from informed positions that take other groups into account.

Together, the many values of a free press help to make the channels of public communication more accurate and reliable. One purpose of a free and truth-seeking press is to reveal bogus claims by individuals and special-interest groups who pretend to be arguing for the public good. Another purpose is to reduce the amount of spin and manipulation of public communication by powerful and media-savvy groups. Not being manipulated in communication or in ordinary human relations is an evident good. But it becomes especially important when it involves public policy decisions that affect many citizens.

A list of reasons for valuing a free press prepares us to confront the minefield of free-press debate. It tells us that without freedom to publish, journalism is a restricted, tepid enterprise that fails a democratic public. However, to get a clearer view of where freedom to publish stands we need to see how we have arrived at today's debates. History shows the limits of the idea of a free press as a philosophy of journalism. Of special historical importance is the fact that as the battle for a free press began to ebb in the second half of the nineteenth century, journalists themselves realized that freedom was not sufficient for good journalism and not sufficient for modern democracy. What was needed was a media ethics that incorporated freedom as one of several primary principles.

Seventeenth century: weakening controls

Citizens in developed liberal democracies sometimes forget how long it took to create a press that was reasonably free of control. Much of the history of Western journalism, from the 1600s onward, is the history of editors agitating for increased freedom to inform and advocate through the revolutionary mechanism of the printing press. They sought freedom from restrictive press laws and state systems of censorship.

In seeking freedom of expression, journalism joined a prior and more comprehensive movement toward liberal society. First came the call for freedom of religious conscience. The Reformation, and the wars of religion, ended with a degree of tolerance towards freedom of religious conscience. Freedom of religion was a beachhead for the establishment of other freedoms.

As we have seen, printer-editors in Amsterdam, London, and other major centers in the seventeenth century experimented in selling news to the public while inventing a basic ethical vocabulary. These editors were quite unlike today's professional reporters employed by large media corporations. They were an eclectic group of religious dissidents, reformist editors, entrepreneurial publishers, government officials, and academics. Many took up journalism to advance their ideas, their group, or their personal interests. Some published illegal broadsheets to challenge absolute monarchs, an established church, or the censors. These publishers were not watchdogs for liberal society. Many of the editors demanded the right to publish their "truth," and sent those who disagreed to the devil. The claims by editors to publish impartial truth and report facts were prompted, in part, by the press's lack of freedom. Editors made these claims to persuade nervous government officials and skeptical readers that their new publications were reliable and safe for society.

The dominant authoritarian approach to the press was weakened by a two-fold development – a decline in absolute government and the inability of officials to stem the tide of new publications which, in turn, stimulated public demand for more publications. It was in England that this weakening of authoritarian control went the furthest. A freer press emerged at times of political turmoil such as the collapse of central authority during the English Civil War, and periods of strong opposition to the Stuart monarchy. The restoration of the Stuarts under Charles II in 1660 ushered in another period of controls on the press, including a law that made reporting on Parliament a crime. But the movement toward a less authoritarian society did not die. In 1689, England became a Parliament-restrained monarchy under a Bill of Rights. At the same time, the amount of publications continued to swamp the censors causing delays for printers. As the public sphere and its publications expanded, it was clear that the press licensing system had to be dismantled. In 1695, the English Parliament allowed the Printing Act to expire. England became the first country in Europe to end the licensing and censorship of the press.

The seventeenth-century news press in England was instrumental in the creation of a freer public sphere. An unlicensed press flew in the face of the authoritarian view of printing as a privilege granted by the king. By the end of the century, the idea of public involvement in politics, supported by a freer press, was given philosophical justification by Locke with his idea of a social contract based on popular consent.

Eighteenth century: liberty of the press

In England, the end of press licensing allowed the newspaper to become a medium for the emerging Enlightenment public sphere. There was a virtual explosion of many new types of newspapers in London and across Britain, feeding an almost insatiable demand for news of war, commercial information, critical reviews, and political comment. In London, publishers circulated dailies, weekly journals, and tri-weekly newspapers. By 1709, London had 12 tri-weeklies, a bi-weekly, 20 weekly journals and, on March 11, 1702, the first daily newspaper – Samuel Buckley's *The Daily Courant*. London had 6 dailies in the 1730s, 9 dailies in the 1780s, and 14 dailies in 1792.

The same freedom of the press was not matched across the English Channel where the press continued to labor under absolute government and authoritarian press controls. Yet in Enlightenment France and elsewhere, monarchs could control but not repress the growth of newspapers. For example, no fewer than 1,267 periodic journals were established in France between 1600 and 1789, many dealing with scientific and artistic matters.[4] And as in England prior to 1695, many more illegal (or unlicensed) papers circulated, attacking the king and the central government as the country moved towards revolution.

The eighteenth-century idea of newspapers addressing a public and creating public opinion was a new and formidable challenge to authoritarian

---

[4] Burke, *A Social History of Knowledge*, 47–48.

philosophy. Freedom of the press was advanced as the freedom of editors to protect the liberties of citizens and to represent the public. Newspapers claimed to be the tribunes of the public. In England, from 1720 to 1723, John Trenchard and Thomas Gordon published anonymously the famous "Cato" letters in the *London Journal*. The 144 letters provided a theoretical basis for ideas about freedom of conscience and speech against "wicked ministers" who "enslave their country."[5] On February 4, 1720, the fifteenth "Cato" letter presented its famous argument that freedom of the press was "inseparable from public liberty." Cato wrote: "Freedom of Speech is the great Bulwark of Liberty; they prosper and die together: And it is the great Terror of Traitors and Oppressors." Cato's arguments, republished in the American colonies by Benjamin Franklin, played a role in the acquittal of John Peter Zenger in 1735 for criticizing the governor of New York. Zenger's lawyer, Alexander Hamilton, argued that the people had a right to expose and oppose arbitrary power by speaking and writing the truth. He told the court that the case was "not just the cause of the poor printer … It is the best cause; it is the cause of Liberty."

Across the turbulent eighteenth century, a restless public sought greater political representation and social change. The idea of a free press was articulated in a host of places – in judgments by jurists, in famous conflicts between editors and government, and in the philosophical writings of Hume, Jefferson, Erskine, and Condorcet. From the 1760s onward, the strongest demands for freedom to publish come from a new generation of journalists pushing for far-reaching reform and, in some cases, revolution. The cry was for "liberty of the press." The press was aligned against a common enemy: corrupt, unrepresentative, and tyrannical government. In the USA Tom Paine campaigned for the "rights of man" and the American Revolution. In England, the liberty of the press was a central issue in the infamous clashes between an unpopular Hanoverian monarchy and John Wilkes, MP and editor of the London weekly, *The North Briton*.[6] Wilkes used the intoxicating ideal of the liberty of the people to ride a wave of dissent

[5] Hohenberg, *Free Press, Free People*, 38.
[6] The weekly *North Briton* was born on June 6, 1762. Wilkes and Charles Churchill were the editors. The paper was an answer to *The Briton*, edited by Smollett and financed by Lord Bute. The name of the *North Briton* referred to the belief among some reformers that the Bute administration employed too many "northern" Scots. The *North Briton*'s 45 numbers, from June 1762 to April 1763, contained strident criticism of government.

to notoriety, public office, and journalistic immortality. On April 25, 1763, the famous No. 45 issue of the *North Briton* criticized the king's speech to Parliament for repeating the alleged falsehoods of Bute and other allegedly corrupt ministers. The government charged Wilkes for seditious libel, raided his premises, seized documents, and threw him into jail. "My Lords," Wilkes cried at his trial, "the liberty of all peers and gentlemen, and what touches me more sensibly, that of all the middling and inferior set of people, who stand most in need of protection, is in my case this day to be finally decided upon a question of such importance as to determine at once whether English liberty shall be a reality or shadow." When the charge was dismissed, a crowd of Wilkes supporters left the court shouting "Wilkes and Liberty."

Although Wilkes was subsequently convicted of libel in another court, the case of No. 45 began a series of court actions where juries refused to convict publishers of libel. Eventually, truth was recognized as a defense against common-law libel and the charge of criminal (or seditious) libel was less frequently applied. Courts even imposed fines on officials for using "general warrants" to round up publishers and seize materials. Gradually, the legal basis for a free press was being established.

Eventually this freer press played major roles in the American and French Revolutions. By the end of the eighteenth century, the press was a socially recognized institution, a power to be praised or feared, with guarantees of freedom in the post-revolution constitutions of the USA and France. The free press was called a fourth estate – one of the governing institutions of society.[7]

Nineteenth century: achieving negative liberty

The press of the seventeenth and eighteenth centuries in Western Europe and in the new societies of North America sought to reduce the interference of rulers, Parliament, and the church. In the nineteenth century, negative liberty as achieved across most of Europe as press controls were eliminated and more liberal societies were established.[8]

---

[7] Ward, *The Invention of Journalism Ethics*, 89–173.

[8] For a detailed history of this path to liberal theory see my *The Invention of Journalism Ethics*, chapters 3 to 6. Quotations in this section of the text are taken from these chapters.

The nineteenth-century press of Britain, the United States, France, Canada, and other British colonies had a strong liberal orientation, born of conflict. Between 1815 and 1880, newspapers won a struggle for freedom from harsh laws and crippling taxes. Their struggles were part of the liberal movements that sparked revolutions across Europe in 1848. The revolutions showed that the European newspaper had survived Napoleon's clampdown on free speech. In England, as the onerous taxes on newspapers were slowly removed, a popular press began to grow.

The Enlightenment press of the eighteenth century was not the full-blooded liberal press of the nineteenth century. The latter arose when the ideas of an ascendant liberalism were applied to the press. Press liberalism of the nineteenth century magnified the importance of an uncensored press. The press must not only be uncensored but also *maximally* free of pre- and post-publication restrictions. Service to the public was interpreted as service to the construction of a liberal society. The liberal press pushed the idea of a fourth estate to the limit. *The Times* described itself as a "perpetual committee of the legislature" since, unlike Parliament, it "sat" every day.

One result was the articulation of the liberal theory of the press. According to this theory, a liberal press is a privately owned, self-regulated, free press that protects individual rights, informs citizens, acts as a watchdog, expresses public opinion to government, and helps to oil the economy. The theory drew inspiration from Milton, Locke, and Paine. The liberal theory was given its definitive nineteenth-century form by J.S. Mill and journalists such as John Delane, C.P. Scott, and Walter Bagehot. As both the British Empire and American ideals spread in the nineteenth century, the idea of a free press accompanied Western liberalism to become a dominant value in countries far from London and New York City.

As noted, classical liberal-press theory was often libertarian, reflecting the libertarian spirit of the times. In economics, liberalism supported laissez-faire defined by a free economic marketplace without excessive government interference. Liberalism also supported a free marketplace of ideas. Only a free press could be a watchdog on government. This liberal view assumed that there was a sort of "hidden hand" in both the marketplace of the economy and of ideas that led in the long run to the victory of the most progressive ideas.

The tenets of liberalism were attractive to publishers and editors. A free marketplace of ideas made a newspaper of opinion possible. Liberalism sought to remove government restrictions on the operations of newspapers. Free trade stimulated economic activity, increasing circulations and advertising.

Liberalism produced two types of liberal press: an elitist newspaper in England and an egalitarian, popular press in the USA. *The Times* and the *Morning Chronicle* in London were elite liberal papers of the mid-1800s, followed by the *Daily Telegraph*. The story was different in the USA where journalists and the public were more ready to draw a direct link between a liberal and a democratic press because of the more egalitarian character of society and a popular press. Beginning in the 1830s, the new penny papers of New York, Boston, and elsewhere claimed to be informing all classes for greater democratic involvement.

However, by the end of the 1800s, the popular press was dominant on both sides of the Atlantic in the form of a mass commercial press operated by Hearst, Pulitzer, and others. The mass commercial press was devoted to the business of news. Newspapers now had the technological ability to gather, edit, print, and distribute the news to thousands of readers morning, noon, or night. The mass circulation paper employed a hierarchy of editors and reporters working to immovable deadlines, constructing news according to standard styles. Making papers "pay" changed the aim of a newspaper from the dissemination of opinion by an editor to the dissemination of news for profit through advertising and large circulations. By the 1890s, the largest American papers produced weekend editions of over 100 pages, almost half advertising. In New York, Pulitzer employed over 1,300 at his *World*, which made profits of $500,000 per annum in the late 1890s.[9]

It is difficult for us to appreciate the enthusiasm generated by the mass newspaper. London commuters in the 1880s fought over newspapers at railway stations. "Newspapers have become almost as necessary to our daily life as bread itself," effused Mason Jackson. The newspaper was not just ubiquitous. It was apparently omnipotent. The newspaper was praised lavishly as an instrument of progress and educator of public opinion. The power of newspapers over public opinion seemed obvious. "The true

---

[9] Mott, *American Journalism*, 546.

Church of England at this moment lies in the Editors of its newspapers," Thomas Carlyle wrote in 1829. Editor Charles Peabody said the press "raised the tone of our public life; made bribery and corruption … impossible."[10]

This was the great liberal hope for the newspaper. But that hope was perched on a vulnerable assumption: a free press would be serious, public-minded, and progressive. It would elevate public opinion, and provide important political information. It would lead to the construction of rational public opinion and, thereby, to the triumph of liberal ideas. A free press would practice journalism in the public interest. It would put the interests of the public ahead of factions and the economic interests of the newspaper itself.

The need for ethics

Disillusionment and ethics

At the turn of the twentieth century, trends in the free press challenged this great liberal hope. The result was disillusionment with the libertarian views that freedom to publish should be the sole (or dominant) value of journalism, and that the idea of restraint was dangerous.

The heart of libertarian theory was a belief in a self-correcting marketplace of ideas and the presumption that this marketplace approach was an adequate philosophy for news media. Just let the press be free and a self-governing, rational public sphere would come into being, in the long run. A free public sphere moves discussion towards truth and wise public policy. The precariousness of these libertarian ideas became evident in the late 1800s as the mass commercial press disappointed many of its supporters. A torrent of criticism of the press emerged at the start of the twentieth century.

Disillusionment arose from two sources. First, the hope that an unregulated press would be a responsible educator flagged as the commercial press was accused of being sensational and spending its editorial resources on everything from high-society scandals to race-track results. The idea that a free press would be an independent voice for the public good was undermined by an increasing dependency on profits and advertisers. This dependency

---

[10] Ward, *The Invention of Journalism Ethics*, 214–219.

was so powerful that it distorted the marketplace of ideas. The business of news meant that business would run the press. Critics worried about the new chains of newspapers that were consolidating the power of the press. The press was said to be a tool of the new press barons. It seemed that the press had exchanged control by government for control by advertisers, publishers, and large corporations. A commercial press seemed to be no better for journalism, liberal society or democracy than a partisan press dependent on political patronage. So much for the hidden hand of the marketplace.

A second source of disillusionment was skepticism about journalism's capacity to report truthfully about the complex modern world that emerged after the First World War, a world that included such difficult-to-understand events as the Great Depression. There was a growing awareness that reporters' stories were distorted not only by the reporter's subjectivity and bias but also by manipulative forces in the public sphere, such as the growing number of public-relations agents. The belief that reporters could obtain the truth by reporting their observations, citing facts, and quoting officials came to be regarded as naive.

At the turn of the twentieth century, naivety was replaced by skepticism about the libertarian philosophy of the press. If public opinion could be irrational, or manufactured, there was reason to question the belief that a marketplace of ideas, led by a free press, leads necessarily to progressive ideas in the public interest.

Inventing professional ethics

So, what should be done? The main response, within journalism, was to develop an explicit ethics for practitioners, often in the form of a code of ethics. Ethics was conceived of as a set of principles that journalists would voluntarily honor as a form of self-regulation. But what needed to be self-regulated, and why? What needed to be regulated was what journalists had long fought for: their negative liberty; their freedom to publish. The topic of ethics was how journalists should *use* their freedom. The assumption was that one should not simply use one's freedom to publish in any way one liked. Journalists had an ethical obligation to use their freedom to achieve desirable social ends such as an informed citizenry and to avoid undesirable consequences such as providing unreliable information or recklessly harming reputations.

What sort of ethical principles? Journalists felt that it was evident from the problems of the press that journalists needed to be independent of political and business pressures. Therefore, they should aspire to report in an objective and impartial manner. Their first allegiance was to the public. Also, news should be distinguished from opinion so that readers could ascertain the facts surrounding an event without having the presentation of the facts slanted by bias. Reporters should stick to the facts. Finally, journalists should raise themselves to the level of a profession with a distinct public-interest mandate to raise the standards of journalism and to counter business pressures. In sum, journalists should discipline their freedom with the principles of objectivity, balance, fairness, and impartiality.

Between the 1880s and the 1920s, journalists created a modern professional ethics. The construction of this ethics began among the growing ranks of journalists as they formed themselves into professional associations. Across the USA, state and national associations, such as the Society of Professional Journalists, wrote codes of ethics that stressed professionalism, independence, truth-seeking, and objectivity. The codes became the content for the first ethics textbooks and for courses in journalism schools. In Canada, England, and the United States, high-level commissions investigated the impact of a powerful free press on democracy, giving more impetus for talk of media ethics and the development of its principles.

The creation of a formal ethics shows how modern journalists struggled to fit their freedom into their overall commitment to responsible informing of the public. Before this era, the question of the relationship of freedom to other journalistic values was not a major issue among journalists. The first task was to secure a free press. However, from the late 1800s onward, freedom comes to be seen as being one of several basic values. Freedom fits into journalism as a necessary condition for good journalism. Practitioners were asked to balance freedom with other ethical considerations such as minimizing harm and reporting without bias. Yet the incorporation of freedom into ethics was not always smooth. Freedom continued to be viewed by some as external to ethics, as a force to be controlled by commitments to ethical principles. These attitudes exist today.

The project of ethics worked against the original impulse of libertarian theory. Ethics was thought to be needed because a free marketplace of ideas was not enough. Ethics was born in the acknowledgment among

many journalists, academics, and members of the public that libertarianism was an insufficient philosophy of the press. Democracy needed
journalists to adhere to ethical principles. The turn towards ethics was a
recognition that journalism would need more than freedom to achieve its
high-minded goals of a liberal and democratic society.

The project of ethics carried forward across the 1900s and into the present century, with new principles and ethical aims added with almost every
decade. One motivation for articulating new duties was the evolving nature
of journalism and society. Both liberalism and media ethics attempted to
respond to the emergence of pluralistic societies that demanded a liberalism that went beyond libertarianism. In journalism, the power of the
press grew as new forms of journalism, on the radio and the TV, made
news media a central informer of modern democratic society. In social
philosophy, pluralistic societies encouraged the development of a "social"
liberalism that stressed not just liberty but also equality. Social liberalism
endorsed programs to create equal opportunity among citizens, and eventually encouraged a politics of recognition that demanded fair representation of minorities in society and in the media.

Liberalism had already begun to change at the turn of the twentieth
century when liberal philosophers such as Thomas Green and then John
Dewey argued that it was not enough to protect negative liberty. Talk of
freedom in the abstract was meaningless if some citizens had a greater
opportunity to develop their capacities and exercise their freedoms than
others. Not everyone started from the same position in life due to the
circumstances of birth, economic class, ethnic group, or gender. It was
not enough to protect individuals from undue government interference
in their lives. The opposite was true: liberal society needed government to
interfere in the marketplace and in society to protect the disadvantaged,
to challenge monopolies, and enforce a constitution that made sure the
pursuit of individual goods occurred within the law.

A pluralistic society stimulated further elaboration of media ethics. New theories of a responsible press examined in the previous chapter – social responsibility theory and communitarian approaches, among
others – were advanced. Meanwhile, members of the new academic disciplines of mass communication and media ethics joined the chorus for an
ethical "repair" of the press. Media ethics came to include such ideas as
the responsibility of media to fairly represent struggling minorities, and

to advance social justice. The watchdog role enlarged from the monitoring of government to the monitoring of private centers of power such as large corporations.

It must be emphasized that *nothing* like this – a system of media ethics with ever-increasing duties and social concerns – was envisaged by the partisan journalists who fought for a free press in the eighteenth century, or by the libertarian press in the nineteenth century. The idea of a free and democratic press, based solely on libertarian grounds, had failed.

Journalism and democracy

Only libertarianism?

This overview of freedom and ethics leads to a difficult question: what *is* an adequate philosophy for today's media? Should we retreat back to a simpler libertarian approach? I think libertarianism remains an inadequate philosophy for news media. The challenge is to reconceive the balance between freedom and responsibilities in a way that speaks to the issues of today's multi-media journalism. The best way to do this is to return to the theme of the aim of journalism and show how our press values should be balanced to promote that aim. Given media's importance for citizens, a plausible candidate for the aim of journalism is the promotion of democracy, or at least a certain kind of democracy. The central questions are: What type of news media does democracy need? How should the value of freedom and the norms of responsible journalism be related to promote democracy? Theoretically, the task is three-fold: (a) to say in some detail what form of democracy should be the goal of journalism; (b) to show how the values of media ethics can be understood to support this form of democracy; and (c) to explain how freedom of the press figures in such an account of media ethics. We need to analyze, once again, the link between a free press and democracy.

Some people do not delve into this link because they assume that a free press and democracy are inseparable, in the same way that nineteenth century liberals assumed that a free press would naturally lead to rational public opinion. History is clear here. Liberalism paved the way for democracy but they are not identical movements; nor do they follow identical philosophies. Liberalism as a movement existed before the rise of genuine liberal democracies. Also, many liberals in the past were not democrats. They wanted greater freedom for their social class, e.g. the middle class, but they balked at giving the vote to all citizens. Similarly, a free press aided the development of democracy. Yet a free press and a democratic press are not identical. Forms of media are tools that can be used in many ways, and a free press may not be used to promote democracy.[11] Our confidence that freedom is so important and so necessary lulls us into a false confidence that a free press entails a democratic press. But is that so? It wasn't obvious to the critics of the free commercial press more than a century ago. Why so today? It is always possible to ask: "to what extent is our free press democratic?"

Confidence in a necessary link between a free press and democracy has grown of late, not declined. The advent of the Internet appears to have created a new and more dynamic marketplace of ideas. Social media enthusiasts and a good number of online writers have become the new libertarians. I call them the libertarians of the Net. Like libertarians in the past, the new libertarians believe that the public sphere requires primarily – or only – a free media available to many citizens. According to this view, the restraints of journalism ethics are not especially relevant for cyberspace. Ethical rules belong to a fading era of traditional, professional journalism. Libertarianism of the Net poses one of the clearest, strongest challenges to media ethics today. After almost a century of professional media ethics, the primacy of freedom of expression is put forward again with renewed strength.

Democratic journalism

Let's start by being careful how we use key terms. A free press means a press that is relatively unfettered by government and law in its news-gathering and publications. A democratic press is a free press that substantially advances democracy. By democracy I mean a constitutional liberal democracy. A constitution is a social contract that defines the terms by

---

[11] That the media can be used for ill or good in the world is evident from studies of how media can support human rights around the world, or inflame ethnic tensions and prompt abuses of human rights, or even genocide. For a study of the link between a free press and human rights, see Apodaca, "The Whole World Could Be Watching."

which different groups can peacefully and fairly coexist, enjoying the benefits of co-operation. A constitution, among other things, balances freedom and justice. It protects basic liberties for all while making sure the pursuit of liberty by any individual or group is restrained by law. For example, a constitutional regime places restrictions on what majorities can do to minorities. Therefore, a constitution is rooted in principles of liberty, equality, and justice. Moreover, a liberal democracy should be participatory and deliberative. Citizens not only vote but can meaningfully participate in public deliberations. To ask if a press is democratic is to ask to what degree the press contributes to this ideal of liberal democracy.

Democracy is the goal of journalism because, as Dewey argued, democracy is a precondition for the richest kind of communal life and human flourishing.[12] Democracy is free, equal, and respectful participation in social life. It is a way of relating to others, of carrying out projects, of designing institutions, of educating, of persuading and deciding. In education, democracy means perfecting the critical powers of citizens so they can make meaningful choices and participate in a democracy defined not solely by competing interests but also by deliberation on the common good. Politically, it means that institutions act to promote freedom and equality in society, and act according to principles of justice endorsed by citizens. A democratic community is a community that promotes Mill's "experiments in living." The question of how to live is open and not fully known until we engage in democratic deliberation and politics.

A democratic approach to journalism starts from the obvious but often overlooked point that a free press is not the goal of journalism. Not even a marketplace of ideas is the end of journalism. To think otherwise is to confuse means with ends. Freedom and a marketplace of ideas are means to something else, such as liberal society, or the free flow of information. Another basic point is that a democratic approach sides with those who think that ethics is crucial to journalism. Democratic journalism theory is one form of media ethics. What is distinctive about democratic journalism theory is its belief that the most important ethical values are to be explained and justified with reference to democracy. Journalists are said to have a positive duty to promote democracy, not just an obligation to be accurate or a negative liberty not to be interfered with. As we will see, to

---

[12] Dewey, *Democracy and Education*, 16.

accept democracy as the ultimate journalistic goal implies that journalists honor certain values and practices not mentioned (or stressed) by other approaches.

But what sort of democracy? At this point, media ethics needs help from theories of democracy. Two models of democracy are especially relevant: participatory and deliberative.

Participatory democracy

Variants of democracy are divided into two main types: (1) direct or participatory democracy where citizens are involved in making decisions about public issues; and (2) liberal or representative democracy where elected officers represent the interests of citizens within the rule of law.[13]

The roots of participatory democracy go back to classical Athens. But the term more accurately refers to a form of democracy defined by writers from the 1970s onward, such as Carole Pateman and C. B. Macpherson.[14] These writers complained that liberals had not paid sufficient attention to how inequalities of class, sex, and race hinder active participation in contemporary democracy. These inequalities limit the extent to which citizens can claim to be free and equal. For Pateman and others, liberals err when they try to separate the state from the private life of citizens. The state is an integral part of the social system that maintains inequalities in participation. For Pateman, society and the state must be democratized by making parliament, state bureaucracies, and political parties more open and accountable.[13] Macpherson thought the idea of participatory democracy was essential to the future of democracy. He asked whether anything more than occasional participation by citizens, such as voting every four years, was possible in complex societies. Ideally, democracy provides many more opportunities for participation. It gives people a sense of political power and agency, encourages a concern for collective problems, and makes citizens more knowledgeable by playing a part in the governing process. Citizens need to participate in the regulation

---

[13] Held, *Models of Democracy*, 4.
[14] Pateman, *Participation and Democratic Theory*; Macpherson, *The Life and Times of Liberal Democracy*.

and monitoring of activities in key social institutions, in politics, in the workplace, and in local communities. Many participatory political parties – parties responsive to and directly accountable to their memberships – should exist. Also, as Held maintains, society should redistribute resources to allow marginal groups to participate, minimize unaccountable bureaucratic power, and ensure an "open information system to ensure informed decisions."[13]

These views have implications for what democracy requires of its free press. An "open information system" implies a democratic journalism that provides diverse and accessible channels for public communication. Here is where the libertarians of the Net have a valid point. The Internet and new forms of communication provide better access to the public sphere. The political value of new media is the many voices online.

Praise for the democratization of the media via the Internet rests on a participatory model of democracy. Enthusiasm about the potential of new media has created a "democratic media" movement where citizens are no longer passive consumers of news but actively help to shape the news and public discussion. Shayne Bowman and Chris Willis, in their book, *We Media*, see the future of journalism as participatory journalism, which they define as: "The act of a citizen, or group of citizens, playing an active role in the process of collecting, reporting, analyzing and disseminating news and information. The intent of this participation is to provide independent, reliable, accurate, wide-ranging and relevant information that a democracy requires."[15] Similarly, journalist Dan Gillmor's influential book, *We the Media*, argues that new media allow "grassroots journalism by the people, for the people."[16] The book chronicles how the Internet is helping independent journalists combat the consolidation of traditional media. Of course, there are good and bad uses of media. Cell phones and Twitter can help citizens report election abuses in developing countries. The same technology can spread malicious rumors around the world in a literal wink of the eye. Writers like Gillmor emphasize the positive potential of new media. What these writers share is the old liberal belief in a marketplace of ideas.

This enthusiasm for the new, digital media takes a wrong turn when it becomes an extreme libertarian viewpoint that thinks ethical standards

---

[15] Bowman and Willis, *We Media*, 9.   [16] Gillmor, *We the Media*.

are not relevant to the wired world, and not central to democracy. Ignoring the libertarian view for the moment, let us take the fact of participatory media seriously and ask: isn't a participatory, interactive new media what we mean by democratic media?

It depends on whether you believe that participatory democracy is the correct model of democracy. And it depends on whether you believe that a high level of citizen participation in media is all that is needed for democratic media. Another model of democracy, deliberative democracy, contends that the answer to these questions is no. Participatory media is not sufficient for a democratic media.

Deliberative democracy

What is missing in the participatory model of democracy is the notion of deliberation. Deliberation is more than simply participating in events, communication, or decisions. It is a special and important way of participating. Philosopher Michael Walzer defined deliberation as: "a particular way of thinking: quiet, reflective, open to a wide range of evidence, respectful of different views. It is a rational process of weighing the available data, considering alternative possibilities, arguing about relevance and worthiness, and then choosing the best policy or person."[17] The model of deliberative democracy argues that citizen participation in the media (and elsewhere in society) should aim to be deliberative. The theory of deliberative democracy is relatively recent.[18] For deliberative theorists, the problem with modern democracy is not only that too many citizens are not able to participate in their society in equal measure with other citizens. The problem is that the mode of participation is often non-deliberative.

The source of deliberative democracy theory is a deep dissatisfaction with current forms of political decision-making and declining citizen interest in civic life. Instead of deliberative citizens, the public is said to be increasingly self-interested, emotional, and unreasonable. Too many citizens treat other perspectives with disrespect and prefer simplistic, ideological approaches to complex issues. Politicians practice a politics that takes voters' current

---

[17] Walzer, "Deliberation, and What Else?" 58.
[18] Joseph Bessette was the first to use the term to refer to a distinct variant of modern democracy. See his "Deliberative Democracy: The Majority Principle in Republican Government."

opinions as given, or they try to get out in front of the latest swing in opinion polls. Public opinion is manufactured through manipulative, non-deliberative practices, from emotive "attack" advertisements during elections to heart-tugging media campaigns for new products, from automobiles to life insurance. News media are thought to be part of this growing non-deliberative public sphere, resorting to "hot talk" radio shows, eight-second sound bites and a blurring of news and entertainment. The trend, then, is away from deliberation, which is the key to wiser and more inclusive decisions.

True democracy requires not just participation but substantial amounts of public deliberation that is "fact-regarding" (based on facts as opposed to opinion or doctrine), "future-regarding" (not myopic or short-sighted) and "other-regarding" (not selfish; takes the interests of others into account.).[19] Deliberation requires impartial reasoning, defined as reasoning where no one group or view has special status. Political legitimacy is not just about the ballot box or majority rule but also about the process by which decisions are reached – by the "giving of defensible reasons, explanations, and accounts for public decisions."[20] The source of political legitimation is not existing citizen preferences but what those preferences would be if citizens were fully informed through deliberation. A legitimate political decision is a decision that survives a deliberative testing as to whether it advances the public good.

Theorists of deliberative democracy, such as James Fishkin, propose new mechanisms for public deliberation such as citizen juries and deliberative polls where representative samples of the population are asked to study an issue over several days before reaching a judgment.[21]

Also, deliberative democrats promote e-government initiatives that allow citizens to access government documents and participate online in discussions of issues.

Deliberative journalism

The ideal of deliberative democracy provides a goal for a free and democratic press. On this view, news media have positive duties to create

---

[19] This characterization of deliberative democracy was put forward by Offe and Preuss in "Democratic Institutions and Moral Resources."

[20] Held, *Models of Democracy*, 237.

[21] Fishkin, *Democracy and Deliberation*.

deliberative spaces in the public sphere. They should offer programs on current issues that encourage deliberative exchanges among people of differing views. A deliberative space allows the sort of reflective, evidence-based communication that Walzer defined as deliberation. Without a public culture of deliberation, without institutional practices and media coverage that encourage citizens to come together to deliberate, democracy declines into the irrational rule of the insufficiently informed, whose desires and views are the result of manipulation by powerful elites who distort and dominate channels of communication. Only under conditions of deliberative democracy can we speak about the free and reasonable agreement of citizens, and of rational public opinion.

By now, it should be clear why the model of deliberative democracy regards free expression and citizen participation in media as a necessary but not sufficient condition for democracy or democratic journalism. Our society is a communicative society of the highest order. It has more accessible forms of communication for sharing information than at any other time in history. Yet it may still fail to be a deliberative democracy. It may be a society where non-deliberative exchanges are the norm and the most important factor in political decisions.

We should not confuse media participation with a diverse press or a deliberative democracy. A marketplace of ideas in any era, no matter how sophisticated, can be limited in participation and dominated by an elite group of powerful media organizations. Although internet access grew by 362 percent from 2000 to 2009, especially in the Global South, the internet still covers only a quarter of the world's population. The threat of domination is also present. Citizens need to pay attention not only to the actions of large traditional media corporations but also to the business motives and growing power of self-described participatory media such as YouTube, Google, Twitter, and any other new media entity that will appear in the years ahead.[22]

Talk about the diversity of voices on the Internet ignores the fact that the Internet allows monopolies of information. For instance, many of the most popular news sites in countries such as the United States, Canada,

---

[22] For a critical analysis of the democratic claims and motives of Twitter and other entities of the "participatory Web" see Tamara Shepherd's "Twittering in the OECD's 'Participative Web.'"

and Britain belong to mainstream news media – the same companies that dominate traditional news media. Globally, about a dozen Western conglomerates dominate the world of media, film, and similar cultural products. This has sparked a debate whether we are entering the golden age of a diverse global public sphere or we are witnessing its colonization. It is not enough for a robust democracy for individuals to have a voice. One must also pay attention to whether certain voices are stronger than others.

Nor does the democratization of media lead necessarily to greater deliberation or concord among participating citizens. The lovely idea of many voices connected globally ignores the plain fact that the world is anything other than Marshall McLuhan's global village. A media-linked world can create great tensions among cultures. Democracy is not based simply on the freedom to express oneself on the topics of the day. How one expresses oneself and how one interacts with others who also wish to express themselves are crucial. In other words, how citizens use their new and increasing freedom to publish is as important as the fact that they now have such media capabilities. The same question that dogged professional journalists – how will you use your freedom for democracy – can now be asked of citizens.

The question of how one uses one's voice is clear when we realize that a celebration of a diversity of voices online has little to say about who these voices are, and how such voices have to interact to address issues democratically. It says nothing about the type of information available for discussion, the obstacles put up by governments to free speech, or the selfish (or intolerant) attitudes that can thwart attempts at fruitful online discussions. Conversation, offline or online, may lead nowhere or somewhere. It may promote informed rational discussion or emotional shouting. Moreover, the issues that confront countries in a global world, from climate change to health-care reform, are so complex that deliberation and study is needed, not just random exchanges of views. Organized, reasoned debate, not ideological ranting or simplistic analysis, is desperately needed in public communication. To make things worse, many powerful agents have a stake in how that public discussion turns out. Millions of dollars are spent on attempting to influence and manipulate public deliberation. To assume that interactivity is by itself sufficient for democracy is as naive as thinking, in the late 1800s, that a mass commercial press was the answer to the woes of democracy.

Therefore, democracy needs not just participation and lots of voices but citizens who are willing to participate in fair and respectful communication among citizens, and willing to follow facts where they lead. From a deliberative democracy perspective, there is still a role for critical, well-informed, and fair journalists to play in objectively informing citizens and critically directing the conversation. Against the libertarians, deliberative democrats argue that the nature of today's public sphere rules out a rejuvenated laissez-faire attitude that thinks simply getting more voices to connect is the answer. We need to deliberately use media in democratic ways, not assume democratic discourse and wise choices will happen.

The conclusion is that good journalism deliberates, and helps citizens deliberate. The manner in which journalists talk to their audience, frame their topics, and structure discussion is paramount. A non-deliberative approach can be seen and heard on television and radio every day. It is the tired format of talking heads screaming at each other. Or it is the arrogant talk-show host who frames the topic in the most simple and provocative manner. Hot talk is a modern example of why a free press is not enough for democracy. If all of talk radio was divided evenly between clones of conservative Rush Limbaugh and extreme liberals on the other, would this make news media democratic and deliberative?

Democratic journalists and citizens approach public discussion differently. The aim is not to simply express my view; it is not about portraying those who disagree with me as unpatriotic enemies who must be crushed. It is not a winner-takes-all affair. Deliberation is not a monologue. Democratic discourse is social and co-operative. It is about listening, learning. It expects robust disagreement, but it also seeks areas of compromise and new solutions. Democratic journalism challenges character assassination, flimsy facts, and loaded language like "socialist." Democracy is about how we speak to each other, engaging in public reasoning. It needs the democratic virtues of tolerance, reciprocity, and the glorious ability of humans to transcend their perspective. When fundamental issues threaten to confuse and divide us, it is time for objective and deliberative public journalism. Without this type of democratic journalism a reasonable public cannot come into existence.

Public use of reason

The arguments of deliberative democracy find support in the philosophy of John Rawls. Rawls believed that citizen participation must take into account the pluralism of our times. A central issue for the future of pluralistic democracies is how citizens with different interests and different conceptions of life can live together in freedom and relative harmony. How can they arrive at common principles and policies?

To respond to this challenge, Rawls developed his idea of political liberalism.[23]

Democracies do not accept the imposition of principles from one religion or philosophy on the entire body politic. Therefore, citizens from different groups need to find a way to identify an overlapping consensus on political principles for running their country, sharing benefits, protecting basic rights, and operating institutions. These principles must be applied every day to new and thorny issues. Therefore, inclusive and reasonable deliberation about principles should take center stage. The quality of communication among citizens is of special importance. Rawls echoes the warning of deliberative democrats that how citizens approach the discussion of issues, and how they speak to each other, is crucial. Without public means of deliberation, discourse can be hi-jacked by loud and intolerant voices. Media manipulation becomes an extension of power, an undemocratic way of dealing with the differences among us.

Rawls argues that a special sort of discourse is crucial when citizens deal with fundamental issues. He calls it the "public reason."[24] It is reasonable discourse by people willing to transcend their own interests and ideology to consider what is fair to others, and to base their decisions on objective evidence.

If we follow Rawls in this line of thinking, the question about a democratic press becomes this: how do journalists promote public reason in pluralistic societies? Journalists promote public reason when they fulfil two crucial functions of democratic media – an informative and a deliberative function. Journalists have a duty to improve the informational and deliberative health of citizens just as public health officers are responsible for the physical health of citizens. We have already discussed the deliberative

---

[23] Rawls, *Political Liberalism*, 131–172.   [24] *Ibid.*, 212–254.

approach to journalism, so let's consider the informative function. The informative function is based on the view that citizens need the best possible "content" or information upon which to deliberate. Informative journalism is not just reporting any sort of information. It is a combination of three types of journalism that require skill and disciplined inquiry. First, accurate, contextualized reporting on events. Second, investigative journalism, as the necessary exploration of what goes on below the surface of society. And third, informed interpretation of major social areas. Intelligent context and depth of investigation – these are two qualities of democratic journalism.

And I will mention a fourth: objectivity. The informative function is best fulfilled when journalists adopt the attitude of what I call "pragmatic objectivity."[25] This is not a traditional objectivity of reporting just the facts. It is about adopting an objective stance and then evaluating stories according to a set of norms. Journalists adopt the objective stance when they are disinterested. They are disinterested when they do not prejudge a story in advance but follow the facts where they lead. They are willing to put a critical distance between them and their views. Journalists then have to test their stories with a set of criteria, such as the empirical strength of their reports and their coherence with existing knowledge. Pragmatic objectivity includes the critical evaluation of claims to fact, knowledge, and expertise. Objectivity is not neutrality or perfect knowledge of reality. It is a flexible imperfect method, a way of testing stories and reducing bias. If journalists carry out these three forms of journalism objectivity, they carry out a major task of democratic media. They express views grounded in knowledge, experience, research, and a critical but open mind. They provide a reliable base for all subsequent analysis and comment. We will explore objectivity in more depth in the next chapter.

What does democracy require of its press? The question sounds out of date. An updated version is: what does democracy require of its public system of communication and all of its participants, from professional journalists to citizen bloggers? What can we realistically hope for? Our hope for democracy in this expanding universe of media cannot be that all communicators will have the skill to do democratic journalism or the motivation to deliberate. What we can hope for is that our societies will be

[25] Ward, *The Invention of Journalism Ethics*, 261–316.

able to maintain a core of deliberative public journalism across all media formats – from newspapers to radio to TV to blogs. If our media system is to be democratic, a core of professional reporters need to work with citizen journalists. The complexity of dealing with today's issues leaves plenty of room for both professional journalists and citizen communicators who have knowledge, research abilities, and a democratic spirit. The ideal of deliberative democratic journalism must be the core of our media system.

Conclusion

This chapter has not attempted to provide an extensive discussion of the many issues of press freedom. It has analyzed two fundamental questions: what place does media ethics have in this connected world? And how does freedom fit into that scheme?

We found that the origin of media ethics starts with the realization that a free press is not sufficient for good journalism or democracy. The battle for a free press culminated in the perceived need for ethics, an ethics of professional journalism. The achievement of media freedom was followed by an attempt to channel that freedom.

The chapter examined one way of using that freedom, to promote democracy. It noted that the idea of promoting democracy was more complex than sometimes thought. There are many forms of democracy, and many ways to advance it. So media ethics today has to decide what forms of democracy it wants to promote. One form is participatory democracy, made popular by the Internet and its participatory and interactive forms of media. But the chapter showed how media ethics, while recognizing the value of participatory media, needs to aim for something higher – the use of participatory media in promoting deliberative democracy.

The future of democracy appears to require a core of journalists, professional and non-professional, practicing deliberative journalism across all media platforms. Journalism goes beyond simply exercising its freedom to publish to an ethical concern for how it facilitates public discourse in a pluralistic society. Journalists not only have freedom to publish; they have duties to use their freedom to foster reasonable political discourse. A libertarianism that thinks democracy only requires a free and diverse media, offline and online, is not enough. The best fit of freedom in today's media is a freedom that continues to defend negative liberty while pursuing deliberative journalism.

In the next chapter, we will analyze the principles of truth-telling and objectivity in terms of their contribution to democratic journalism.

Questions for discussion

1. Historically, media ethics formulated principles for a small number of types of news media, such as the newspaper and television news. However, over the past decade many new types of media have emerged. Is it possible for media ethics to formulate principles for the many kinds of news media today?

2. Does the public have an ethical responsibility to use new forms of communication, e.g. blogs, Twitter, wikis, in a responsible manner? If so, what would responsible use mean?

3. Should bloggers, tweeters, and online communicators follow an ethics? Should they follow the same rules and guidelines as mainstream journalists?

4. What is meant by "mixed media"? Hasn't media always been mixed? If news media is mixed, should this change its ethical principles? Why or why not?

5. What are some examples of journalism today, especially online, that operate under rules and values different from the traditional mainstream media of newspapers, public broadcasters, and so on?

6. Given the wide range of media today, is it necessary any longer for reporters to strive to be objective? Are citizens informed equally well by a news media where journalists put forward their views honestly, rather than attempt to be balanced and impartial?

7. Does the diversity and accessibility of the Internet constitute a new marketplace of ideas that is freer and more effective than the former marketplace of ideas before the Internet?

8. From an ethical perspective, does it matter what form of media one uses? For example, does it make a difference if a person's privacy is violated or their reputation damaged by a blogger or by a reporter for the *New York Times*? Aren't both the blogger and the *Times* reporter wrong to act this way?

9. If democracy is the ultimate political aim of news media, what form of democracy should be the goal? Is deliberative democracy too unrealistic and demanding both for citizens and for news media? If deliberative democracy is not the appropriate goal, what *is* the right aim?

10. Are citizens too busy, or too apathetic, or too ill-equipped to engage in complex discussions and deliberation about social issues? What should be the role of the press in large, impersonal societies with substantial numbers of citizens who have "tuned out" politics?

11. Is there still a role for journalists as gatekeepers of information? Are there other roles that journalists need to assume today, given the developments in media and society?

4   Reaffirming truth and objectivity

I have argued that media ethics is not antithetical to the freedom to publish. Media ethics recognizes freedom as a necessary condition of a democratic press. Without freedom, a robust journalism cannot exist. Yet media ethics also values how that freedom is used. It values the use of media to promote fair and wise decisions in the public good. The last chapter considered one way that media freedom should be used – to promote deliberative democracy. Deliberative democracy is the ultimate aim of responsible news media.

This chapter examines two principles that are essential means to realizing democratic journalism and deliberative democracy: (1) the pursuit of truth, and (2) striving to be objective in the pursuit of that truth. Many other values are important to journalism but they are important insofar as they help to foster an objective and truthful press.

For media ethics, the two principles must work in tandem. Journalists cannot properly pursue truth without seeking to be objective. This is not to say that, in some cases, a subjective method can never hit upon a truth. For example, a newspaper columnist may correctly speculate upon meager evidence that the prime minister will resign. However, overall, journalists pursue the truth best by adopting an objective approach to stories.

The principle of truth has a number of components. Truth serves as an ideal, or a goal, of inquiry. The pursuit of this ideal includes both truth-seeking and truth-telling. Truth-seeking in journalism is the gathering information and sifting through conflicting claims in the construction of a story. In truth-seeking, considerations of evidence, facts, and methods should loom large. Truth-telling is what follows truth-seeking. It refers to the way in which journalists present and publish stories. Truth-telling revolves around such questions as to whether the journalist should always publish everything they know to be true, the courage to publish controversial truths, the harm caused by publishing certain facts, and the balance, fairness, and tone of the truth-telling.

Truth-telling and truth-seeking require journalists to exercise virtues of two kinds: (1) the virtues of moral character such as truthfulness, honesty, sincerity, and transparency about one's methods, and (2) the cognitive virtues of being disinterested in determining the truth, of being willing to follow facts where they lead, of having a respect for objective methods, and fairness, and an abhorrence of manipulative techniques of communication. The pursuit of truth also requires skills and knowledge. The good journalist skillfully employs empirical methods in gathering, researching, and evaluating information.

Therefore, the pursuit of truth implies many principles, values, and skills. Journalists will either not pursue the truth, or not pursue it properly, unless they bring to their work this web of attitudes, skills, values, and virtues. This chapter makes truth and objectivity the two primary principles. Media ethics is simplified by centering many of its norms on these two principles. Norms are justified as means to truth and objectivity. Truth and objectivity are the twin pillars of media ethics. They are pillars because, without them, media ethics lacks a foundation and journalism lacks ethical character.

Truth and objectivity in journalism

Reaffirming truth and objectivity

This chapter reinterprets and reaffirms truth and objectivity. Why is this necessary?

The simple answer is that the pillars of truth and objectivity show signs of serious wear and tear as ideals within and without journalism. So much skepticism and misunderstanding about these terms has grown up that their moral force has eroded. To many, these concepts are antiquated, due to at least three factors: first, a corrosive subjectivity and a post-modern skepticism. Truth is said to be only the subjective opinion of individuals. Objectivity is depicted as a suspect concept of Western imperialistic culture. Second, a cynicism about the motives of news organizations. Citizens are increasingly skeptical about claims by journalists to be truthful and objective. Third, a belief that non-objective journalism is best for today's interactive and online public sphere, as discussed in Chapter 3. The result is an intense debate about these principles of journalism.

In this climate, a reaffirmation of old journalistic understandings of truth and objectivity is a conservative strategy that won't succeed. A reaffirmation must be based on a new interpretation that corrects misunderstandings. Media ethics needs to explain in some depth what the pursuit of truth means, and what objectivity entails.

Prima facie, it may appear nonsensical to question truth and objectivity. How could media ethics *not* include truth? Is it permissible for journalists to tell lies or publish false rumors? How can journalists inform citizens if they don't follow objective standards? This reaction to doubts about truth and objectivity has its heart in the right place. But it is too quick. What media ethics needs is a thoughtful explanation and defense of the twin pillars. Criticism needs to be taken seriously. Some of the critics make valid points and show the limits of current thinking about truth and objectivity.

Surprise at skepticism about truth and objectivity forgets that objectivity, as an explicit doctrine for news media, is relatively recent. For most of the 400 years of modern journalism, journalists were expected to be partisan, not impartial. Moreover, a full-blooded affirmation of truth-seeking and objectivity is hardly universal. Support for truth-seeking journalism is weak in authoritarian societies. In democracies, at times of insecurity, citizens support a patriotic journalism that restrains truth-telling and takes the side of government. Perhaps other values, such as care or civic engagement, are more important than truth and objectivity.[1] Any reaffirmation must keep the *problem* of truth and objectivity in mind.

This chapter will shed light on the problem by examining the evolution of journalistic truth and objectivity, and by providing new conceptions. The chapter begins by outlining how truth and objectivity came to be principles of media ethics, and how they came under attack. The chapter argues that, to fend off attacks, media ethics needs to develop better theories of its core principles. As examples of such theories, it proposes the notions of pragmatic truth and pragmatic objectivity.[2]

---

[1] Steiner and Okrusch, "Care as a Virtue for Journalists."

[2] Some of the ideas in the chapter are drawn from my previous work on truth and objectivity, such as "Truth and Objectivity," "Multi-Dimensional Objectivity for Global Journalism," and *The Invention of Journalism Ethics*.

Roots

Claims to report the truth objectively have long roots in journalism. Newsmongers in the agora of classical Athens claimed to tell the truth about military battles and strange social practices in other countries. As noted, printer-editors in the seventeenth century claimed to provide accurate and impartial reports. Editor Daniel Border of London opened his *The Faithful Scout* in 1651 with a flourish: "Having put on the Armour of Resolution, I intend … to encounter falsehood with the sword of truth. I will not endeavour to flatter the world into a belief of things that are not; but truly inform them of things that are." In the same period, the editor of the *Moderate Intelligencer* insisted, "I am no Romance-Monger to present the world with Tragi-Comedies of my own invention."[3]

Despite these homilies to truth, editors acknowledged that journalistic truth-telling was a cumulative affair. News came late by post, from uncertain or conflicting sources, and in dribs and drabs. In 1643, Henry Walley, editor of *The True Informer*, said: "Truth (in the newsbooks) is the daughter of time." In France, Cardinal Richelieu, wary of inflammatory pamphlets, granted an exclusive privilege for news publication to Theophraste Renaudot and his *Gazette de France*. "In one thing," wrote Renaudot, "I yield not to anyone – in the search for truth."

In the 1720s, London editor Nathaniel Mist portrayed his *Weekly Journal* as a moral educator that, like the theatre, instructs while providing pleasure. It is a "History of the present Times" guided by "a love of truth." Pierre-Louis Roederer, French revolutionary politician and journalist, said in a 1796 essay that newspapers reached more readers than books and taught the same truth "every day, at the same time … in all public places." By the end of the century, editors claimed their right to be considered a fourth estate because, unlike the government, it printed the truth to protect liberty. During the nineteenth century, the libertarian press believed a marketplace of ideas led to truth.

As we saw in Chapter 3, modern media ethics was built upon the principles of truth and objectivity. The doctrine of objectivity was a response to the newspaper's enthusiastic pursuit of news in the late 1800s. News

---

[3] Many of the quotations in this section are cited in Chapters 3, 4, and 5 of *The Invention of Journalism Ethics*.

encouraged a naive empiricism that thought that journalists could reliably and truthfully inform the public by simply going out into the world and observing, without an explicit methodology or strict ethical principles. However, this empiricism was soon on the defensive for producing unreliable or sensational stories. At this point, journalists developed the idea of news objectivity as an explicit method of reporting. Journalists began to speak of a truthful report as an objective report, defined as a news story where the reporter excluded her own opinion and reported only the known facts.

In North America, "objectivity" arrived as an explicit, common term after the First World War, espoused by leading editors and widely practiced in newsrooms. The term occurred in numerous press codes, articles, and textbooks. One of the earliest known uses of journalism "objectivity" is found in Charles G. Ross's *The Writing of News,* published in 1911: "News writing is objective to the last degree in the sense that the writer is not allowed to 'editorialize.' "[4] Objectivity reached its zenith in the 1940s and 1950s. Brucker saluted objective reporting as one of the "outstanding achievements" of American newspapers.[5]

The recognition of truth and objectivity as fundamental principles was evident in two major codes of ethics – the 1923 code of the American Society of News Editors (ASNE) and the 1926 code of the Sigma Delta Chi, forerunner of the Society of Professional Journalists (SPJ). The ASNE code, the first national code, stressed responsibility, freedom of the press, independence, truthfulness, impartiality, and decency. The ASNE code said that anything less than an objective report was "subversive of a fundamental principle of the profession." The first two principles of the Sigma Delta Chi code were: "truth is our ultimate goal," and "objectivity in reporting the news is another goal, which serves as a mark of an experienced professional. It is a standard of performance toward which we strive."[6] Today, truth remains the fundamental principle of the SPJ. As we've seen, its code tells journalists to: "seek the truth and report it."

In the second half of the century, investigative journalism, advocacy journalism, and broadcast journalism challenged the twin pillars of truth and objectivity. Journalists sought to escape from the restricting idea of

---

[4] Ross, *The Writing of News,* 20.
[5] Brucker, *Freedom of Information,* 21.
[6] Pratte, *Gods within the Machine.*

truth-telling as requiring complete neutrality and reporting only the bare facts. As the century closed, internet-based journalism questioned objectivity.

However, not even social media enthusiasts or libertarians of the Net argue that truth is not important to their work. The dispute tends to be about how best to serve the truth, not whether online journalists should reject truth in total. We will explore these ideas in depth in Chapter 6.

Journalism "theories" of truth

The prevalence of truth claims does not entail that journalists have constructed elaborate theories of truth. For the most part, the opposite is true. Journalists have tended to rely on commonsense notions about what is true and how one determines what is true. Often the methods of truth-seeking amount to not much more than the typical routines of reporting, such as checking a fact or getting a second source for a story.

In some ways, the lack of theory is not surprising. Journalism is a practical craft. Journalists are not philosophers. Many journalists do not see what is to be gained from engaging in theoretical discussions. The strategy for journalists-in-a-hurry when discussing issues about truth is to get along with a minimum of theory. Where truth is discussed seriously the focus is often not on conceptions of truth but on situations where journalists report falsely or fabricate sources.

Given these facts, an inquiry into truth in journalism should not begin by asking: what philosophical theory of truth is articulated in codes of ethics? Instead the inquiry should be more indirect. It should seek to expose the assumptions about truth that we find in journalistic discourse and practice. It asks: when journalists talk about truth, what assumptions do they make? What theories do they unconsciously or consciously use? Philosophers have offered conceptions of truth such as realism, which understands truth as a correspondence of belief and world. Pragmatic theories emphasize the usefulness of hypotheses, such as the solution of problems, as evidence of true belief.[7]

Coherence theories emphasize how a true belief must fit with other beliefs about the object (or topic) in question.[8] For example, a chemist

---

[7] See Kunne, *Conceptions of Truth*, and Blackburn, *Truth: A Guide*.
[8] See Rescher, *Coherence Theory of Truth*.

mixes the contents of two test tubes, observes a green tint, and says "there was copper in it."[9] The truth of that statement is not based solely on the perception of a green tint. The statement does not faithfully describe the object in isolation of other beliefs. "There was copper in it" is true because the perception is supported by, and coheres with, a set of other beliefs from chemistry about the relationship between copper and the color of test-tube liquids under certain conditions. Similarly, Darwin's idea of natural selection is true because it coheres with an enormous amount of observations and beliefs about the natural world. While realism refers us to the external world, coherence theory refers us to the background assumptions and conceptual schemes that stand behind our belief in a proposition. Truth refers to (a) beliefs which fit well the best available conceptual scheme on a topic; or (b) to theories (or explanations) that offer a more coherent account than rival systems. The idea of truth for coherence theory is holistic, involving the convergence and coherence of many beliefs.

Realism has been the most prevalent view in journalism. But at a cost. As we will see, the stress on realism has caused journalists to ignore the importance of coherence in their methods. Realism in philosophy refers to a family of theories developed from antiquity onward.[10] Common to all kinds of realism is the idea that truth is the proper alignment of belief and the world. Beliefs are made true by an objective reality external to my mind. If I say "gold is malleable" what I say is true if and only if gold actually *is* malleable.[11] "Gold is malleable" refers correctly to an external object that has the property in question. Nothing else is relevant to the truth or falsity of my statement than the fact that gold is malleable – not my ethnicity, not my knowledge of gold, not the coherence of my statement with other statements, not the time or place in which I live. The existence of malleable gold in the world is the truth "maker."[12] For the realist, there exists an independent, external world containing an immense number of objects, properties, relations, facts, and law-like behavior which await correct description. What is truth? Truth is the way the world is. To have

---

[9] Quine, *Word and Object*, 10–11.

[10] Theories of truth are so varied and sophisticated that this section only attempts to place journalism truth within the realist camp. For a taxonomy of theories of truth, including the varieties of realism, see Haack, *Evidence and Inquiry*, 188–190.

[11] Alston, *A Realist Conception of Truth*, 5.

[12] *Ibid.*, 5–6.

true beliefs is to believe something about the world as it is. Truth and what is real are intimately linked: to say that my belief is true is to say it describes a real object. Aristotle famously expressed the realist attitude in his *Metaphysics* when he defined truth as "to say of what is that it is, or of what is not that it is not."[13] Propositions are true or false depending on whether they accurately predicate a property of an object – whether propositions correspond with reality or the facts.[14]

For realists, truth is not the pursuit of truth. Truth is not how we come to know reality. It is the result of inquiry, when inquiry goes well. It is not to be confused with the process of acquiring knowledge of the world. Truth is not about the methods by which we pursue truth. There may be truths about the world that humans may never know or will not discover for centuries. Moreover, truth is not identical to "evidence" or justification. The pursuit of truth, through inquiry and the collection of evidence, is fallible. A belief, considered true at time t_1 may be shown to be false at time t_2 in the future. At any given time, we may be well justified in believing a hypothesis, given our evidence and careful inquiry. But the hypothesis may turn out to be false. The conception of truth as the alignment of belief to object of belief does not entail that we know with absolute certainty when that fit is achieved. In many cases, we may be unable to determine which of several rival beliefs (or theories) are true. Truth is an elusive, difficult ideal.

Realists have used a variety of metaphors and concepts to explain how true beliefs fit reality, or the object of belief. One of the oldest ideas is that of a *correspondence* between idea and object (or word and object, sentence and fact).[15] The belief that snow is white is true because it corresponds with the way snow is in the world. A correspondence theory has the difficult task of specifying how the items in the mind and in the world correspond, or line up. Is the correspondence mental? For example, do ideas

---

[13] Aristotle, *Metaphysics*, 749; 1011b22–30.

[14] Aristotle discusses a proposition's "correspondence with reality" or "facts" in *On Interpretation* (47, 48, 18a30–40, 19a30–34). In *Metaphysics*, Book Alpha the Lesser, Aristotle identifies the search for truth with the search for causes (712–713, 993b1–30). In *Nicomachean Ethics*, Aristotle says that both theoretical and practical intellect aim at truth but the practical intellect seeks "truth in agreement with right desire" (1024, 1139a30–31).

[15] See Kunne, "Varieties of Correspondence," *Conceptions of Truth*, 93–174. For a classical discussion, see Russell, *The Problems of Philosophy*.

in my mind refer somehow to physical objects? Or is the correspondence linguistic. Do terms of language (or sentences) denote objects, properties, or facts?

Realists differ on the reality that true beliefs describe. What one means by saying "a true belief describes reality" depends on what you think reality is. Three views have dominated discussions of truth – transcendental, scientific, and common sense. Transcendentalists believe that truth is about a transcendent reality. It could be a realm that transcends the ordinary world of observation, such as a spiritual or metaphysical reality that cannot be known by common sense. Truth, in this sense, is often thought to be objective and certain knowledge, as opposed to uncertain and changing opinion. Plato was such a realist. Truth, for Plato, was not the shifting belief of ordinary people about the quasi-real objects of perception. Truth is about absolute ideas of forms of the good, of justice and so on that are grasped by the intellect. The ideas are perfect standards which are only partially realized in this world.[16]

Scientific realism is the view that reality is the world as known through scientific inquiry and empirical methods. The scientific world often corrects or goes beyond what is known by commonsense, such as the world of quantum physics. True beliefs are scientific beliefs that accurately describe the world as it is. Common sense realism is concerned with beliefs that fit with the world of common sense, such as our beliefs about how other people tend to behave or about the properties of ordinary objects such as tables and chairs. In our everyday lives, when we are not engaged in philosophy, we tend to be commonsense realists.[17]

Journalists' discussions of truth tend to be based on a non-technical understanding of truth. That is, a commonsense realism. According to this view, journalists can often determine truth or falsity about a claim, an event, or a dispute by using their common sense. Common sense in this context means observing people and events, collecting facts, relying on what past experience has taught, using official documents and studies,

---

[16] Cornford, *The Republic of Plato*, 217–218.

[17] There are "minimalist" forms of realism that do not think it is necessary to answer technical questions about how ideas correspond to objects. Instead they believe it is sufficient to define truth simply as what is the case. A statement (proposition, belief) is true if and only if what the statement says to be the case actually is the case. Alston, *A Realist Conception of Truth*, 5.

and relying on the testimony of multiple sources. Most journalists also make the distinction between truth and justification, between seeking truth and actually achieving it.

Commonsense realism in journalism holds that a story in journalism is true if it faithfully describes some object, event, or state of affairs; otherwise it is false. A true story corresponds with the way the world is, or the way an event occurred. A false story does not correspond. Similarly, a news photograph is true if it faithfully captures an external event. If not, it is false. To many journalists, the ideas of faithful description and correspondence are self-explanatory. They do not call for technical elaboration or philosophical defense.

In recent years, however, journalists have added a large dollop of scientific realism to their understanding of a truth story. This was inevitable given the rise of science as an authority on the nature of things. Increasingly, it is more accurate to say that journalists believe that what is true is not just the world of common sense but also the world as explained by good science. Increasingly, journalists report on the leading edges of scientific research. They accept as true what scientists believe about such newsworthy issues as climate change, the genetic basis of diseases, the risk and benefits of new drugs, and the effects of economic and social policies on the public. In journalism today, the commonsense and scientific images of the world converge, reflecting the same convergence in society at large. The transcendental approach makes little headway among journalists.

Rise and decline of objectivity

Traditional news objectivity

To summarize our discussion: journalists have tended to approach the topics of truth in a practical fashion, following a commonsense realism supplemented by scientific expertise. However, journalists have developed more detailed views about how to test what people claim to be true. The most elaborate and influential view is the doctrine of traditional news objectivity. Traditional news objectivity is a conception of how to objectively report the news developed by American print journalists in the early 1900s and adopted by their Canadian colleagues.

What sort of objectivity was news objectivity? The short answer is: it was a narrow form of epistemological objectivity that required a strictly neutral reporting of "just the facts." To understand that statement we need to examine the notion of objectivity. Two senses of objectivity have dominated Western culture: ontological and epistemological. Both senses play a part in defining traditional news objectivity.[18]

Ontological objectivity is close to a realistic theory of truth. What is objective is what is real. An objective belief or statement is about some reality. It comes to much the same thing to say that an object really exists in the world apart from the mind or to say that my belief about the object is true. Ontological objectivity, like realism, is about the reality of the objects of belief.

Something is ontologically objective if it denotes an independently existing object, property, fact, lawful regularity, or state of affairs. My car in the driveway is ontologically objective. My belief that my car is in the driveway corresponds to this fact and is an example of an ontologically objective belief. The law of gravity is ontologically objective. My belief in the law of gravity is also ontologically objective. On the other hand, something is ontologically subjective if it is non-existent or exists only in the mind, such as perceptual illusions or hallucinations. For example, I may have a dream in which I believe that there are a hundred pink flamingos in my bedroom. The pink flamingos are not ontologically objective. They are a product of my imagination. My belief is ontologically subjective. To take another example, my belief that a friend's tree in her backyard is dark brown in color is not an ontologically objective belief because that is not the case – the tree is actually light brown.

Epistemological objectivity focuses not on the object of belief but on the processes by which the belief was formed. It is about the pursuit of truth – about how we seek it, and should seek it. While ontological objectivity is about truth and reality, epistemological objectivity is about the best methods and ways of justification for truth-seeking. This form of objectivity is epistemological because of the emphasis on the process of belief formation and evaluation.

---

[18] Ward, *Invention*, 14–18; Megill, *Rethinking Objectivity*, 1–20.

Therefore when we talk about objectivity in an epistemological sense, we are talking about the objectivity of our attitudes, beliefs, judgments, and methods of inquiry. Our beliefs are epistemologically objective if they satisfy the norms of our best practices and standards; otherwise they are subjective or less objective than they could be.

Ontological and epistemological objectivity do not always agree. Since inquiry is fallible, a belief that appears epistemologically objective (e.g. following the best methods available at the time) could later be shown to be false or ontologically subjective.

The attempt to be epistemologically objective occurs in many areas, such as academic research, the administration of institutions, in law, and in journalism. For instance, a scientific study into the genetic causes of brain cancer may be rejected as not epistemologically objective because it failed to comply with standard practices for testing hypotheses. A study of the effectiveness of a new drug may be rejected as subjective because it failed to follow objective methods, such as using a double-blind test where both the patient and doctor do not know which pill is the new drug and which is the placebo. An opinion poll on the popularity of the main political parties may be epistemologically objective, as far as its methods allow, because it employed objective data-gathering techniques, such as a proper representative sampling of the public. The jury's verdict was epistemologically objective to the degree that it was based on objective rules of evidence, fair judgment, and proper court procedure. The administrator's hiring decision was objective to the degree that it followed fair and objective criteria of evaluation for the new job opening.

In science and other domains, inquirers combine both senses of objectivity, arguing that the results of the work followed objective standards *and* faithfully describe an object or phenomenon in the world. Journalists claim that a news report is objective, ontologically and epistemologically. Ontologically, they claim they describe things the way things are. Epistemologically, they support their claims by appeal to their facts and methods. Suppose a team of journalists investigate an allegation that a city mayor has illegally used public funds. It finds the allegations to be true and publishes its findings. The journalists defend their controversial report by saying that they used objective methods (epistemologically objective) which led to objective truth (ontologically objective) – funds were, in fact, used illegally.

This discussion of the senses of objectivity clarifies what is meant by claiming that traditional news objectivity was a narrow form of epistemological objectivity. When journalists developed the doctrine of traditional objectivity they combined the ontological and epistemological senses of objectivity, but the emphasis was strongly on the latter sense. Objectivity was primarily a *method* for making stories more reliable. Traditional objectivity was a narrow form because objectivity was reduced to reporting facts. A report was objective if and only if it reported only the facts and eliminated comment and interpretation by the reporter. An objective report must be neutral between rival views about the topic or issue in question.

Traditional objectivity was a realism of the fact. It expressed a great confidence in the human ability to know the facts and separate them from other things. Truth-telling was the reporting of facts conceived of as hard, uninterpreted nuggets of information about the world. Facts were facts about objects, events, or states of affairs open to the observation of journalists and recorded in official documents. Facts guaranteed ontological objectivity; they were the "truth makers" that disciplined our wishes and biases. Anything beyond the facts was subjective opinion or speculation. If reporters included their interpretations, reports were subjective. External facts alone checked subjectivity.

Journalists before the late 1800s had claimed that their reports were factual and unbiased. But their claims did not amount to the strict methodology that defined traditional objectivity in newsrooms. It was no longer enough for reporters to simply claim that their writing was neutral and based only on facts. Objective reporters had to *show* that their reports were factual by following a set of rules and adopting certain attitudes. The difference between objectivity and the preceding empirical realism was the strictness of its norms of objectivity. Traditional news objectivity was realism disciplined by a method. Objective reporters were to be *completely* detached; they were to eliminate *all* of their opinion; they were to report *just* the facts. The traditional language of journalistic objectivity was a language of self-denial, restraint, and exclusion. Objectivity was a policing action against the agents of error and bias – the reporter's desire to interpret, theorize, campaign, and judge. It disciplined journalism's empiricism by subjecting reporting to standards of factuality and neutrality.

Traditional objectivity was never just an ideal. It was a system of norms that restrained and governed practice. The standards of factuality, balance, and neutrality were operationalized in newsrooms by rules on newsgathering and story construction: all opinion must be clearly attributed to a source, accompanied by direct quotation and careful paraphrasing; reporters must verify facts by reference to studies and numerical analysis; and news reports must be written from the detached tone of the third person; all stories were to balance the rival points of view on the issue, or "to get the other side." Phrases in a story that indicated a bias or the reporter's viewpoint must be eliminated, or translated into more careful, neutral language. Instead of writing, "the police chief was angered by the reporter's question," the objective reporter wrote, "the police chief appeared to be angered by the reporter's question." Instead of writing that a state's program to stimulate employment had failed," the objective reporter wrote that "the state's employment program appears to have failed to reach its aims, a major study of the program has concluded."

Objectivity was justified as a method for producing more accurate, truthful reports and more independent professional journalists at a time of growing skepticism about the press. As we saw in Chapter 3, objectivity was part of journalism's "turn to ethics" in the early 1900s. Objective reporting, it was argued, was crucial to egalitarian democracies. Commentary was not enough, and biased (or manipulated) reporting tainted the information supply. Citizens needed objective news about their government to make political judgments for themselves. Journalism, Walter Lippmann claimed, only served democracy if it provided objective information about the world, not "stereotypes."[19]

In sum, traditional objectivity combined ontological and epistemological objectivity but its distinctness lay in its epistemological stress on rules and methods. Traditional objectivity advanced a strict, reductive form of objectivity that reduced objective reporting to one dimension of good inquiry – reporting facts. Traditional objectivity applied to only one type of journalism: a completely factual and neutral form of "straight" reporting.

Skepticism and decline

The heyday of traditional objectivity was from the 1920s to the 1950s in the mainstream broadsheet newspapers of North America. The doctrine

---

[19] Lippmann, *Public Opinion*.

was so pervasive that, in 1956, press theorist Theodore Peterson said objectivity was "a fetish."[20] The second half of the century is a story of challenge and decline due to new forms of journalism, new technology, and new social conditions. Far-reaching doubts about objectivity and truth gathered strength across the rest of the twentieth century. There have been three types of complaint: first, objectivity is too demanding an ideal for journalism and hence objectivity is a "myth." Second, objectivity, even if possible, is undesirable because it forces writers to use restricted formats. It encourages a superficial reporting of official facts. It fails to provide readers with analysis and interpretation. Objectivity ignores other functions of the press such as commenting, campaigning, and acting as public watchdog. Third, objectivity restricts a free press. A democracy is better served by a diverse, opinionated press where all views compete in a marketplace of ideas.

Objectivity was challenged from its inception. Henry Luce, who founded *Time* magazine in the 1920s, dismissed objectivity: "Show me a man who thinks he's objective and I'll show you a liar," Luce declared.[21] He argued that events in a complex world needed to be explained and interpreted. The new magazine "muckrakers" of the early 1900s rejected neutrality in reporting. The emergence of television and radio created more personal forms of media where a strict objective style seemed inappropriate. In the 1960s, an "adversarial culture" that criticized institutions and fought for civil rights was skeptical of objective experts and objective journalism. Other journalists, such as Norman Mailer and Tom Wolfe, practiced a personal journalism that looked to literature for its inspiration. As discussed in Chapter 3, the final decades of the twentieth century gave birth to online communication, which favored an interpretive journalism skeptical of professionalism and objectivity.

In academia, doubts about objectivity arose in the middle of the century. Post-moderns and others questioned the ideals of truth and objectivity in Western culture and science. Thomas Kuhn's influential writings were interpreted as showing that scientific change was a non-rational "conversion" to a new set of beliefs.[22] A sociology of knowledge explained

---

[20] Peterson, "The Social Responsibility Theory of the Press," 88.
[21] Baughman, *Henry R. Luce and the Rise of the American News Media*, 29.
[22] Kuhn, *The Structure of Scientific Revolutions*.

knowledge by reference to social causes.[23] All knowledge was "socially constructed."[24] Philosopher Richard Rorty attacked a "Platonism" that believed objective knowledge was a "mirror" of nature.[25] Post-modernists such as Lyotard and Baudrillard questioned the ideas of detached truth and philosophical "meta-narratives" – large historical narratives that make sense of human experience.[26] Butler describes the illusive sense of post-modernism as a "realism lost" where people live in a "society of the image" or "simulacra."[27] Feminists portrayed objectivity as the value of a patriarchal society that "objectifies" women.[28] Media scholars treated objectivity as the dogma of corporate media.[29] Objective routines protected journalists from criticism.[30]

The questioning continues. Journalist Martin Bell rejected objectivity for a journalism of "attachment."[31] Jon Katz, an online columnist, said journalists should "abandon the false god of objectivity" for new forms of communication.[32] A lead article in the *Columbia Journalism Review*, entitled "Rethinking Objectivity," repeated the complaints cited above.[33] A public policy center in the United States published a "manifesto for change" in journalism, which noted how objectivity is "less secure in the role of ethical touchstone" while norms such as accountability are increasing in importance.[34]

Skepticism, within and without journalism, caused journalists to be less confident about asserting their objectivity and their ability to report the truth. Journalism codes of ethics dropped objectivity from their principles. Journalists replaced objectivity with the apparently more modest norms of being accurate and fair. Leading journalism textbooks maintained the importance of truth but they described truth-seeking as a difficult and uncertain process of verification.[35] At the same time news reporting moved away from reporting just the facts. Even the former bastions of traditional

---

[23] Barnes and Bloor, "Relativism, Rationalism and the Sociology of Knowledge."
[24] Hacking, "The Social Construction of What?"
[25] Rorty, *Philosophy and the Mirror of Nature.*   [26] Connor, *Postmodernist Culture.*
[27] Butler, *Postmodernism: A Very Short Introduction*, 110–111.
[28] Hawkesworth, "From Objectivity to Objectification."
[29] Hackett and Zhao, *Sustaining Democracy?*   [30] Tuchman, *Making the News.*
[31] Bell, "The Truth is Our Currency."   [32] Katz, "No News is Good News."
[33] Cunningham, *Rethinking Objectivity.*   [34] Overholser, *On Behalf of Journalism*, 10–11.
[35] Kovach and Rosenstiel, *The Elements of Journalism.*

objectivity – the news agencies, the major American broadsheets – began reporting in a way that included more room for the reporter's perspective and "voice."

Responding to the challenge

The chapter so far has examined how journalists came to establish truth and traditional news objectivity as pillars of modern media ethics, only to face a century of questioning about their definition, application, and usefulness.

Where does this leave media ethics today? It makes the clarification of these principles an important matter. How shall we use media freedom responsibly if we lack plausible principles of truth and objectivity? Rather than abandon truth and objectivity, or adopt the prevailing skeptical attitude, the rest of the chapter responds to this difficulty by doing three things. It restates why truth and objectivity matter. It argues that journalism (and media ethics) must develop more sophisticated concepts of these principles and better explanations of how the principles operate in media ethics. Finally, it puts forward the concepts of "pragmatic truth" and "pragmatic objectivity" as examples of more sophisticated concepts.

Why truth and objectivity matter

The assumption that we can distinguish between truth and falsity, between the objective and subjective, is embedded in our everyday lives. We could scarcely get out of bed in the morning and get through the day without knowing some things to be true. It is true that today is a certain date on the calendar and that Moscow is the capital of Russia. It is true that my car exists and it will start when I insert the key into the ignition. It is true that I have an office in the university (which truly exists). I wouldn't get on an airplane unless I believed that the laws of aerodynamics were true.

Truth has great utility. Engineers use truths about materials and physical forces to build bridges. If a bridge under construction collapses, we assume there is some reason for it, some error. Physicians operate upon our bodies confident in the truth of their tests and diagnosis. Socially, truth-telling is central. I believe a family member when she says she is financially in trouble and needs help. I believe a faculty member speaks the truth when he says he can't make an important meeting because he is ill. I believe a friend when he promises to repay a loan from me. Unless we could trust people to tell the truth on most occasions, social co-operation and communication would founder.

Truth is tied in complex ways to mental health and human growth. When people say ruefully that they have deceived themselves, what are they deceiving themselves about if not some difficult-to-acknowledge truth, such as the fact that they are, below the surface, quite selfish, unhappy; or they have deviant sexual desires; or they no longer love their partner.[36] A troubled person may not begin to heal psychologically until they open themselves up, often painfully, to truths about themselves.

The utility of truth has biological roots. Our species would not have flourished unless our sensory organs were not efficient in monitoring a perilous environment and detecting things that were real and threatening – from the fleeting image of a tiger in the woods to signs of an impending violent storm. Our species survived because it was good at tracking what was true or false, subjective or objective.

Beyond biology, truth plays a central role in anchoring our most basic concepts. Without the distinction of truth and falsehood, other distinctions cannot be made, such as the difference between accuracy and inaccuracy, bias and non-bias, rational persuasion and propaganda. What is being biased other than not being disposed to recognize some truth? What is being inaccurate journalistically if not to publish something false? Truth and falsity are *not* expendable concepts.

Humans need to care for truth in general, not just specific truths.[37] Truth, taken in bits and pieces, is instrumentally valuable, from the engineer's truths about the tensile strength of materials and the doctor's truths about the causes of disease to a police investigator's facts about a case. To care for truth in general is to care about extending and deepening the truths we know, and to take joy in simply understanding significant truths previously unknown or obscure. To care for truth in general is to be willing to protect our hard-earned truths from error, ignorance, and misrepresentation. To care for truth in general is to encourage a society that

---

[36] For a clear and emphatic defense of the utility of truth, see Frankfurt, *On Truth*. For a debate on its usefulness, see Rorty and Engel, *What's the Use of Truth?*

[37] Frankfurt, *On Truth*, 94–96.

is intolerant of what Frankfurt frankly called "bullshit," an indifference to the truth and its manipulation.[38] Caring for truth in general grounds our more particular love of specific truths and our curiosity about facts. Caring about truth sustains an interest in accumulating specific truths.[39]

The love of truth supports the organized, rigorous pursuit of truth. Truth acts as both a presupposition and an ideal of rigorous inquiry. Truth is a presupposition because one must assume its existence before embarking on any serious study. One inquires about phenomenon x to find out some truths about x. "Every man is fully satisfied that there is such a thing as truth, or he would not ask any question," wrote C.S. Peirce.[40] Moreover, the idea of truth is required to believe anything, for to believe that p is to accept that p is true.[41]

Truth is crucial in the regulation of inquiry. A commitment to truth demands that we inquire honestly, accurately, diligently, and with disinterest. Disinterestedness is not a callous unconcern for people or events. Disinterestedness is not allowing personal interests to distort truth-telling. Truth is not a comforting illusion. It is a hard taskmaster. A commitment to truth will not allow us to acquiesce in wishful thinking or platitudes. As Nietzsche said: "Truth has had to be fought for every step of the way, almost everything else dear to our hearts … has had to be sacrificed to it."[42] Moreover, truth serves as a real-world restraint on our other goals. The quest for solidarity and solutions to problems is important. However, we should want our pursuit of solidarity and problem-solving to be based on well-evidenced truths.

The goal of truth persuades us to follow methods of inquiry. We don't pursue just any sort of truth in any sort of way. Inquiry seeks important and secure (or well-evidenced) truths.[43] The pursuit of significant truth is difficult and requires discipline. The world is so complex that it often resists our attempts to discover or change it. We seek methods of discovery

---

[38] Frankfurt, *On Bullshit*.   [39] Frankfurt, *On Truth*, 98.

[40] Quoted in Haack, *Manifesto of a Passionate Moderate*, 22. In the same way, the assumption of an external world is not an inductive inference from experience. It is a precondition for any inquiry.

[41] Haack, *Evidence and Inquiry*, 192.   [42] Nietzsche, *The AntiChrist*, 50.

[43] There are goals for inquiry other than truth, from biological survival to intellectual pleasure. See Alston, *A Realist Conception of Truth*, 231–264.

and standards of evaluation because truth is not directly accessible.[44] Scientists, professionals, and others would not follow methods and standards unless they were "truth-conducive."[45] If justificatory procedures are not "truth-acquiring," why prefer rigorous scientific methods to other dubious methods of acquiring beliefs, such as brainwashing or consulting oracles?[46] Part of the concept of justification is that justification "counts toward truth."[47]

The commitment to truth is also a commitment to objectivity, ontologically and epistemologically. As we discussed with respect to realism, to seek the truth is to seek what really exists in the world. Our beliefs and theories are true if they are ontologically objective. Similarly, to care for truth is to be willing to pursue it in epistemologically objective ways. It is a contradiction for someone to claim that they are rigorously pursuing truth if they are unwilling to follow methods that reduce bias and subjective tendencies in our thinking. The idea of "subjective truth" – that truth is just what each person thinks it is – is nonsense, and an abuse of the term "truth." Subjective truth is better called opinion. Truth is about real things whose truth is independent of anyone's perspective; a truth that can be approached by other inquirers using objective methods.

Application to journalism

These arguments for the importance of truth and objectivity apply to journalism as a form of inquiry and communication.

Conceptually, truth and objectivity are no more expendable in journalism than elsewhere. Without clear notions of truth and objectivity, media ethics lacks the resources to distinguish between good and bad journalism and lacks the authority to critique dubious practice. If journalists dismiss truth and objectivity as impossible, or as a cultural myth, they open the doors to

---

[44] Bonjour, *The Structure of Empirical Knowledge*, 7–8. Rules for conducting inquiry are related, but not identical with, objective criteria of justification. The standards of justification differ from rules of inquiry in the same way that criteria for judging a meal as nutritious differ from directions for cooking. Haack, *Evidence and Inquiry*, 204.

[45] Alston, *A Realist Conception of* Truth, 242. See Moser, *Knowledge and Evidence*, 42–43.

[46] Williams, *Truth and Truthfulness*, 127–129.

[47] Audi, *The Structure of Justification*, 300–301.

subjective and misleading journalism. Who can criticize a biased journalist or critique subjective reporting if we doubt the ideal of truthful, objective journalism? On what basis do we critique journalism if we question the difference between truth and falsity, between subjectivity and objectivity? How can we complain about biased reporting if we no longer expect journalists to be objective? If everything is simply one's perspective, why bother constructing stories according to careful methods and demanding criteria? Who is to say what is good or bad journalism? Journalists also need to care for truth in general, in addition to specific truths, because the former grounds the long-term allegiance of journalists to truth. Care for truth encourages journalists to protect hard-won truths, to avoid temptations to water down the truth, and to create a society that is intolerant of "bullshit."

The love of truth supports good inquiry in journalism, as elsewhere, as a presupposition and a goal. Unless journalists presuppose truth, why should they inquire seriously into anything? If one believes that there is no truth to be found, that everything is just whatever people think or "spin," then the motivation for rigorous journalistic inquiry will flag. A commitment to the goal of truth, that hard taskmaster, is good discipline. It does not let journalists rest content with sloppy or lazy journalism.

The commitment to truth is also a commitment to objectivity, ontologically and epistemologically. Journalists seek to know what really exists or has happened in the world. Their beliefs and theories are true if they are ontologically objective. Similarly, to care for truth in journalism is to be willing to pursue it in epistemologically objective ways. Journalists are not pursuing truth properly if they are not pursuing it according to objective methods that restrain bias, subjectivity, and partisanship.

Finally, truth and objectivity matter for journalism because they are essential to journalism's important role in society. As Frankfurt rightly states:

> Any society that manages to be even minimally functional must have, it seems to me, a robust appreciation of the endlessly protean utility of truth. After all, how could a society that cared too little for truth make sufficiently well-informed judgments and decisions concerning the most suitable disposition of its business? How could it possibly flourish, or even survive, without knowing enough about the relevant facts to pursue its ambitions successfully and to cope prudently and effectively with its problems?"[48]

[48] Frankfurt, *On Truth*, 16.

Journalists form one of the most important groups for ensuring that the public have the truthful information of which Frankfurt speaks, through a dogged insistence on accuracy, honesty, and clarity in reporting. Standing behind those norms is a deep and non-cavalier respect for truth and objectivity.

Those who are skeptical about truth, should ask whether it is important that journalists determine whether a country really has weapons of mass destruction, or whether the government is telling the truth when it claims that the food supply system is safe. Is it not important that journalists speak truth to power, and that they take responsibility for their own power by refusing to spread unverified rumors? Truth motivates courageous journalism. For instance, a global gathering of journalists in Toronto in 2006, which recognized international journalists who had fought for press freedom, was entitled, "now try writing the truth."

Without journalists who have the virtues of honesty, sincerity, disinterestedness, and a passionate desire for the truth, without journalists who have the research capabilities and methods of good inquiry, journalism is an unreliable source of information for the public. Without these virtues and methodological skills, journalism is not only unreliable but likely to be used to advance the personal, ideological, or partisan interests of subsets of the general public. Without a journalism that is committed to truth and objectivity, the public has the unattractive choice between sincerely produced falsehood (or error) and intentionally produced propaganda. Together, truth and objectivity, properly understood, counter-balance the pressure in journalism to twist the truth, to bias the evidence, to force an unwarranted interpretation.

Truth-seeking and truth-telling, the two acts that make up the pursuit of truth, are constitutive of good journalism because truthful communication on essential public issues is the goal of democratic journalism. Untruthful communication is the tool of tyrants; misleading persuasion is the tool of propagandists; an inability to distinguish between reliable and unreliable communication is the mark of an undemocratic society.

In summary, the pillars of objectivity and truth need to be sustained as principles for the practice of journalism and in all professions across society. It is not necessary to adopt a rigorous objective stance toward everything in life. In much of our daily lives, whether we are choosing a restaurant or cheering for our football team, we can be quite subjective and partisan. However, truth and objectivity loom large where we are dealing with knowledge-seeking and fair decision-making. In society, the public expects its legislatures, government agencies and institutions to make decisions based on true information that are defensible from an objective point of view. We expect the same of judges, labor arbitrators, teachers, referees, and peacekeepers. There is no reason why the same expectations should not apply to journalists.

Few people would care to live in a society that has no respect for the concept of truth or objectivity, a society that sees no virtue in aspiring towards truth or adopting an objective stance. Few critics of truth and objectivity would want journalism to abandon truth and objectivity *tout court*. It is one thing to discuss the myth of objectivity or the illusion of truth in academia; it is quite another to live in a society that lacks these ideals.

Need for theory

Journalism and society have evolved to a point where the journalist's strategy of getting by with a minimum of theory is inadequate. Commonsense realism and an appeal to facts fail to address the most pressing questions about journalism. Dodging theory fails to address questions about journalism's role in a larger and more complex communication sphere.

What is the way forward? We cannot return to the past. The answer is not to develop a stronger defence of traditional objectivity. Traditional news objectivity is, by all accounts, a spent ethical force, doubted by journalists and academics. Few news organizations, let alone the former bastions of objectivity, report in a neutral "just the facts" manner of the past. In addition, traditional objectivity cannot be adapted to major forms of journalism old and new. For example, traditional objectivity is inconsistent with agenda-setting investigative journalism that rejects neutrality and seeks not just to report but to reveal wrongdoing. What can traditional objectivity say, by way of guidance, to other forms of journalism, such as online blogging or advocacy journalism, which are gaining in popularity?

A narrow traditional objectivity cannot respond adequately when other values than just reporting facts, such as reforming society, are advanced as alternate principles of journalism.

On the other hand, the way forward is not a curt dismissal of the criticisms of truth and objectivity as merely academic – the mumbo-jumbo of people who know nothing about the practical realities of a newsroom. The future of media ethics, and a credible journalism profession, is to articulate its values in ways that are plausible and defensible to thoughtful people, skeptics, and scholars. Media ethics cannot be based on weak concepts.

Still, it may appear that the lack of defensible theory does no harm in practical enterprises such as journalism. In defense of their anti-intellectual attitudes, many journalists would say that when they cover breaking news they have little time for theory, little time for a philosophical debate about truth or objectivity. This reply is based on the obvious fact that, in some situations, doing philosophy is inappropriate. But how far does this piece of common sense go? Not far. A responsible approach to practice requires journalists to develop thoughtful theories and ethical frameworks for difficult situations, such as when to reveal one's confidential sources, when to report a country's military secret, or when to treat subjects of stories with compassion. Journalism is an ad hoc practice relying on seat-of-the-pants judgments if journalists do not approach problems with ethical aims, principles, and the skill to apply principles. Seat-of-the-pants judgments are often wrong, and inconsistent. An anti-intellectual attitude does journalism no good, inhibiting its moral development.

If journalism is not prepared to address questions about its role and ethics, it will surely lose its bearings. It will be unable to maintain the support of a skeptical public and to provide in-principle arguments against unethical practitioners. In addition, it will struggle to say which of the new forms of journalism honor the principles of journalism, let alone how the principles need to change to apply to new practices. For instance, if truth-seeking defines good journalism, then a lack of clarity about truth seeking also makes the notion of good journalism unclear. If journalists defend their truth-telling and objectivity with inadequate or outdated notions, they will be unable to articulate what they stand for when they engage in dialogue with academics, scientists, professionals, and the general public.

Good theory helps journalism avoid fruitless debates. For example, the endless debate over objectivity in journalism is due to the fact that both the proponents and critics of objectivity presume an implausible and superficial view of news objectivity. They presume incorrectly that

objectivity requires complete neutrality and the elimination of all interpretation. Deeper thinking about news objectivity would show that there
are better versions of objectivity operating in other disciplines that don't
demand a positivistic ban on interpretation or complete neutrality.

Finally, a minimum of theory leads to confusion about what the pursuit
of truth demands in concrete situations. What happens when journalistic
truth-telling comes up against other values, such as minimizing harm,
protecting vulnerable people, and not jeopardizing the security of one's
country? Should journalists publish everything they know? Does truth-
telling require publishing the names of rape victims or the identity of
children caught up in family tragedies? Does truth-telling require journalists to publish the names of every source for a story? What if the main
source for a story on motorcycle gangs needs anonymity to avoid reprisals
from bikers? A journalism that can only talk about truth and objectivity
superficially lacks the intellectual resources to formulate correct editorial
policies, especially where a weighing of values is required. Media ethics,
therefore, requires more sophisticated theories about the role of truth and
objectivity. Journalism is practical; it is a practice; but it should not be a
blind practice, uninformed by reflection and theory.

A plausible theory of truth and objectivity must answer six related
questions.

First, what is the status of truth and objectivity in today's journalism
practice and media ethics? Historically, have these principles played a central role in the media systems of different cultures? Is the value of truth
and objectivity dependent on one's view of the political and social functions of journalism?

Second, what concepts of truth and objectivity are most appropriate for the practice of journalism? If a simple correspondence to facts is
not adequate, what are the leading candidates for a more sophisticated
concept?

Third, what is the relationship between truth and the virtues of honesty, sincerity, and transparency?

Fourth, what is the place of truth and objectivity in media ethics? Is truth
an absolute principle that always trumps other values? Is it permissible for
certain forms of journalism to ignore objectivity or adhere to its precepts
in varying degrees? What is the relationship between truthful, objective

journalism and democracy? How do we distinguish truthful journalism from propaganda, ideology, and special interest communication?

Fifth, what economic, political, and institutional structures encourage truthful journalism? To what degree do media ownership and commercial pressures obstruct good journalism? What are the real-world obstacles to truth-telling in journalism?

Sixth, what is the future of truthful, objective journalism in a digital era? How can journalists responsibly use social media and online publication?

Pragmatic truth and objectivity

What would a more sophisticated conception of truth and objectivity for journalism look like?

In what follows I propose the ideas of pragmatic inquiry and pragmatic truth to serve as a more adequate concept of truth in journalism. I also propose the idea of pragmatic objectivity to accompany the notion of pragmatic inquiry and to provide a more adequate concept of objectivity in journalism.[49]

Pragmatic inquiry and truth

"Pragmatic"

The term "pragmatic," which in the following sections will modify "inquiry", "truth," and "objectivity," is used to signal that these are concepts defined with the practical domain of journalism in mind. I use "pragmatic" in the dictionary sense of being concerned about "matters with regard to their practical requirements or consequences."[50] The pragmatic has a close association with the practical defined in Chapter 1 as a domain where the dominant aim is sound judgment to guide action. Truth and objectivity in news media are sought because they result in fairer and better-grounded actions.

---

[49] Pragmatic truth and objectivity were first introduced in Chapter 7 of my *The Invention of Journalism Ethics*.

[50] Barber, *The Canadian Oxford Dictionary*. By "pragmatic" I do not mean sacrificing principles to obtain results.

Therefore, "pragmatic" is used because the discussion is about (a) inquiry conducted by practical disciplines, (b) practical reasoning to reach informed judgments and decisions, and (c) truths specific to practical domains. We find pragmatic inquiries and pragmatic norms of truth and objectivity everywhere: in professional practice, in disciplines such as applied ethics, and in practical enterprises such as police investigations, journalism, jury trials, forensic accounting, medical diagnosis, and commissions of inquiry into social problems.

Use of the term, "pragmatic," signals that we are dealing with practical enterprises where the methods, standards, and aims are different from theoretical and academic pursuits. In practical enterprises, such as journalism, we may not obtain certain knowledge or proof of truths but instead settle for high probability or strong evidence. Pragmatic truth in journalism is not the sort of abstract truth we find in logic and mathematics. Pragmatic truth in journalism can't aspire realistically to be as rigorous as truth in science. But this does not mean it is futile to develop a theory of truth for journalism. It means that we should develop a theory appropriate to the practice in question. Other practical disciplines, from law to medicine, have developed methods of evaluation appropriate to their own practices that increase the likelihood of reaching the truth or of reaching good outcomes.

Inquiry and interpretation

The redefinition of truth begins by conceiving of journalism as a form of inquiry which should follow appropriate methods and employ normative criteria for assessing the results of inquiry. The "results of inquiry" is the story before publication.

What idea of inquiry should shape our view of journalism? One approach is to see journalism as part of the human impulse to inquire into the world to achieve certain purposes. Pragmatism, as a philosophy, celebrates constructive activity in a contingent world. Humans give meaning to their lives through purposeful activity.

Inquiry, in its broadest sense, is the natural activity of a highly evolved organism that is motivated to explore, understand, and control phenomena as it navigates a perilous natural and social environment. Both theoretical knowledge and practical truths (and wisdom) are outcomes of that exploration. In practical enterprises, careful observation is part of inquiry, but inquirers are not passive spectators. The practical inquirer's knowledge is not a list of facts produced by a passive observation of the world. Inquirers are active, purpose-driven agents operating in a social setting, whose inquiry is influenced by pre-existing conceptual schemes and skills. They go out into the world to test hypotheses, to solve problems, to find the best means to ends. Ideas are mental tools that organize and predict experience. They evaluate methods according to whether they achieve goals.

For practical ventures like journalism I prefer to speak about interpretations rather than beliefs since journalism stories are more naturally understood as interpretations. To interpret is to perceive, understand, or explain something in a specific manner. In its simplest form, an interpretation places an object (event, phenomena) under a descriptive or explanatory category. Interpretation is a judgment that x is F or is understood *as* F. We perceive x *as* a lion in the dark, we interpret x *as* a mocking gesture, we conceive of light *as* quanta of energy. We interpret stimuli effortlessly and almost without notice. A few black streaks on the sea's horizon are seen as smoke from a ship. What we believe to be true is the result of much interpretation, hypothesis, and theory. Theories are complex interpretations of phenomena or events. Knowledge itself is the interpretive accomplishment of rigorous inquiry.

Psychologically, the interpretation, as an explicit judgment, is only the tip of the iceberg. Interpretations are the "final result" of much thinking and conceptualization. The central mental 'tool' of interpretation is the conceptual scheme. A conceptual scheme is a set of ideas that help us to interpret experience. My conceptual scheme of living creatures, which uses the categories of animals, mammals, fish, and so on, helps me understand the complexity of life on earth. The normative conceptual scheme of utilitarianism helps its adherents decide on courses of action. Simple statements such as "this is a sparrow" and "there was copper in it" depend on conceptual schemes for birds and natural elements.

Interpretation is ubiquitous because humans do not have direct, cognitive contact with reality. Even our seemingly direct perceptions of objects are the result of much processing of stimuli by our perceptual system. The information-processing brain interprets the stimuli according to our categories, beliefs, and expectations. Our awareness of the world is mediated by conceptual schemes.

If we adopt this perspective, all statements, even factual statements, are interpretations, strictly speaking, because they always contain some element of conceptualization, theorizing, and evaluation. Statements of fact differ from other statements by having *less* interpretation, not because they contain no interpretation. Statements of fact are more responsive to empirical stimuli than theoretical statements. We readily assent or dissent from statements of fact in the presence of the appropriate stimuli because they contain a minimum of theory and speculation.

Pragmatic truth

What type of truth is implied by pragmatic inquiry? It is a conception of truth that provides a goal for active, interpretive inquiry, working through the mediation of conceptual schemes. The goal is true interpretations, or interpretations that come as close to truth as possible. Pragmatic truth is the result of successful inquiry by situated inquirers employing their best available conceptual schemes to interpret the world or some part of the world. For practical enterprises, the realistic conception of truth as beliefs that align with the world remains an important presupposition and regulator of inquiry. Pragmatic inquirers seek interpretations that describe and explain real objects and properties in the way that they exist. Truth remains a presupposition of pragmatic inquiry and a goal that motivates serious investigations using challenging methods.

However this realist notion is combined with a coherence approach to truth. Recall that the coherence theory states that a true belief must cohere with other beliefs about the object in question.[51] Truth refers to (a) interpretations that fit well with the best available conceptual scheme on a topic, or (b) theories (as complex interpretations) that offer a more coherent account than rival systems. The idea of truth for coherence theory is holistic, involving the coherence of many beliefs. This stress on coherence fits very well pragmatic inquiry's idea of interpretations as the product of conceptualization and theorizing. If our knowledge of reality is never direct but always mediated, then coherence among ideas must be important

---

[51] See Rescher, *Coherence Theory of Truth*.

to articulating and defending true interpretations.[52] Logic and other methods evaluate the internal consistency of the ideas within a theory. We ask such questions as, "does my theory have internal contradictions?" "Does my argument follow logically from true premises?" "Does my interpretation contradict or support a recent major study on this topic?" "How does my interpretation explain these apparently contradictory facts?"

However, it would be a mistake to define pragmatic truth as simply a coherence of ideas. Coherence among ideas is, by itself, insufficient for truth. A novel may create a fictional world where the beliefs and actions of the main characters cohere. Non-fictional inquiry needs a strong sense of realism. Ideas need to be tested against the real world through a variety of means – observation, prediction, noting how ideas are useful in solving real-world problems, and so on.[53] These means check the external reference of ideas to the world. They test interpretations for empirical validity and give them a solid footing in the real world. Combining coherence with realism discourages wishful thinking and ideologies.[54]

Pragmatic truth defines truth as a faithful description of the way the world is through both an empirical fit with external objects and a logical coherence with existing knowledge.

Pragmatic pursuit of truth

Our description of pragmatic inquiry and truth has implications for how we should pursue the truth. We should pursue interpretations that are as true as possible – interpretations that are empirically valid and internally coherent.

The task requires the coming together of three elements: (1) the inquirer must have a certain character. That is, she must exhibit certain virtues

---

[52] Lynch has argued that there is such a thing as "truth in context" – or truth within conceptual schemes, Lynch, *Truth in Context*, 101–139.

[53] Note here that I am including pragmatic ideas about truth – solving problems – to be part of a realistic stress on testing ideas against objects and situations in the real world.

[54] By "empirical validity" I do not mean "proven" or known absolutely to be true. These concepts are too strong for pragmatic inquiry. Empirical validity is a concise way of saying that the interpretation is, empirically considered, a candidate for a true interpretation because it is supported by strong evidence and good empirical methods.

and attitudes toward truth-seeking; (2) the inquirer must use skillfully the best available methods of inquiry; and (3) the inquirer must evaluate the results according to objective standards of justification.

Earlier, we noted the importance of character. It was argued that journalists will not properly seek truth unless they care for truth in general and come to inquiry with a disinterested attitude and other virtues. We have also noted the importance of proper method. Pollsters should use good methods to measure public opinion; genetic scientists should follow accepted protocols for investigating genes in the brain. Courts of law need to follow strict rules of procedure.

The evaluation of results involves two things. First, making sure that inquirers used the best available methods, and used the methods skillfully and properly. Good methods are methods that are known to be truth-conducive by reducing subjectivity and bias, and by encouraging an objective analysis of results. A double-blind test of a new drug is a good method because it reduces subjectivity. Assessing polling results by referring to the study's margin of error encourages an objective analysis of the data.

The second part of evaluation is testing the results by using broad standards of justification. These standards spell out what is meant by empirical validity and coherence. As a whole, they define what it means to inquire rationally. The standards include the rules of induction from facts and standards for what counts as well-evidenced belief. The standards can be general or specific, or somewhere in between. The most general standards come from logic, such as the principle of non-contradiction or the logical ban on circular arguments. An example of a mid-level standard of empirical validity are criteria that determine whether a correlation between two variables – such as the correlation between abuse of human rights and the existence of a free press – is statistically significant.

Just as realism and coherence combine to define pragmatic truth, realism and coherence combine to justify interpretations. Susan Haack has explained how empirical and 'coherent' factors combine in her *Evidence and Inquiry*. She calls her approach "foundherentism" – a theory that thinks justification requires both empirical foundations and a coherent set of beliefs. Empirical foundations are basic empirical beliefs verified by perception and sound empirical methods. For Haack, a "foundherentist" allows for "persuasive mutual support among beliefs and for the contribution of experience to empirical justification." The justification of beliefs is analogous to the construction of a jigsaw puzzle where many different pieces must fit together.[55] The goal of inquiry is "substantial, significant, illuminating truth"; the goal of justification is to make sure the interpretation is actually true, or likely to be true. Justification ratifies the results.

The pursuit of truth is holistic through and through. Interpretations rarely confront the world as individual statements. Since interpretations are often part of larger theories and are the products of conceptual schemes, verification is rarely a simple matter of testing one statement of belief against a specific fact. An interpretation approaches the test of empirical experience and coherence as part of a larger set of beliefs. Interpretations must in some way agree with the way the world is. But such agreement is not directly knowable by a special intuition or direct perception. Instead, the alignment of belief and the world is judged *indirectly*. The truth is that interpretation which is best supported by the use of good methods and a holistic testing of the results of inquiry.

The process of justification, then, is multi-directional and multi-dimensional. Support flows to the interpretation from many sources. Justification consists of mutual support from experience, observation, empirical methods, statistical and mathematical analysis, and logical relations among ideas. Judgments of what is justified are often a matter of degree, a matter of seeing how well these various standards are honored in specific studies and interpretations. We should not think of a well-supported interpretation as a house resting upon a foundation of (only) empirical facts. A better analogy is that of an arch, where many types of blocks mutually support each other and are essential to maintaining the structure.

The pragmatic pursuit of truth is situated. We always start from some point, some perspective, some purpose, and some conceptual schemes. The fact that human inquirers are situated means that we need to be tolerant of the non-absolute and fallible nature of our pursuit of truth. There is no guarantee that our most fundamental and seemingly secure beliefs won't be revised at some later point. Fallibilism walks between absolutism and extreme skepticism. Both absolutism and extreme skepticism agree that, if there are no absolute truths, than there is no knowledge. There is only

[55] Haack, *Evidence and Inquiry*, 1–2.

relative opinion. If there are no guarantees of certainty, then it appears that no claim is more objective than any other. Inquirers who accept falli-bilism employ only a limited skepticism. They question particular beliefs and interpretations while maintaining the rest of the conceptual scheme. The pursuit of truth is fallible, situated and yet non-arbitrary.[56]

The aim of inquiry, at least in practical domains, is not the impos-sible aim of some universal, transcendent truth that exists apart from all human perspective and interest. Nor does pragmatic inquiry require that we wipe our minds clean of all presuppositions and start fresh from abso-lute propositions. The aim is to construct substantial and significant inter-pretations by partial transcendence of one's current situation through well-designed inquiry, questioning, imagination, and interaction with other ways of thinking.

Pragmatic inquiry and journalism

Given this description of pragmatic inquiry and truth, we reconceive the practice of journalists. Journalists are regarded as active, situated inquir-ers who should aim at constructing well-tested interpretations. Truth-seeking in journalism proceeds via the interpretation of events.

Journalists are not idle observers of the passing show of life. Journalists cannot be, and should not try to be, passive recorders of facts. Journalism is a cultural interpretive activity. The journalist's mind is not a repository of facts; it is an active mind that tests interpretations in the public sphere. If all statements are interpretations, all journalism statements (and stor-ies) are interpretations. Journalists, like other inquirers, interpret events with the assistance of conceptual schemes. Journalists place events or issues under some frame of understanding. Journalism is situated inquiry. Journalists start from a practice in a certain culture, and they bring to their reports their conceptual schemes, perspectives, and interests.

Interpretation in journalism is ubiquitous and unavoidable. A report say-ing the police chief was "stung" by accusations of wrongdoing and "strug-gled" to reply is an interpretation. Rival descriptions of an armed stand-off between natives and police as an "illegal native act" or a "legitimate

---

[56] For a pragmatic conception of fallibilism, see Putnam's *Pragmatism*, 21, and *Words and Life*, 152.

affirmation of native rights" are rival interpretations. If I report that, "the defense minister is a zealous, misguided opponent of any budget cuts that might hurt retired soldiers," I mix facts and evaluation. Journalists interpret both the language and behavior of leaders. What is the meaning of an awkward handshake between the prime minister of Israel and the leader of the PLO? Headlines also summarize and interpret. On January 24, 2003, Canadian newspapers reported the comments of Prime Minister Jean Chretien on whether he supported an American plan to attack Iraq. The *Globe and Mail* headline read: "PM to Bush: Hold Off On War. The *Toronto Star* blared: "Chretien Supports U.S. Push For War."

Deciding on the "angle" for a story, its most important facts, and the most credible sources is a selective process. Deciding on the news of the day is an interpretive exercise influenced by newsroom culture, news judgment, and the form of media. News is not a natural kind. News is information deemed to be novel or significant, according to the interests of the journalist, his news organization, their readers, and society at large.

To be sure, there are occasions when journalists attempt to strip away most of the interpretation in their reports. For example, reporters may attempt to write careful, factual descriptions of what is said during important court trials. They may balance comments from both sides of the case. Yet vestiges of interpretation always remain, whether it is the choice of a news hook or a judgment about the most important facts. Such exercises are properly described not as non-interpretive reports but as reports that restrain interpretation, extrapolation, and unwarranted inferences. They are reports that hover close to the level of observation. Even the "just the facts" stories of traditional objectivity were (and are) interpretations. Pragmatic inquiry understands traditional objectivity as the demand that journalists reduce the amount of interpretation by only using statements that are responsive to empirical stimuli. For pragmatic inquiry, there is no escaping interpretation.

Pragmatic inquiry reconceives journalistic truth as a species of pragmatic truth. The conception of journalistic truth is that of a true interpretation – a journalistic interpretation of an event, person, or trend that comes as close as possible to capturing how these things are in the world. Journalist interpretations should seek to be both coherent and empirically valid, like other types of interpretation. Interpretations should have support from facts, logic, and other elements of good inquiry. At its best, journalistic inquiry brings several methods to bear on a topic from common observation and the computer-assisted analysis of statistical information to the interrogation of multiple witnesses and the search for coherence among its results and existing knowledge. As journalists investigate an issue over time, new facts are added, false claims revealed, more perspectives are considered. Through this winnowing process, journalism truth resembles a 'protean thing which, like learning, grows as a stalagmite in a cave, drop by drop over time."[57]

The journalistic pursuit of truth is a fallible process. In journalism, the practitioner occupies a precarious epistemological situation. His reports are based on limited data, imperfect methods, conflicting values, and changing conditions. He is assailed by self-interested rhetoric from all sides. Therefore, it is wise for a theory of journalism objectivity to talk about imperfect procedures and standards that *point* in the direction of truth.

The pursuit of journalism truth requires, like all good inquiry, the convergence of three elements: good character, good method, and good evaluation. Journalists need to have certain truth-seeking virtues. They need to employ the best methods available. And they need to test their interpretations with the same candor that they apply to other people's interpretations. Journalistic testing of results is multi-dimensional and multi-directional. An interpretation hopes to receive support from many sources of evidence. Justification of a journalistic interpretation is like an arch of mutually supporting blocks.

Pragmatic objectivity

What place does objectivity occupy in pragmatic inquiry? Its role is in the evaluation (or testing) of the results of inquiry. Traditional news objectivity thought that this evaluation was one-dimensional: statements were tested by facts. If statements went beyond the facts, the statement was regarded as subjective. In the rest of this section, a multi-dimensional conception of evaluation will be put forward called pragmatic objectivity. The conception builds upon the premises of pragmatic inquiry and pragmatic truth.

---

[57] Kovach and Rosenstiel, *The Elements of Journalism*, 44.

Traditional news objectivity went wrong when journalists, seeking to discipline the rush for news, adopted a popular but flawed version of objectivity – a stringent positivism of just the facts. In addition, writers used the misleading metaphor of the objective journalist as a recording instrument who passively observes and transmits facts. When positivism and the passive model of journalism collapsed, so did traditional objectivity.

The moral is that we need a notion of objectivity that is compatible with the idea of journalism as an active, interpretive, cultural activity. The task of truth-seeking and truth-telling in journalism is not to eliminate active inquiry and interpretation. The task is to develop fallible but important methods for testing interpretations.

The fact that all of journalism consists of interpretations doesn't mean that anything goes. Interpretations can be better or worse, they can be well-evidenced or not, they can be far-fetched or false. The idea of objectivity as testing interpretations exists in many domains. Philosophy of science regards scientists as active investigators of nature, whose theories and hypotheses are interpretations that face the objective test of facts, logic, and coherence with other knowledge.[58] Philosophical hermeneutics seeks an interpretation of texts against the background of a larger "fusion of horizons."[59] The idea of objective interpretation or "interpretive sufficiency" grounds a basic method of qualitative research in the social sciences.[60] Longino developed a concept of scientific objectivity "by degree" that depends on whether the social practices of disciplines are open to "transformative criticism" and dialogue.[61] In law, there are sophisticated theories of objective interpretation.[62]

Pragmatic objectivity is part of this movement toward a more nuanced approach to truth and objectivity. It believes that journalistic interpretation, like other forms of interpretation, can be subjected to criteria of evaluation. Pragmatic objectivity is multi-dimensional. It attempts to evaluate the many dimensions of a story with a plurality of evaluative criteria. The claim of objectivity is not absolute but rather a fallible judgment about a belief or report, based on a holistic weighing of several standards.

---

[58] Thagard, *Conceptual Revolutions.*   [59] Gadamer, *Truth and Method*, 305.
[60] See Christians, "Preface" and Denzin and Lincoln, *Handbook of Qualitative Research.*
[61] Longino, *Science as Social Knowledge*, 76.
[62] See Marmor, *Law and Interpretation.*

The criteria are a melding of standards from both the empirical (or realist) and coherence strains of pragmatic inquiry.

Among the standards of pragmatic objectivity are norms for any rational inquiry and standards specific to journalism. The reason for these two levels is because, as I argued in *The Invention of Journalism Objectivity*, there is a general conception of objectivity for all rational inquirers which then gets articulated into standards and rules specific to certain domains. For example, the double-blind method in drug trials is an application of the general demand for objective evaluation to health research. The rule in law courts against hearsay evidence is a particular application of the general standard to consider only reliable empirical evidence.[63]

How would pragmatic objectivity work in a newsroom? Journalists would construct stories according to a certain attitude, and then test the story according to evaluative criteria. The stress on correct attitude stems from my previous comment about the importance of certain virtues and attitudes in the pursuit of truth.

The attitude is what I call the *objective stance*. It consists in moral virtues such as honesty and intellectual virtues such as caring about truth in general and caring for specific truths. An objective inquirer must be willing to place a critical distance between oneself and the story, to be open to evidence and counter-arguments, to fairly represent other perspectives, and to be committed to the disinterested pursuit of truth for the public. One is "disinterested" in not allowing one's interests to prejudge a story. This is not neutrality. It is the attitude of a critical inquirer.

However, it is not enough to have an objective attitude. One has to apply this attitude by using criteria to test stories for objectivity. There are five kinds of criteria.

First, there are criteria that test for *empirical validity*. These criteria test the story for carefully obtained and collaborated evidence, and the accurate presentation of that data. Empirical validity is broader than reporting facts. It includes placing the facts in context. For example, a story on the rate of breast cancer in an ethnic group will include the rate of breast cancer in the general population. The accurate presentation of numerical information is one of the challenges of objective reporting. Testing for empirical validity also means noting the methods used and how they were

[63] Ward, *Invention*, 283–285.

used, as noted above. Journalists not only need to make sure they use their own methods properly; they also need to evaluate the methods of scientists and other inquirers. Objectivity requires taking a critical approach to both the results and the methods of inquiry that are the subject of press releases and news conferences.

Second, there are criteria that test for *completeness and implications*. Where appropriate, journalists should check to see if the story contains all important facts, avoids hype, and reports on both the risks and benefits (or the positive and negative consequences) of a new policy or scientific discovery for society.

Third, there are criteria that test for *coherence*. These criteria test the story for coherence with existing knowledge and the views of credible experts. Journalists respect these criteria, for example, when they compare the clinical trial of a drug with existing studies.

Fourth, there are criteria of *self-consciousness*. An objective story is self-conscious about the frame it uses to present a study or event, and the sources chosen. Have powerful sources manipulated the media to present the story in a certain light? Is the story on crime in poor city areas not also a story about social inequalities or government inaction? Is the media's depiction of a war as a march towards freedom ignoring the war's economic motivations?

Fifth, there are criteria that test for *intersubjective objectivity*. Objectivity in journalism encourages inquirers to share ideas and facts with other people – other journalists, experts, and citizens. Through this interaction, mistakes are spotted, counter-evidence noted, other interpretations brought forward. The objective reporter is open to varying perspectives.

Some people may be surprised that I include such things as context and self-consciousness as elements of objectivity. This is partly because of our cultural baggage. We assume, at least in journalism, that objectivity is *not* multi-dimensional. It reduces to facts. But the language and the frames that journalists use can be as responsible for subjective reports as a lack of facts. Objectivity is a complex method that reflects the many dimensions of rational inquiry and evaluation. As mentioned above, journalism's emphasis on commonsense realism obscures the importance of coherence both in the pursuit of truth and in evaluating stories for objectivity.

In sum, journalists are objective to the extent that they adopt the objective stance and test their interpretations with the standards that fall under the five kinds of criteria. Satisfaction of these criteria enhances the credibility and depth of the story, while adding to the likelihood of its truth. In the end, the judgment as to whether an interpretation is pragmatically objective will be a matter of degree, according to how well the story satisfies the criteria. To evaluate a story as objective, we must weigh, holistically, a group of criteria. In most cases, the judgment will be relative – story *x* is more objective than story *y*.

Pragmatic objectivity is not the whole of media ethics. But together with pragmatic truth, it is the main guide for truth-seeking in journalism. Also, pragmatic objectivity fits well with other ethical principles such as fairness, transparency, and accountability. Fairness, transparency, and accountability can be seen as values that support and encourage more truthful stories. An unfair representation of a point of view, or an unfair depiction of an individual, usually results in an inaccurate, untrue, and non-objective story. The demand that journalists be accountable for their stories and transparent about how they construct stories encourages the virtue of honesty in journalism. The demand promotes accuracy and truthfulness. Lack of transparency provides "cover" for inadequate methods and biases. We will examine these other principles, such as minimizing harm and transparency, in future chapters.

Relevance of pragmatic objectivity

Earlier, we examined why truth and objectivity matter and how pragmatic inquiry is a good model for thinking about how journalists seek truth. We now examine why pragmatic objectivity is a more adequate conception than the traditional objectivity of the early 1900s. We examine why multidimensional objectivity has features that recommend it as a principle for today's journalism. Again, there is room only to indicate the plausibility or potential of the reformulated principle.

It is interesting to consider multi-dimensional objectivity as a unifying methodological principle for many kinds of journalism. Multi-dimensional objectivity is a flexible method that can be applied in different degrees and in different ways, according to the form of journalism in question. Even if journalists seek different goals – report the world, interpret it, or change it – responsible journalists can make multi-dimensional objectivity a method for testing whatever stories are produced, for whatever reasons.

The form of objectivity that I have described is not identifiable with any one form of journalism, one style of writing, or one aim of journalism.

Traditional news objectivity lacked this flexibility. Only one form of journalism could satisfy its strict fact-value dualism – a facts-only, rigidly neutral, form of reporting. Objectivity was not applicable to forms of journalism that were more interpretive, such as features or reporter's perspective pieces.

By rethinking objectivity as a holistic method for testing interpretations, objectivity can evaluate many kinds of journalism. For instance, the criteria of empirical validity, coherence, and openness to perspectives can be used to evaluate investigative journalism, despite the latter's rejection of neutrality. In fact, good investigative journalism is a clear case of using objective methods to ferret out the objective truth about what happened behind closed doors.

In the same vein, criteria such as coherence and self-consciousness are important elements of good interpretive journalism in the form of background pieces, analysis, and column writing. To be sure, the emphasis in this writing will be on argumentation and theorizing. But that does not mean that the objective stance, and its intellectual virtues and criteria, cannot be a part of the journalism process. Why shouldn't informed column writers not follow the facts where they lead, not fairly represent rival views on an issue?

Earlier, we noted that pragmatic objectivity is compatible with fairness, transparency, and accountability. We can add to this list the values of respect and human solidarity – features that critics, especially feminists, communitarians, and spokespersons for minorities, have said are lacking in much of the news media. One cannot embrace the criteria of pragmatic objectivity, with their emphasis on self-consciousness of media frames and openness to perspectives, without favoring a journalism that values fair representation of all groups and that seeks to build bridges among these groups in pluralistic democracies. Moreover, pragmatic objectivity, by encouraging informed interpretation, supports deliberative democratic journalism.

Not all forms of journalism need to enforce the norms of objectivity to the full extent. It depends on the communicative intent and the nature of the medium. Satirical journalism is probably the form of journalism where the objective method is weakest. Satirical journalism seeks to state a truth or expose hypocrisy beneath the rhetoric of modern life and its politics. Often it does so through exaggeration and unfair portrayals, for dramatic effect. Yet in an open public sphere, satirical journalism plays an important role. Other forms of journalism are closer to objectivity in spirit, such as investigative journalism.

Multi-dimensional objectivity is compatible with many motivations for doing journalism. Whether journalists want to act as watchdogs or impartial observers, they should be able to accept the idea of testing their interpretations. Some forms of journalism may lay more stress on some rules and criteria of objectivity than on others. Since pragmatic objectivity does not require neutrality, it can be adopted by forms of activist and advocacy journalism. A reporter for the *Jewish Chronicle* in Toronto or a gay rights magazine in New York can be committed to the advancement of their group and also committed to stories that satisfy at least some of the criteria of multi-dimensional objectivity such as coherence, accuracy, self-consciousness, a fair representation of the views of other groups, and so on. A commitment to achieving group goals can weaken one's commitment to telling the whole truth where facts may damage the group's public profile. But that danger aside, it is also possible for reporters for these forms of attached journalism to refuse to distort the facts and to seek a degree of multi-dimensional objectivity in their reports.

Multi-dimensional objectivity is also a plausible candidate for a principle of global journalism. The ethics of global journalism will be explored in Chapter 7. What can be said at this point is that multi-dimensional objectivity is well suited for foreign reporting in a global age. Multi-dimensional objectivity is a stance and a method that, if practiced, would lead to better coverage of global issues from poverty to social justice. The objective stance is *just* the sort of attitude you would want in global reporters since it asks journalists to put a distance between themselves and their beliefs and parochial attachments. Also, the criteria of coherence, self-consciousness, and intersubjective testing are key values for a responsible global journalism.

Traditional news objectivity advised journalists not to let their own biases, or the biases of groups within their own country, distort the accuracy and fairness of their reports. With a global approach to journalism ethics, objectivity becomes a global objectivity that asks journalists to not allow their bias toward their country distort reports on international issues. A journalism that follows multi-dimensional objectivity would be less prone to be swayed by narrow forms of ethnocentrism and xenophobia. Journalists would be less swayed by narrow patriotism wherever the national interests of their country comes into tension with other national interests. It is not implausible, then, to claim that multi-dimensional objectivity can cross borders and put itself forward as a unifying principle for global media ethics.

Conclusion

This chapter has examined the place of truth and objectivity in media ethics. It has argued that these two values should remain central to media ethics, although their meanings have to be substantially updated and redefined.

The first half of the chapter followed the rise and decline of truth and objectivity as principles of responsible news media. This skepticism has eroded the moral force of the principles, leaving an ethical vacuum. If truth and objectivity are in doubt, what other principles might guide journalists?

The second half of the chapter sought to reaffirm the notions of truth and objectivity by reviewing why these notions still matter for democratic journalism. It was argued that journalists need to deepen the theoretical basis of media. The chapter then set out to contribute to this goal by advancing the notions of pragmatic truth and multi-dimensional objectivity – concepts appropriate to the pragmatic enterprise of journalism. These concepts were said to be more adequate and relevant to today's global media than the traditional concept of objectivity for yesterday's media.

In the next chapter, we analyze the restraining principles of media ethics – principles that call on journalism to minimize harm when they pursue the truth.

Questions for discussion

1. What is your definition of truth? What is the difference between a concept of truth and the truth in a certain situation?
2. Do you think journalists can claim to report the truth, or to be objective? Why or why not?

3. Explain the difference between truth and justification? How could this distinction be used to describe the practice of journalism?

4. Explain the difference between a realist and a coherence theory of truth. Which theory of truth do you think is the most persuasive?

5. In the chapter, journalists are said to be commonsense realists. What does this mean? Are most people commonsense realists? Are you a commonsense realist?

6. What is meant by the term, "traditional objectivity"? Why is it referred to as "one-dimensional"?

7. Traditional objectivity was (and is) more than an ideal for journalists. It also had rules and standards. What were some of these rules and standards?

8. Give an example of a news story that attempts to stick only to the facts. Give an example of a story that goes beyond the facts. What's the difference between the two?

9. Why is pragmatic truth called "pragmatic"? What is meant by the claim that journalism needs a form of truth "appropriate" to its practice? Do you agree?

10. What are the distinctive features of pragmatic truth in journalism? How do these features differ from other approaches to truth?

11. What is it for a theory of truth to be "holistic," according to this chapter?

12. Why is multi-dimensional objectivity called "multi-dimensional"? What are its main criteria for evaluating a story?

13. Discuss, using an example, how one would apply the criteria of "multi-dimensional objectivity."

5   Media harm and offense

The power of news media can be abused. Abuse leads to misinformation, erroneous judgments, and harmful consequences for individuals, groups, and countries. Therefore, ethics promotes the responsible use of media freedom and power. Responsible use means restraining the freedom to publish by considering the harm that stories and images may cause.

I assume that previous chapters have explained sufficiently why media have responsibilities. I now concern myself with what those responsibilities are, how they are expressed by restraining principles, and how the principles should operate in situations. In particular, I examine the restraining principles of avoiding harm and offense.

In the first three sections of the chapter, I discuss the importance of avoiding harm for ethics and I examine contending principles for restricting liberty, including the liberty of the press. I formulate and argue for three principles of restraint for media: (1) avoiding unjustified harm to others; (2) avoiding unjustified "profound offence"; and (3) minimizing harm where harm is justified. The three principles take their inspiration from John Stuart Mill.

In the remaining sections, I apply the three principles to cases that involve the potential harm of reporting kidnappings and publishing state secrets. I also consider cases that require journalists to minimize harm when they publish graphic and offending images.

Harm in ethics

Universality of avoiding harm

Almost all moral systems, secular or religious, identify harm as an evil to be avoided if at all possible. Among the professions, similar injunctions to avoid harm prevail. In medicine, health-care providers adhere to the dictum: "first, do no harm." The need to avoid harm is evident if we reflect on a few examples, such as the harm caused by torture or the damage of malicious rumors to people's careers and reputations. The content of moral codes is a list of harms to avoid: do not murder, do not steal, do not break promises, do not lie, do not injure others. Positive-sounding rules such as "respect for life" and "work for peace" express our hope that humans can avoid the harms caused by war and disrespectful treatment of people.

Harm avoidance is part of our species' evolutionary history. The early detection of harms in the environment was (and is) required for survival. Culturally, harm is central to moral education. Causing harm and preventing harm – such as injuring another child – are our earliest understandings of what is good or bad, right or wrong. Our learning of ethical norms begins with experiences of harm in the form of pain, hurt feelings, deprivation of a need or desire, or an arbitrary exclusion from a group. In ethical theory, writers refer to harm when defining ethics. Earlier in this book, we quoted sociologist Steven Lukes as saying that moral norms include "avoiding harm to others and promoting their well-being."[1] Two contemporary moral philosophers, W.D. Ross and Bernard Gert, made harm a central ethical notion.

Ross, in *The Right and The Good*, made "non-maleficence" one of our prima facie ethical duties. Under "non-maleficence" Ross included all the duties that fall under "not injuring others." Other kinds of prima facie duties are the duties of fidelity, e.g. to keep promises, and the duties of justice, gratitude, self-improvement and beneficence. Non-maleficence concerns how my actions will impact others in the future.

Ross thought that non-maleficence was more important than beneficence. Beneficence is a positive duty to assist others, to do them good.[2] Non-maleficence is a negative duty not to harm others. To not harm others is not the same as to fail to do someone good. Ross said non-maleficence is ethically prior, "as a duty of a more stringent character" and "as *prima facie* more binding."[3] That is why we do not kill one person to keep another alive; nor steal from one person to give alms to another.

Gert makes preventing evil central to ethics. Evil is similar in meaning to harm. Gert defines an evil as "that which all rational persons will avoid" while the good is that which is "irrational to give up or avoid."[4] Examples

---

[1] Lukes, *Moral Relativism*.   [2] Ross, *The Right and the Good*, 21.
[3] *Ibid.*, 22.   [4] Gert, *Morality*, 106.

of evils are death, pain, disability, disease, injury, and loss of freedom. For Gert, "morality is primarily concerned with protecting and preventing people from suffering harm, not with self-realization or promoting benefits."[5] The moral guide to action is summarized in an ancient command, "Eschew evil; do good." Gert says that another way of expressing this command is: "Always be just; be kind when you can."[6]

In *Common Morality*, Gert argues that rational people agree on a common morality of rules and ideals. Morality protects people from harm. The moral rules, such as "do not kill" and "keep your promises" are a "public guide" for the conduct of all moral agents.[7] All moral agents agree that killing, causing pain or disability, or depriving someone of freedom or pleasure is immoral unless there is adequate justification.[8] Moral rules are concerned with harm prevention and reduction.

Indeterminacies

Although harm is a central concept, using the idea in ethical reasoning is complicated by several factors. One factor is a lack of consensus on a definition of harm. Socrates thought that the only real harm was moral harm – neglecting the virtuous development of one's soul. Bentham thought harm was the experience of pain.

Definitional disagreements lead to disputes about whether something causes harm. Does pornography really harm its consumers? My criticism of you as an incompetent employee offends. But does it harm you? If a TV station broadcasts the video of a soldier killed in the streets of a foreign city, does it harm the parents of the soldier, who do not want their child's death made public? Even where people agree that an activity causes harm, they may disagree as to what society should do. If a newspaper photo of a movie star looking fat and sad on a beach causes harm, should there be laws that censor such photos? If pornography harms consumers, should pornography be made illegal?

Another factor is that harm assessments are often uncertain predictions about the consequences of actions. How can journalists predict the consequences of publishing a story? How can they predict with confidence

[5] *Ibid.*, 384.   [6] *Ibid.*, 384.
[7] Gert, *Common Morality*, 6.
[8] Gert provides a list of the "common" moral rules in *Common Morality*, 20.

how readers will respond? Can a reporter predict that publishing a story on the collapse of a bank will cause a stockholder to commit suicide? In other areas of life, claims about harms may be on firmer ground. Claims about the harm of water pollution can refer to scientific studies.

A final indeterminacy concerns deciding what to do when avoiding harm conflicts with other values. In some cases, the balancing of values is easily resolved. If an angry husband comes to my door with a weapon asking if his wife is in my house should I tell him the truth – that she has taken refuge in my basement? No, I should lie. Protection is primary here. Other situations are not clear. Should a journalist not report, on the eve of a major battle, that her country's armed forces are dispirited and in disarray, thereby giving energy to the enemy? Should a Catholic bishop not disclose that a priest in his diocese has been sexually abusing boys because the truth, made public, will do irreparable harm to the priest and the church? Moreover, when is it ethically permissible to cause harm to prevent a greater harm – to choose a lesser evil? Is torture justified to stop a terrorist attack on a major city?[9]

Contending principles

To clarify these issues, ethicists have defined harm and proposed principles for avoiding harm. The purpose of these inquiries is practical. The principles are supposed to help citizens decide which actions are harmful and which actions should be restricted. A principle of harm, then, is a liberty-restricting principle. To avoid (or reduce) harm is to restrain liberty – the liberty to act, or the liberty to publish. Questions about restraining actions are part of larger discussions about the proper extent of liberty in society. Theories of where to draw the line between liberty and restraint reflect the social and political views of their authors. The principle of harm put forward by John Stuart Mill in the mid-1800s favored the emerging liberal society of England. More traditional thinkers have advanced conservative notions of harm avoidance that allow government greater scope to interfere with the actions of citizens. We are faced with contending liberty-restricting principles, including contending principles of harm.

---

[9] See Michael Ignatieff's *The Lesser Evil.*

The debate among contending principles has implications for debates over media harm. What principle of harm should be embraced by media ethics? Should we accept a libertarian approach that makes minimizing harm a secondary concern of a free press? Or should we adopt a conservative view that asserts a stronger principle of harm more restrictive of media practice?

Whatever theory you adopt, the principle of harm that you apply to media should be consistent with the principle of harm you apply to society as a whole. If your principle of harm for society says no citizens should do activities of type y – say, because it causes physical harm to others – then presumably you will also hold that media practitioners should avoid practices that cause similar physical harm. If it is wrong for me, as a citizen, to destroy your character by spreading rumors behind your back at the office, then presumably it is also wrong for the media to maliciously ruin someone's reputation by using the printing press or Internet. Our moral and political philosophy should inform our media philosophy.

Therefore, to develop a systematic approach to questions of media harm, we face a two-fold task: (1) we need to choose liberty-restricting principles for all citizens, whether citizens are engaging in journalism or not. These principles should include guidelines on when to avoid or reduce harm. (2) Then we need to use these principles to define and justify restraining principles for media. Restrictions on media are based on more general moral and legal restrictions that society places on all citizens.

In the rest of this section I undertake (1). I formulate and argue for three liberty-restricting principles for media based on a moderate liberal perspective.

Liberty-restricting principles

Liberty-restricting principles call on citizens to restrain their behavior in specific ways. Liberty-restricting principles may seem to be the dark tools of authoritarian societies. They are not. All societies, even societies devoted to liberty, require liberty-restricting principles. A political philosophy of liberty must have two sorts of principles: principles that identify and explain the basic liberties and principles that explain where the liberties end. A political philosophy is largely characterized by how it draws the boundary between liberty and authority. Imagine the task as that of drawing a clear

line around how much liberty should be allowed citizens. On one side of
the line is the sphere of liberty; on the other side of the line is the sphere
of restraint and authority. Move the line of liberty in any direction and it
changes both the extent of liberty and the extent of authority. One cannot
clarify the limits of liberty without clarifying the limits of authority.

A liberty-limiting principle can have ethical or legal meaning, or both.
Legally, it may justify statutory prohibitions enforced by penal sanctions.
Ethically, a principle may give us reason to regard some behavior as unethical and rightly subject to moral condemnation. Society has many ways
to restrain behavior. It can imprison those who violate the laws. Or it can
bring social and ethical pressure to bear, including the force of public
opinion and public criticism.

Most people would agree that a person's liberty can be questioned (or
restrained) when it interferes with the freedom of others – or harms others.
To put it proverbially, my liberty to act ends where my fist meets your nose.
However, beyond such intuitions, it is not easy to describe the relationship
between liberty and harm. It is not adequate to simply say that people should
not be allowed to harm others. As noted, there are serious disagreements
over what constitutes harm. Also, people justifiably cause harm to others
in many areas of society, from judges who sentence criminals to years in
prison to journalists who accuse politicians of wrongdoing. Therefore, a liberty-restricting principle needs to say what sorts of harms are justifiable.

Liberal and non-liberal principles

Legal scholar Joel Feinberg lists a number of liberty-restricting principles.[10] A society could adopt one, or a combination, of these principles.
Whatever it chooses will have a profound effect on its laws, how open a
society it is, and on public debate about controversial behavior. I divide
liberty-restricting philosophies into two categories – a liberal approach
and a non-liberal approach.

Liberal principles

The liberal approach to liberty-restricting principles is a minimalist
approach in three ways: (1) it limits the number of restrictions on liberty

---

[10] Feinberg, *Harm to Others*, 26–27.

to a minimum; (2) it favors a narrow view of what counts as harm so liberty is not unduly restricted; (3) it confines restrictions to actions that do harm to others. It is suspicious of views that argue for laws to prevent people from doing harm to themselves, because of bad choices or faulty morals. Liberal principles tend to be "other-regarding" principles. They are principles concerned with the impact of actions on others.

Liberals have been inclined to accept one, or both, of the following two principles:

> *The harm-to-others principle*: citizens should not use their liberty to do unjustifiable harm to others. The liberty of persons can be legitimately restricted and/or morally condemned if it helps to prevent (eliminate, reduce) unjustifiable harm to persons other than the actor.
> *The offense principle*: the liberty of persons can be legitimately restricted or morally condemned if the actions cause serious offense to others.

Beyond the harm and offense principles, liberals do not go. The strong liberal position is that society should be guided by only one liberty-restricting principle, the harm-to-others principle. Harming others is the only valid reason for legal restrictions or ethical criticism.[11] This view is the standard position of many libertarians. A moderate liberal position thinks the harm-to-others principle is the main liberty-restricting guidelines for society but it is not sufficient, by itself. The moderate position accepts two principles: the harm-to-others principle and some version of the offence principle.

The liberal approach is distinct in its skepticism about paternalism. Paternalism is not a popular word in many liberal circles. It is often used in a derogatory manner, as an illegitimate interference in my conduct. To be treated paternalistically, is to be treated like a child. It is insulting. Another person presupposes that I am not smart enough to make my own decisions: a doctor withholds information from me because he doesn't think I can make the right decision on my care if I know all of the facts. Or a religious group prevents me from gambling because they think it is bad for me. Despite its derogatory connotations, issues of paternalism are not always simple and paternalism is not always wrong. Even in liberal societies, the courts and many citizens acknowledge areas where

---

[11] *Ibid.*, 26.

paternalism can be a legitimate source of restraint on others. For example, parents have a right – one might say a duty – to act paternalistically toward their young children to prevent them from injury and harm. State officials may intervene to prevent someone from harming themselves if they have lost the cognitive ability to think clearly about themselves, due to severe depression, mental illness, or Alzheimer's disease.

Issues surrounding paternalism become more difficult when we move from personal relationships, such as the relationship of parent and child, to legal paternalism, where the state enforces laws based on a paternalistic concern. Roughly defined, person A treats another person B paternalistically when A interferes with B's freedom for B's own good – to protect or promote B's health and safety, economic interests, or moral well-being. In such a case, A may interfere with B's freedom by disregarding either B's judgment or preferences.[12] Legal paternalism refers to interferences backed by laws and legal sanctions, such as laws intended to reduce personal harm. Laws that require automobile drivers to wear seat belts is an example. Legal moral paternalism is especially controversial, since it approves state action designed not to prevent physical harm but to improve a person's character or to prevent a person from engaging in immoral conduct. The goal of legal moral paternalism is to "make persons better off morally."[13]

It is not accurate to say liberal thinkers reject all interferences based on grounds of paternalism. They recognize that young children and mentally ill people may require paternalistic treatment by others or the state. But liberals want to reduce the number of areas where such paternalistic arguments are used. In particular, the liberal approach is especially skeptical about paternalistic intervention in people's lives based on some other person's (or the state's) conception of what is good for them, morally.

Liberals emphasize the autonomy of individuals in deciding what sort of life they wish to lead, whether or not such choices eventually cause them harm or hardship. Each individual is to be given as much freedom as possible to judge what is best for themselves. Citizens in liberal society should question state laws that would force people to live their lives according to some external moral standard. Intervention is justified only where such choices harm other persons. For the liberal, the fact that one's

---

[12] Husak, "Legal Paternalism," 388.   [13] Ibid., 409.

actions may bring some harm to oneself, morally or otherwise, does not automatically justify state intervention.[14]

Non-liberal principles

Non-liberal approaches to restricting liberty reject the idea that society should only intervene where someone's conduct harms others. Non-liberal approaches are non-minimalist in three ways: (1) They do not strive to keep the number of restrictions on liberty to a minimum. The non-liberal approach thinks the liberal principle of harm is not sufficient. Other principles are needed. (2) They favor a wide view of what constitutes harm. It may count as harmful actions that a liberal would not call harmful, e.g. verbally offending someone's religious belief. (3) Paternalism is accepted as a source of justification for restrictions on liberty. The state or society may know better than an individual what is good for them, and is entitled to intervene in the life of the individual. Actions that harm the actor morally, physically, or intellectually are valid concerns of society and its liberty-restricting principles. Some non-liberal approaches think the state can not only force a person to avoid harm to themselves, but can also force them to do good – to work towards certain social ideals or values.

Non-liberal approaches to the restriction of liberty embrace the paternalism principle:

> *The paternalism principle (legal and moral):* the liberty of persons can be legitimately restricted and ethically criticized if it protects or benefits the actor. The paternalism principle has two forms:
> - Negative paternalism: The liberty of persons can be legitimately restricted or morally condemned if it is necessary to prevent harm (physical, psychological, moral, or economic) to the actor himself. For example, society may interfere with liberty to prevent "moral harm" to the individual. Certain actions or activities should not be tolerated, even if the action causes neither harm nor offense to others. Therefore, society may enact laws that prevent people from gambling or drinking alcohol to excess, prevent people from watching pornography or engaging in homosexual acts in private.

---

[14] Liberals would add a qualification. Intervention in preventing harm to oneself may be required where the person is a child or a mentally disturbed adult.

> In communitarian societies, citizens are expected to not violate a
> common religious or moral code.
>
> • Positive paternalism: citizens may be required to act in certain ways if
>   it is necessary to improve (elevate, perfect) the character of either the
>   actor or the citizens generally, or both. Here, the emphasis is not so
>   much on avoiding immoral acts but on doing morally good acts, such
>   as attending religious services at designated times, or giving a portion
>   of their wealth to charity. Women may cover their body with gowns
>   to advance the virtue of modesty. These positive duties are based
>   on the view that the state can legitimately promote, and enforce,
>   moral, religious, and other views of the good life or the good society.
>   One purpose of law and public morality is to perfect individuals and
>   society.

Support for the prohibition of alcohol consumption in the USA in the early
1900s was based, philosophically, on a non-liberal approach to state intervention that combined negative and positive paternalism. On the negative
paternalistic view, the state should prevent people from harming themselves by drinking alcohol; on the positive paternalistic view, society has
a right to impose restrictions that would improve or perfect individual
citizens.

I support liberal resistance to, and skepticism of, the non-liberal
approach to restricting citizens' liberties and in restricting news media.
At the very least, such an approach to restricting liberty should not be
dominant in society. In what follows, I argue that the best approach is
a moderate combination of the harm-to-others principle and a greatly
limited version of the offense principle. Any paternalistic interventions
should be exceptional. I begin with the harm-to-others principle, as articulated by Mill.

Restraining principles for media

Mill as starting point

A discussion of the problem of liberty and authority, of freedom and harm,
should start from Mill's principle of harm in his classic *On Liberty* of 1859.
Mill's powerful defense of liberty has shaped subsequent formulations
and amendments of the harm principle. Even critics of liberalism need

to deal with Mill. Mill wrote *On Liberty* to explain when it is legitimate for society to use its powers of condemnation, law, and coercion to limit the liberties of citizens. The problem is where "to place the limit" which achieves "fitting adjustment between individual independence and social control."[15] How should liberty and authority coexist? Mill starts with a liberal view of society. Individuals have basic liberties that must be protected from undue social or political interference because they develop the capacities of citizens and allow citizens to freely pursue their plans of life.

Mill formulates his harm principle as follows: "That principle is, that the sole end for which mankind are warranted, individually or collectively, in interfering with the liberty of action of any of their number, is self-protection. That the only purpose for which power can be rightfully exercised over any member of a civilized community, against his will, is to prevent harm to others."[16]

Mill, as a liberal, wants to reduce the range of paternalism as a liberty-restricting principle argues that neither government nor society should intervene in people's lives on the grounds that society supposedly knows what is good for individuals. Each person is to be free to pursue their own lives as they see fit, rightly or wrongly, stupidly or wisely. An individual is not accountable to society where her actions only help or harm herself, or "in so far as these concern the interests of no person but himself."[17] Society can show its dislike of such actions through advice and persuasion, or by avoiding the person in question but it is not entitled to use the force of law. However, for actions that harm others, the individual is accountable and may be subject to social restrictions.[18]

However, Mill's eloquence on liberty from the interference of others should not lead us to think that Mill rejects all and any paternalistic actions. For example, *On Liberty* makes it clear that not all societies can or should be structured according to his harm principle. Mill states that the harm principle is meant to apply "only to human beings in the maturity of their faculties" and it does not apply to those who require the care of others and who must be protected against their own actions and external injury. His liberal approach also doesn't apply to "backward states of

---

[15] Mill, *On Liberty*, 11.   [16] *Ibid.*, 16.
[17] *Ibid.*, 106.   [18] *Ibid.*, 106.

society in which the race itself may be considered as in its nonage." Mill adds: "Despotism is a legitimate mode of government in dealing with barbarians" provided the state's actions actually improve citizens. Liberty, as a principle, only applies "anterior to the time when mankind have become capable of being improved by free and equal discussion." Otherwise, at best mankind can hope for nothing but obedience to a wise ruler.[19] Mill also allows that police and other state agencies can intervene to prevent people from committing crimes and to prevent accidental injury to people. Mill says that a public officer could physically stop a person from stepping onto an unsafe bridge if there was no time to verbally warn the person.[20]

Mill identifies three areas of liberty: (a) of conscience; (b) of the free pursuit of goals; and (c) of free association in pursuit of those goals. The first type of liberty belongs to the "inward domain of consciousness" which includes liberty of conscience, liberty of thought and feeling, and liberty of speech and sentiment on all subjects. Liberty of expression and of publishing opinions, although such actions involve other people, falls under liberty of conscience in the broadest sense since liberty of thought is "practically inseparable" from it. The second type of liberty is freedom in tastes and pursuits. This is the liberty to develop your own likes and dislikes, and to plan and follow your own life plan. It is also the area of "doing as we like," as Mill calls it, without impediment from others. The third area is the freedom to unite with others to reach certain goals.[21] All three areas of liberty are subject to the same restraint: the exercise of such liberties should not harm others and deny other people the right to enjoy their own liberties.

Mill does not justify the principle by saying it is an abstract right. Instead, he argues that liberty has great social utility. Liberty is essential for individuals to develop themselves in creative ways and to develop society through "experiments in living." As Mill says, liberty and the principle of harm promote "utility in the largest sense, grounded on the permanent interests of man as a progressive being."[22] Like those who support paternalistic liberty-restricting principles, Mill supports the development and perfection of humans, but he thinks such perfection is achieved through liberty, not through state intervention. As Skorupski states: "The basic

---

[19] *Ibid.*, 16–17.   [20] *Ibid.*, 108–109.
[21] *Ibid.*, 18–19.   [22] *Ibid.*, 17.

case for liberalism (for Mill) is that human beings achieve the most valuable forms of happiness under liberal morality and liberal law."[23]

Ever since Mill laid down this principle of harm as the limit of liberty, critics have sought to show that it is flawed. Some are skeptical about Mill's distinction between a sphere of personal liberty and a sphere where my actions affect others. Surely, they say, no person is an island; almost any action has impact on others. Still others think Mill's nineteenth-century liberalism has little to say about issues of liberty today. Mill seems to think that hateful or provocative speech is trivially offensive and does not constitute harm. This ignores "group harm" – hate speech that demonizes minorities and impairs their ability to develop in society.[24]

If these criticisms were entirely true, Mill would be a bad starting point. However, before we draw that conclusion, we need to spend more time looking at two concepts that anchor Mill's arguments: the notion of harm and which harms are legitimately restricted. Later, I will propose an offense principle that takes extreme forms of hateful speech into account, yet remains true to Mill's approach.

Harm as injury to interests

Let's start with Mill's notion of harm. Standard dictionary definitions describe harm as a hurt or an injury. Mill himself uses a battery of terms to talk about harm, which include: a perceptible hurt; an injury; what is injurious; an evil; actions "calculated to produce evil to someone else"; a mischief; what is against utility and happiness; a wrong; actions wanting in due consideration for welfare; not injuring the interests of another; and conduct that "affects prejudicially the interests of others."

Harm does not refer to minor annoyances or inconveniences. If I pinch you on the arm as a joke, and you accuse me bitterly of harming you, this complaint is an over-reaction. The pinch may be painful momentarily and my action may annoy you; but the pain of the pinch will dissipate quickly. Causing unpleasant mental states or unwanted experiences by themselves

---

[23] Skorupski, "The Place of Utilitarianism in Mill's Philosophy," 59. One of Mill's recent biographers, Richard Reeves, goes so far as to say that the principle of harm was essentially a "side-show" to Mill's primary message: the growth and development of the distinctive capabilities of humans. See Reeves, *John Stuart Mill*, 268.

[24] See Arthur, "Sticks and Stones."

does not amount to causing harm. Your body odor on the bus displeases me. It does not harm me. My using chalk on a blackboard gives you an unpleasant sensation, but I do not harm you. My unguarded swearing may offend your sensibilities, but I do not harm you. To be harmed is not to be subjected to a "shocking" sight, such as a nude person streaking across a football field.

So what constitutes harm? "Harm" is best reserved for actions that cause serious injury, physical, mental, or otherwise. As Arthur says, "Harms are significant events."[25] It must set back my important interests. Suppose John is a young, emerging star of baseball; a gifted pitcher. One night, while driving my car, I hit John as he traverses a crosswalk; I break his pitching arm. I have done John serious harm. I have prejudicially harmed his interests, his future. Harms can be caused by multiple sources: falling trees, disease, reckless drivers, economic competitors, unfair teachers, corrupt bureaucrats, muggers, and traumatic experiences.[26]

Sometimes, causing harm can be claimed only if an action occurs repeatedly over time. For example, my playing trumpet in my apartment at night may disturb your ability in an adjacent apartment to learn algebra in preparation for an important exam. But my playing the horn once is not sufficient to cause harm. If I persist in playing the trumpet late at night and ignore your complaints, then I harm your interests. The law of accidents, and the law of negligence, is based on evaluating responsibility for non-trivial actions – actions that harm the interests of others.[27] Harms come in degrees of seriousness. My dispute with you over my trumpet-playing pales in comparison to the harm caused by a husband who physically and mentally abuses his wife.

The best interpretation of Mill's concept of harm is what harms our interests. By adopting this strong sense of harm, Mill can reject arguments for restrictions based on a difference of opinion or tradition. He rules out social restrictions on a person's opinions because they do not conform to the majority's views. Mill says that someone may be disgusted by the eating of pork. They may even think it abhorrent to God. But in a liberal society, feelings of disgust do not constitute harm. They are not setbacks to the interests of those offended.

---

[25] *Ibid.*, 402.   [26] *Ibid.*, 402.
[27] Dworkin, *Law's Empire*, 291–295.

Feinberg uses Mill's notion of harm as prejudicially affecting another's interest to explain the moral limits of the criminal justice system. For Feinberg, harms occur when our interests are frustrated, defeated, or set back. By interests, Feinberg means something in which we have a serious stake, similar to having a stake in a company. Genuine harms impede or thwart my future objectives and the development of my capacities. Some of these interests are agent-specific, such as John's interest in being a baseball star, and some are basic interests shared by the species – an interest in security and sufficient food and wealth. Our interests are related to our desires and wants; yet an interest is not any desire, such as a transitory wish for chocolate ice cream. Interests are our ongoing important concerns.[28] Finally, setbacks to interests should be, as Mill says, "definite." Evidence of concrete harm to identifiable persons is preferred to speculation about harm that may affect an indefinite set of persons.

We can disagree with Mill on the types of things that constitute harm to others. We may regard hate speech, false advertising, or violent images as setting back the interests of at least some groups of citizens. But Mill's restricting of harms to setbacks of interests is the only sane attitude for liberal democracies. The alternative is to allow social control on actions that are trivial, cause minor injury, or are mildly offensive.

Which harms restricted?

So far, the discussion has implied that *all* actions harmful to others are to be legally restricted or ethically condemned. This is obviously false. As mentioned above, many professionals do harm to others, legitimately, in carrying out their duties.[29] Police arrest and imprison criminals. Doctors amputate limbs. State prosecutors prosecute citizens. Teachers give failing grades. Employers fire employees. Journalists accuse politicians of wrongdoing. Therefore, we need to distinguish between justifiable and non-justifiable harms.

Mill was aware that the fact that an action is harmful to others is a necessary but not sufficient condition for legal restrictions or ethical condemnation. He says that if an act is harmful to others, there is a "prima

---

[28] See Feinberg, *Harm to Others*.
[29] See Applebaum, *Ethics for Adversaries*.

facie" case for punishment by law or "general disapprobation."[30] For actions "prejudicial to the interests of others, the individual is accountable and *may* be subjected to social or legal punishment, *if* society is of the opinion that such punishment is necessary for its protection (italics author's)."[31] The qualifying terms, "prima facie," "may," and "if," suggest that intervention does not automatically follow from the fact that an action is harmful to others. There are several reasons why this may be so.

First, citizens are allowed to harm others to defend themselves or their country against violent persons or invading armies. Second, causing harm may be justified by one's profession or social duties. Third, some activities are so beneficial to society that the harms are tolerated. For instance, society allows harm-causing competition for jobs and university scholarships. If I compete with you for a job, or compete with you in business, and I am successful and you are not, then my success sets back your interests. Mill says it is in the "general interest of mankind" that people should be able to pursue their interests in a competitive manner "undeterred" by the harmful consequences.[32]

Fourth, it may be practically impossible or counter-productive to legislate against certain types of actions that are harmful to oneself or others. For example, Mill says society should hesitate to legislate against drunkenness, idleness, uncleanliness, or gambling. Citizens who object to this conduct can avoid people who act in this manner, and they can criticize such behavior. Also, society can regulate how such activities occur, for example, by passing laws about the sale and production of alcohol. Prohibition is not necessary; and in any case, it would violate the non-paternalistic approach of liberal society. Moreover, passing a law in some areas, such as alcohol consumption, would encourage some drinkers to persist in their activity as an act of rebellion against an interfering government. The regulation more and more forms of activity can easily be abused by a moral police – citizens and legislators who impose their lifestyle on others.[33] Mill states that where there is no definite harm or perceptible damage, and no breaches of public duties, these "inconveniences" are things a society can afford to tolerate "for the sake of the greater good of human freedom."[34]

---

[30] Mill, *On Liberty*, 17.   [31] *Ibid.*, 106.
[32] *Ibid.*, 107.   [33] *Ibid.*, 96.   [34] *Ibid.*, 93.

Our analysis has identified four areas where people may justifiably cause harm. These areas can be seen as exceptions to the original harm-to-others principle. Or, the exceptions can be added to the original principle to become: *society can rightfully restrict or condemn liberty where actions cause harm to others (setback to interests) and such actions do not fall under one of the four exceptions – self-defense, social duty, fair competition, and practical difficulties in legislation.* Actions that fall under this principle are justifiable harms.

This modified principle is a more accurate interpretation of Mill's harm principle. The sphere of liberty contains not only liberty to act as one likes as long as it does not harm people; the sphere of liberty also contains actions that cause harm, providing they can be justified under the four exceptions. The principle of harm for Mill is not the bald statement: do no harm to others. Rather, it is: do no unjustified harm to others. The sphere of liberty consists of actions without harm to others, plus actions that cause justifiable harm to others.

What about the remaining sphere, the sphere of authority? This is the sphere of unjustified harm to others. For Mill, the most important kind of unjustifiable harm is when people do harm by failing to carry out their duties to others. A person who breaches a duty is a fitting subject for moral reprobation and "justly punished."[35] Duties arise from an agent's special relationship to others and to society as a whole, e.g. the duties of parents to dependents, soldiers to country, police officers to citizens, teachers to students, professionals to clients. A police officer may drink alcohol when not on the job; but if the officer drinks on the job then the officer fails to perform a "definite duty incumbent on him to the public."[36] Mill's stress on duties fits his view of ethics and law. Ethics and law deal with regulating public conduct – actions forbidden or compelled by society. Ethics and the law are "disciplinary codes by which society exercises sovereignty over individual behavior."[37] Moral wrongdoing is an act for which the individual ought to be punished "if not by law, by the opinion of his fellow-creatures; if not by opinion, by the reproaches of his own conscience."[38] Duty may be *exacted* from a person, as one exacts a debt.[39] Failing a duty is a clear case of inviting punishment from society.

---

[35] *Ibid.*, 92   [36] *Ibid.*, 92.
[37] Skorupski, "The Place of Utilitarianism in Mill's Philosophy," 59.
[38] Mill, "Utilitarianism," 101.   [39] *Ibid.*, 101.

Violations of duty to others are often violations of justice. For Mill, justice is that part of morality which deals with duties that involve a right for some person. In *Utilitarianism*, Mill writes: "Justice implies something which is not only right to do, and wrong not to do, but which some individual person can claim from us as his moral right." The rules of justice are the most "sacred and binding part" of morality because they make society possible. The observance of such duties "alone preserves peace among human beings" without which each person would see others as an enemy against which to protect oneself.[40] Mill's view of liberty and authority is that citizens need to balance their love of liberty with their love of justice – their respect for the freedom of others.

The existence of a right differentiates the virtues of justice from the virtues of beneficence. Mill asserts that no one has a moral right to our generosity or beneficence, because we are not morally bound to practice those virtues towards any given individual.[41] Like Ross, Mill thinks non-malevolence and not failing others is ethically prior to helping others. Mill agrees that altruism and benevolence are crucial virtues for society. They deserve praise. But Mill refuses to make benevolence a duty. So long as benevolence is "spontaneous" and not compelled by external pressure, "there cannot be too much of it."

Why is Mill so adamant that we do not have a duty to benefit others? Because it can violate liberty. Such a duty has no clear limits. Must I benefit others on all occasions? If I must benefit others, how much of my income, time, and energy is required? Mill was wary of social reformers like Auguste Comte whose utopian plans required citizens to sacrifice much of their liberty and resources to achieve an ideal society. Mill says it is a contradiction to talk about the happiness of all in an ideal society when it requires the self-sacrifice of each citizen. This amounts to "despotism of society" over the individual.[42]

In summary, Mill draws a line between liberty and legitimate authority. Mill draws the line where actions, belonging to one of the three categories of liberties, (1) cause serious harm to others by prejudicially affecting the interests of others, and (2) such actions do not fall under one of the four justifications. Prime examples of such harms are breaches of public duty.

[40] *Ibid.*, 110.   [41] *Ibid.*, 102–103.
[42] Mill, *On Liberty*, 20.

An action that breaches no other-regarding duty is not morally wrong and should be permitted.

The offense principle

The harm-to-others principle is a foundational idea for liberal democracy. But is it enough to adjudicate the many conflicts among citizens? There are several considerations that suggest it is not sufficient. Some actions, such as shouting profanities during a theatre performance or masturbating in public are distracting and offensive. Offensive actions cause unwanted and disliked mental states or experiences. They range from annoyance, disappointment, disgust, and embarrassment to fear and anxiety.

Many offensive actions do not cause harm, defined as a setback to interests. Viewing someone masturbate in public is offensive but it does not set back anyone's interests. Sitting next to a foul-smelling person on a bus is offensive but not harmful. Such conduct is an inconvenience and a nuisance. However, this is not to say that offensive conduct never requires the restraint of law or social condemnation. Restraint is legitimate where citizens cannot easily avoid such conduct and are forced to endure it, or such conduct disrupts the enjoyment of their property and well-loved activities. People on a bus or in a theater can scarcely avoid foul-smelling passengers or people shouting profanities.

If this is true, we need one more liberty-restricting principle. We need a principle that helps society decide when and how society should restrain, legally and/or ethically, offensive behavior. To make things complicated, there are some types of offense, such as threatening marginalized individuals through hate speech, that have serious and long-lasting consequences for offended parties. Offensive conduct can rise to the level of harm.

To sort out these complications, Feinberg distinguishes between trivial and profound offense.[43] Trivial offenses never cause harm. The conduct may be an inconvenience, an annoyance, or a nuisance. Trivial offenses offend our sensibilities. They include obscene utterances, spitting and vomiting in public, exuding nauseous smells, or playing loud music late at night. The offense is personal. It is me who is affected by the conduct.

---

[43] Feinberg, *Offense to Others*, 57–58.

It is me that has a grievance against the offender. In most cases, trivial offenses can be ignored, avoided, or tolerated.

In some cases, people cannot avoid trivial offenses. They may be subjected to lewd conduct, spitting, or obscene language while confined in a crowded bus or public arena. We seek protection from offensive behavior (or nuisances) because we are *trapped* by them, and we feel it unfair that we should pay a cost to escape them.[44] It is a violation of our autonomy and privacy. In such cases, society is justified in restricting such conduct.[45] The restraint is needed to avoid a nuisance, or not to be forced to undergo unpleasant experiences – not because the conduct causes harm.

Conduct that causes profound offense is more than a nuisance or a momentary attack on one's sensibilities. It offends people's most profound values, symbols, and identities. Examples of profound offense include hateful speech about someone's religious beliefs, race, gender, ethnicity, or sexual orientation. Profound offense includes disrespectful attitudes towards, and actions against, one's cherished national or religious symbols, such as burning a national flag, ridiculing a religious leader, or desecrating the dead. Profound offense occurs when a neo-Nazis group decides to march through a community of Jewish survivors of the Holocaust. Profound offense occurs when the Ku Klux Klan holds a rally in a mainly Afro-American town. It occurs when an art exhibition displays crucifixes turned upside down in tubs of urine. Profound offenses do not need to be personal. They do not require a direct witnessing of the event, nor must citizens be unable to avoid the offence. I can object to the Ku Klux Klan rally even if I do not live in the town and I am not Afro-American. I can oppose disturbing the dead even if the corpses are not my relatives.

What liberty-restricting principle(s) should address these concerns about offending conduct, trivial or profound? There appear to be two types of principles needed – a principle for restricting trivial offense and a principle for restricting profound offense.

Offense principle 1: society can legitimately take measures to prevent or restrict trivial offenses where such conduct is imposed on citizens

---

[44] *Ibid.*, 5.

[45] Feinberg uses the thought experiment of people on a crowded bus confronted with offensive behavior to explain trivial offensive actions. *Ibid.*, 10–13.

such that the latter cannot avoid or ignore such inconveniences or nuisances.

Offense principle 2: society can legitimately take measures to prevent or restrict actions that cause profound offense, especially where such conduct amounts to causing harm to others.

Earlier I noted how Mill warned against a society that tried to censor opinions or restrict conduct that others found offensive. It is true that a liberal, at best, can accept only a limited form of the offense principle where the most serious offensive actions are the subject of regulation. For trivial offenses, the attitude is that citizens in a free society need to tolerate them. In addition, the liberal will give greater priority to the harm-to-others principle. Causing offense is less serious than causing harm. In the main, offensive conduct is not a threat to society or security, nor does it cause a serious setback to others' interests. Therefore, trivial offenses should not be considered crimes and the penalties for most offensive conduct should be less onerous than criminal acts that cause harm.

Therefore, our reasoning has produced three liberty-restricting principles: one principle of harm to others and two principles regarding offensive conduct. They are:

Principle of harm to others: society can rightfully restrict or condemn liberty where actions cause harm to others (setback to interests) and such actions do not fall under one of the four exceptions –self-defense, social duty, fair competition, and practical difficulties in legislation.

Offense principle 1: society can legitimately take measures to prevent or restrict trivial offences where such conduct is imposed on citizens such that the latter cannot avoid or ignore such inconveniences or nuisances.

Offense principle 2: society can legitimately take measures to prevent or restrict actions that cause profound offense where such conduct amounts to causing harm to others.

We end up with a rough map of the zones of liberty and authority. The map indicates the extent the principle of harm avoidance or harm reduction play in society. The zone of liberty includes all actions that (a) do no unjustifiable harm to others and (b) do not constitute wrongful offense (trivial or profound) as described above.

These three principles define a moderate liberal position. It is moderate in allowing restrictions on harm and offense more than a strong liberal position would allow.

Three principles for media

Having identified three liberty-restricting principles, we now have to apply them to the practice of media in a liberal democratic society. Do all three principles apply to media, and do they all apply to the same extent? What do these principles look like after we've translated them so as to apply to media? Here is a reformulation of the three principles for media practice:

> *Principle of harm to others:* society can legally restrict or ethically condemn media practice where the actions of journalists or news organizations cause harm to others (setback to interests) and such actions do not fall under one of the four exceptions – self-defense, social duty, fair competition, and practical difficulties in legislation.
>
> *Offense principle 1:* society can legally restrict or ethically condemn media practices that cause trivial offense, where such conduct is imposed on citizens such that the latter cannot avoid, ignore, or such inconveniences or nuisances.
>
> *Offense principle 2:* society can legally restrict or ethically condemn media practice where it causes profound offense, especially where such conduct amounts to causing harm to others.

Reflection on the three principles leads to the realization that media ethics cannot embrace the three principles as they stand, for two reasons: one, we need to make a distinction between legally restricting and ethically condemning. Two, a free press should not be bound by the offense principle 1, the principle of avoiding trivial offense. With regard to the first reason, it is plausible to argue that media should be both legally and ethically restricted by actions that cause unjustified harm to others. Such laws exist. If I recklessly harm someone's reputation by writing an inaccurate article, I can be sued for libel and subject to ethical criticism. But it is implausible to say the media should be held accountable in the same way for causing offense, trivial or profound. Offense principle 1 should not apply to media. It should have no role in media ethics. A free press could not exist if society could apply legal and ethical restrictions to every article that trivially offended someone's sensibilities. As noted, readers can take offense at almost any image or story that they find shocking. They may be offended by images of gay marriages or by stories about prostitutes, or offended that a story casts their home town in a negative light. In some cases, journalists need to offend citizens to make society acknowledge a serious social problem. Moreover, much of the conduct deemed trivially offensive, e.g. spitting or smelling foul, doesn't apply to the act of publishing. The principle does say that society could consider laws for restricting conduct that causes trivial offense in cases where other citizens can't avoid the conduct. But it is hard to imagine how this clause applies to media. Normally, citizens can avoid or ignore the offending story or television program; or they can cancel their subscription for an offending newspaper. In sum, media law and media ethics should not be concerned with stories that trivially offend. Avoiding harm, and minimizing harm, through publishing images or words, should be the central concern.

What about offense principle 2? Here, matters are more difficult. Media ethics cannot dismiss the issue of causing profound offense as it does with causing trivial offense. Media reports, TV images, and news programs, with some frequency, do cause profound offense to viewers and sometimes to entire ethnic or religious groups. The 2005 publication of the cartoons of Mohammed in a Danish newspaper is an example. The visual depiction of Mohammed caused profound offense among many Muslims. Coverage of people burning the Koran or of war protesters burning the American flag cause profound insult and offense to many people.

How should we respond to these facts? Should we accept a principle that says it is always illegal and ethically wrong for media to profoundly offend anyone or any group? This interpretation is too strong. If adopted, journalists would be tightly confined in what they could say or publish about controversial issues. Coverage would be confined to a rather small and safe zone of inoffensive and politically correct stories. In some countries, restricting all profoundly offensive stories would violate constitutional guarantees of free speech. The best approach is to reject the idea that the publication of profoundly offensive stories should be illegal, while reserving the right to ethically criticize profoundly offensive journalism on grounds of accuracy, truthfulness, balance, and other ethical norms. Stories should not resort to stereotypes or misrepresent the beliefs of groups. They should not recklessly aim to provoke and gratuitously offend, thereby detracting from informed deliberation on the issues. In cases of profoundly offensive stories, media must be sure they are not helping to create or to sustain harmful social attitudes and environments, especially with respect to marginalized groups. If media believe they should publish stories that may profoundly offend citizens or groups, e.g. a story that many leaders of native groups are misusing tribal monies, they should make sure their stories are accurate, well researched, and aimed at addressing legitimate, if sensitive, issues.

Ethical criticism is necessary where stories amount to causing unjustified harm. Consider a small town where the local newspaper starts an anti-gay campaign on its front page. The paper publishes gay-bashing news stories and images. The paper declares that gays violate God's commands, that they endanger society, that they sexually attack children. The paper starts to name the gays and to publish their home addresses. It publishes photos of people on the list. For the town's gay minority, such stories do more than profoundly offend them. The stories cause unjustified harm. The publicity creates a climate of fear and intimidation. It causes extreme anxiety with physical effects on their health. Some gays may stop going to public events. They may be passed over for jobs, and their children shunned in school. These harmful stories cannot be justified under the four exceptions. It is not the social role of journalism to attack minorities. The stories can be criticized for violating a range of ethical norms, from accuracy to balance.

To summarize, some profoundly offensive stories violate ethical principles. This group of offensive stories requires serious ethical attention. Legally, reckless or irresponsible stories should not be censored. But ethically, they should be avoided and where they occur, the stories should be not only condemned but challenged and rebutted.

We can reformulate offense principle 2 as follows: *society may ethically condemn media practice that causes profound offense that amounts to unjustified harm to others – where stories violate ethical journalistic norms and do not fall under one of the four justifications for causing harm.*

Our construction of ethical principles is not over yet. There is a key concern not covered by the principles noted so far – reducing harm where stories cause justified harm. We need to add a principle of minimizing harm for stories causing justified harm.

Therefore, we have three liberty-restricting principles for media:

Principle of harm to others: society can legally restrict or ethically condemn media practice where the actions of journalists or news organizations cause harm to others (setback to interests) and such actions do not fall under one of the four exceptions –self-defense, social duty, fair competition, and practical difficulties in legislation. Or, news media (or journalists) act unethically and irresponsibly if they cause harm to others (setback to interests) where such actions do not constitute justifiable harm.

Principle of minimizing harm: where media can justify doing harm to carry out their social and ethical role in society, media are obligated to consider minimizing the harm caused by publication to vulnerable, young or innocent sources and subjects of stories.

Principle of unjustified profound offense: society is correct to ethically criticize profoundly offensive media stories that cause unjustified harm. Or, news media (or journalists) act unethically and irresponsibly if their profoundly offensive stories cause unjustified harm to others.

My principle of offense signals an extension, not a violation, of Mill's approach to restricting the liberty of the press. My reason for objecting to some profoundly offensive stories is not that they are, in themselves, shocking or offensive, or cause unwanted mental experiences. They are ethically objectionable because the stories cause harm to other people. For example, the anxiety caused by stories against gays in a town is a matter for media ethics because they have harmful effects on conduct, health, and plans of life. My approach has not abandoned Mill's view that, ultimately, there is only one reason why we should restrict, legally or ethically, the actions of citizens or journalists: such actions cause unjustified harm. This approach rejects the idea that laws or ethical rules should be drawn up to deal with offenses which do not amount to harm. When it comes to restraining principles, avoiding unjustified harm and minimizing justified harm should be our foundational principles and the main concern of responsible journalists.

Media harm: cases

We have established three ethical principles as legitimate ways to restrain media practice. We now need to show how these principles apply to cases and situations. In this section we look at cases of media harm and we show

how two of our three restraining principles deal with telling the truth and publishing graphic images. Then we deal with media offense, especially cases that cause profound offense.

Types of media harm

The harm that media can do, through publication, takes five forms: physical harm, monetary harm, harm to reputation, psychological harm, and social harm.

Physical harm

Among the consequences of journalism are harmful stories and violent reactions. A TV broadcast of a video of white police officers in Chicago beating up an unarmed black man may spark violent attacks against police officers. If I reveal the identity of my source on an undercover investigation into biker gangs, I put my source's safety in jeopardy. He or she may suffer a retaliatory attack from the bikers.

Monetary harm

Monetary harm includes negatives effects on one's wealth and future income. Influential film reviewers may damage the revenue that a producer might make from her new film by writing damning reviews. Financial reporters may damage the value of a company's stock by discouraging readers from investing in the firm. Health reporters may harm the profits of a grocery chain by revealing unsanitary practices in its handling of meat products.

Harm to reputation

News media may harm the reputation and career of citizens and organizations. A story may allege that a politician took a kickback of thousands of dollars from the National Rifle Association for voting against a law restricting gun possession. A story may report that an accounting firm fudged numbers in a financial report of a major bank to protect the bank from unhappy investors. Movie stars and other public figures routinely press charges against news organizations for defamatory stories about their drug use or extra-marital affairs.

Psychological harm

Media can have harmful impact on one's mental states or support harmful attitudes. Many people worry that violent TV images desensitizes children (and others) to violent acts; or that pornography supports misogynous attitudes and discriminatory behavior toward women. News media create anxiety or emotional pain when a parent watches a news video that captures the death of her son or daughter. Persons in grief over the death of a family member in an accident can be further traumatized if hounded by journalists seeking a photo or interview.

Social harm

Uninformed or intolerant journalism can cause friction between groups in society, whip up xenophobia, support discriminatory measures against a marginalized group, misrepresent a religion or ethnic group, stereotype ethnic groups, or support an unjust war. Journalists harm society by focusing on sensational or entertaining stories while ignoring serious issues. They can harm citizens by misinforming them or reporting incomplete facts on social issues.

Minimizing harm

Even where journalists can justify the harm they do, they need to take seriously the principle of minimizing harm. The principle is sometimes misunderstood to mean that journalists should avoid causing *any* harm. The principle is not "do no harm" but "minimize harm." The word "minimize" is crucial. If journalists adopted the principle of "do no harm" little journalism would get done.

   Minimizing harm also does not mean that journalists should minimize the harm in the same way for all kinds of people and institutions. The media rightly hold public figures up for closer scrutiny and stronger criticism than private persons with little influence. Minimizing harm does not mean that one should not publish an important comment by a politician made during an interview because it will damage his popularity. It does not mean refusing to publishing facts about an energy company because it would hurt the value of their stocks. Minimizing harm means reducing the impact of the reporting on innocent third parties, confidential sources, or vulnerable people such as children.

Professional journalists have placed minimizing harm in their codes of ethics. Minimizing harm is one of the four principles of the SPJ code. Minimizing harm is described as treating sources, subjects of stories, and colleagues as "human beings worthy of respect." Under minimizing harm, the SPJ code includes such norms as (a) showing compassion to those adversely affected by news coverage, especially children and inexperienced sources or subjects; (b) being sensitive when seeking or using interviews or photographs of people affected by tragedy or grief; (c) recognizing that gathering and reporting information may cause harm or discomfort; (d) recognizing that private people have a greater right to control information about themselves than do public officials; (e) being "judicious" about naming criminal suspects before the laying of charges, and when identifying juvenile suspects or victims of sex crimes; and finally, (f) balancing a suspect's right to a fair trial with the public's right to be informed.

Many news outlets do not routinely report suicides to minimize harm to the family, unless the suicide involves a prominent figure or disrupts public life. Journalists attempt to minimize harm in sensitive situations such as where a distraught and armed person holds a family hostage. In these situations, responsible journalists co-operate with police negotiators so that live reporting does not unintentionally anger the hostage taker, who may be listening to live media reports.

Many newsrooms seek to minimize harm by allowing parents to be present when reporters interview children. Newsrooms agree not to publish the names of victims of fatal accidents until the next of kin have been informed. For funerals of prominent figures, news organizations work with funeral organizers to limit the intrusiveness of cameras at ceremonies. Adherence to minimizing harm prompts publications not to publish gruesome highway accident pictures, and it leads journalists to strongly protect the identity of sources, such as whistleblowers.

These examples of minimizing harm are not contentious. However, there are cases where minimizing harm conflicts with other values, such as reporting the truth. Let's consider several cases.

Truth and minimizing harm

News blackouts

Truth-telling comes up against minimizing harm when it is feared that reporting a story could place the safety of an individual in jeopardy.

In Chapter 2 we discussed the case of CBC reporter Mellissa Fung, who in 2008 was kidnapped by militants while reporting outside Kabul, Afghanistan. The CBC persuaded other media outlets not to report the story. Now that we have examined the idea of media harm we can describe the decision of newsrooms to impose a news blackout on the Fung kidnapping as a case of minimizing harm (or minimizing the potential for physical harm). News organizations came to the conclusion that, in this case, the principle of minimizing harm trumped the principle of reporting the truth *at this time*. The idea was that "no story is worth a life" and journalists should not cause more hardship for a kidnapped person than already exists. Yet the decision is fraught with indeterminacies and problems. Editors are being asked to determine what they will publish based on some possible response by a third party – the kidnappers. In Fung's case, the kidnappers were far from the newsroom and belonged to another culture.

Can we develop a more explicit, general policy for evaluating these cases? First, minimizing harm in such cases needs to be recognized as an *exception* to normal journalism practice. Given journalism's duty to publish the truth, and the tendency of officials to ask for news blackouts in too many situations, journalists need to approach news blackouts carefully. Second, certain procedures should be followed and certain questions should be asked. Journalists should be satisfied, by the facts and the views of experts, that the act of reporting will directly endanger the person kidnapped. They need to ask how not reporting the kidnapping will affect their credibility and the public interest. When the kidnapping is over and the news blackout is revealed, will the public wonder what other stories are not being reported? In some cases, such as a kidnapping of a wealthy person's son in a residential neighborhood, a news blackout may conflict with the media's duty to warn citizens that a dangerous, criminal group is operating in their area.

If experts or officials request a blackout, journalists need to examine who the experts are. Do they actually have expertise in handling kidnappings? Do they represent a group that might have an interest in the case?

If the police ask for a blackout, could the request be based on a desire to cover up the fact that inadequate policing contributed to a successful kidnapping? Initial skepticism toward experts and toward those who ask for blackouts is reasonable.

After the Fung story was reported, the Canadian Association of Journalists developed a list of questions for editors to ask when they receive a news blackout request:[46]

- Have strong, specific reasons been provided to support the blackout request? Are those reasons rooted in specifics of this case or a general assumption that reporting in this type of instance may result in harm? Is that assumption supported by evidence?
- Are we convinced that our actions in reporting the kidnapping could lead to the death of the victim, or dramatically compound the negotiations potentially leading to the release?
- Is the requested blackout short-term or time-limited? If not, will the request be reviewed after a defined period of time?
- Is a special favor being asked to protect a journalist? If so, would we agree to this request if the person being protected were not a journalist?
- Have senior people within our organization as well as news people in the field been consulted about the request, and their various views taken into account?
- Have we weighed the potential harm to individuals against the potential of harm to the public interest and harm to the credibility of the news media?
- How will our response to this request compare to our responses to similar situations in the past, and how may we justify a perceived inconsistency with such precedents?
- Are we committed to making full disclosure about the circumstances of the blackout once the perceived impediment to reporting has passed?

Publishing secrets

Minimizing harm also becomes an issue when journalists have to decide whether to publish classified or secret documents of the government or

---

[46] www.caj.ca/?p=361. Accessed November 5, 2010.

the military. Typically, officials claim that the publication may harm soldiers and security operations or aide terrorists. The media is jeopardizing national security and helping the nation's enemies. Media should avoid harm by not publishing the documents, or minimize harm by not publishing certain facts in the documents.

The problem of truth-telling and minimizing harm is made more difficult by today's online, global media. Consider, for example, the controversy provoked in 2010 by the web site, WikiLeaks (www.wikileaks.org). The not-for-profit site, directed by Australian Julian Assange, activist and former computer hacker, has said from its inception in 2007 that it was dedicated to publishing all manner of secrets. WikiLeaks justified its work on traditional free press grounds – acting as a watchdog on power. WikiLeaks invited whistleblowers to send secret documents to its web site, depositing them in an encrypted drop box. The site uses several servers around the world so that the site can continue to function, even if a government closes down one server in a particular country.

In WikiLeaks' early days, the issue of minimizing harm was not central. Many people celebrated the site's boldness. It had published confidential material on US operations at Guantanamo Bay, extra-judicial killings in Kenya, and an American Apache helicopter attack on individuals (including two Reuters' journalists) in Baghdad. The site garnered media awards from the *Economist* and Amnesty International. In 2010, the web site published two large collections of US military and intelligence field reports of the conflicts in Afghanistan and then in Iraq. The Afghan data was called the "Afghan War Diary" – more than 77,000 field reports of US soldiers and intelligence officers over a six-year period. The reports were used by Pentagon desk officers and soldiers in the field to monitor the daily events of the conflict. Major newspapers and magazines such as the *New York Times*, the British newspaper, *The Guardian*, and the German magazine *Der Spiegel*, published stories based on the Afghan Diary. Late in 2010, WikiLeaks became the top news story in the world when it released confidential notes written by American diplomats around the world, embarrassing the US government.

The publication of the diplomatic cables prompted an ethical and legal debate on publishing confidential documents and the methods (and aims) of WikiLeaks. The US government vowed to use every available legal hook to rein in the web site; right-wing politicians such as Sarah Palin and conservative media commentators in the USA called for Assange to be treated as a criminal and a traitor. Some even suggested that Assange should be assassinated. Companies that did business with WikiLeaks, such as credit card companies, stopped doing business with the web site. The issue even prompted a "hacker war" between critics and supporters of WikiLeaks. Hackers tried to shut down the WikiLeaks web site. In response, supporters of WikiLeaks set up alternate WikiLeaks sites and used computers to attack the web sites of individuals and companies that took action against WikiLeaks.

In the middle of this furor, Assange was arrested and jailed in England based on accusations that he had sexually attacked two Swedish women. Throughout it all, Assange dismissed the accusations as false and politically motivated, and he vowed that WikiLeaks would not only continue to operate but would release many more confidential documents in the future.

For this chapter, what is important about the WikiLeaks case is whether publishing secrets needs to take account of the principle of minimizing harm, and how it could do so. The issue of minimizing harm was brought to the fore by a mistake by WikiLeaks in handling the Afghan reports. It failed to expunge from the reports the names of Afghan informants to the military. Critics argued that the publication of these names placed informants in danger of attacks from the Taliban and other anti-NATO or anti-USA forces in Afghanistan. Indeed, not long after the documents were published, a spokesman for the Taliban in Afghanistan said it had set up a group to find the informants, which the spokesman called "Afghan spies." Although there were no documented cases of informants being harmed, the WikiLeaks failure to minimize harm prompted internal criticism by WikiLeaks staff and supporters, and drew criticism from groups such as Amnesty International. It was clear that freedom to publish was not a sufficient ethical guide for the publication of secrets online.

The Afghan Diary was a clear example of where WikiLeaks could have minimized harm without jeopardizing the principles of a free press. It was possible to expunge the names of individuals from the documents and still publish interesting and important stories about the conflict. In this case, the principles of truth-telling and freedom can coexist with the restraining principle to minimize harm. In contrast, the *New York Times* was careful to expunge the names of informants who might be harmed and escaped criticism on this score. The *Times* properly applied the minimizing harm principle.

In 2010, the WikiLeaks site had the following paragraph: "As the media organization has grown and developed, WikiLeaks (has) been developing and improving a harm minimization procedure. We do not censor our news, but from time to time we may remove or significantly delay the publication of some identifying details from original documents to protect life and limb of innocent people."[47] This statement is insufficient, ethically. Not only is it lacking in details about how they go about removing "identifying details," but the statement says nothing about other possible harm-causing actions by sites like WikiLeaks. For example, it doesn't say whether there is any secret information the site would *not* publish. If so, what is it? Does the site agree there are valid reasons for secrecy in some cases, and if so, what are those cases? Would WikiLeaks publish NATO codes for protection against nuclear attack? Would it publish the security plans of energy installations or airports against terrorist attack? How does the site decide what to publish? Moreover, what is its politics? When WikiLeaks presents data on its web site, does it attempt to be accurate, complete, and fair? Will the site publish secrets from all countries equally, or will they favor reports that support their favored causes or do damage to countries they dislike? If their site makes a major mistake, to whom should the public complain? How?

The publication of the diplomatic cables and subsequent arrest of Assange only raised additional concerns about WikiLeaks' policy on avoiding or minimizing harm. Assange, at times, said he'd try to prevent causing harm to innocent parties; but, at other times, he seemed to downplay the importance of minimizing harm. The moral for media ethics is that we now live in a world of "stateless" web sites run by many types of people with differing motivations. Since WikiLeaks started operating, other sites have appeared with similar aims – to publish confidential documents and reveal secrets. This makes it imperative that these sites take seriously the principle of minimizing harm and, in a transparent manner, indicate the procedures they plan to use to minimize harm.

[47] www.wikileaks.org. Accessed October 30, 2010.

Ethics of images

Discussions of media harm are prompted not only by reports but also by images, both video and photographs. We live in a media-saturated world with an unrelenting flow of images, instantly gathered and shared. There are at least four types of issues raised in any discussion of images: craft, aesthetic, legal, and ethical.

Craft values have to do with the technical competency of the image maker. We can ask these questions: is the photograph well composed? Is it in focus? Is the lighting optimal? Was the picture technically difficult to produce, e.g. the picture captures fast-moving objects such as racing cars? Aesthetic values deal with the impact of a photo upon us. We may find an image striking, fascinating, graphic, dramatic, disturbing, disgusting, or beautiful. For example, in June 1985, the *National Geographic* published a now famous picture by Steve McCurry of a young Afghanistan woman, a refugee, on its cover. Her beautiful sea-green eyes stare out, angrily, at the camera. For years, she was simply "the Afghan girl" but later was identified as Sharbat Gula of the Pashtun tribe. The picture strikes many people as a ravishingly beautiful photograph that says something about the fate of this war-torn country and its people.

Discussions also center on the legality of images, especially how an image was taken or obtained, who owns it, and whether its publication violates any laws, such as laws dealing with national security or personal privacy.

Ethical discussions may originate with discussions about the aesthetic quality or legality of a picture but they go beyond such considerations. Examples of ethical questions about media images are: even if the photo is striking or beautiful, even if it raises no legal issues, should media publish the image? Does the image fit the media's mandate to inform the public on important issues? Is publishing the image consistent with the ethical principles of truth-telling, independence, accountability, and minimizing harm?

Images can run afoul of ethical principles in many ways. For example, images may violate the principles of truth-telling and accountability if the images have been altered so that they change the meaning of the picture, and mislead unknowing viewers. Using commonly available software such as Photoshop, journalists and citizens can easily change the content of the image, omitting or adding an object, or changing the position of subjects in the original picture. Fashion publications and news magazines alter their front-page images to attract the gaze of viewers. Fashion pictures are manipulated to make the model look slimmer, taller, and her skin devoid of any imperfections.

Manipulating photos goes back to the start of photojournalism. Around 1860, a picture of Abraham Lincoln, that eventually became an iconic portrait of the president, was a composite: the head of the president attached to the body of Southern politician John Calhoun. The issue of manipulation gained prominence in the late twentieth century due to the power of computer technology and software for easily changing digital images. Early infamous cases included the *National Geographic*'s decision, for a front cover in 1982, to make the Egyptian pyramids appear closer in the picture than they are in reality, and the June 27, 1994, cover of *Time* magazine that darkened a police mug shot of accused wife murderer and football star, O. J. Simpson. Both alterations, when made public, drew criticism for violating the principles of truth-telling and accountability. Over the ensuing years, a string of photojournalists were fired by news organizations for altering their images without the knowledge of their editors or the public.

Not all altered photos are obviously wrong. Photojournalists distinguish between technical improvements to their images, such as making an image lighter in color, and changes to the content of the pictures. Magazine editors argue that altering images for their front covers is perfectly acceptable because their covers are works of art to attract readers. The public is aware of these practices, so no one is deceived. The code for the Society of Professional Journalists addresses these issues by making a distinction between news photos and other types of images. It states: "Journalists should … never distort the content of news photos or video. Image enhancement for technical clarity is always permissible. Label montages and photo illustrations."

In the rest of this chapter, we will encounter other ethical issues in the use of images, including the use of graphic and offending images.

Minimizing harm and images: cases

As in the case of reporting news, minimizing harm acts as a restraining principle on the use of images. Ethics requires that the image is truthful and not misleading, and the publication discloses any change to the image.

The principle of minimizing harm adds one further and important consideration: will the image cause harm to anyone? Can the harm be justified under one of the four exceptions, such as social role? For example, graphic images of the crash of a military helicopter may be painful to the parents of the soldiers who died in the crash but it is the media's job to cover such events.

However, even if we can justify harm-causing images on general grounds, media practitioners need to ask a more specific question: should we minimize harm by altering the image or by using an alternate image? Media need to ask: are there vulnerable or innocent people in the picture? What effect will publication have on their lives? Should we choose a less graphic picture of the victim of a terrible car accident? In many cases, minimizing harm supports altering the image, despite what was said above about not altering images. For example, a TV program that interviews a whistleblower may alter the voice and blur the face of the interviewee to maintain anonymity and prevent harm.

Case: "playing" addict

One difficult area is where the motivation to expose harmful conditions in society conflicts with the motivation not to harm innocent individuals. Often the harm in question is caused by a social problem such as the sexual abuse of children. Typically, journalists want to interview and use images of people actually affected by a social problem. Yet this personal approach can raise questions of media harm.

For a salient example, return to a case in Chapter 2 which was used to illustrate the four-step method for making ethical decisions. The case was that of a newspaper considering whether to publish a photo of the children of addicted parents. The children are playing addicts by sticking fake needles into their arms. We can now understand the case as raising the question of whether and how to minimize harm.Proponents of publishing the photo may argue that reporting the unvarnished truth is consistent with the journalistic role of reporting the truth. It also fits with an aim of journalistic truth-telling – the alleviation of social ills. Journalists who want to prompt reform may argue that the image will prompt child protection agencies to protect children in such situations. Proponents of publishing the photo may say that, although the image may cause some harm, the image may help to prevent a greater harm – of children being negatively affected by the addiction of their parents.

Yet the principle of minimizing harm restrains such reasoning. It asks journalists to consider whether the image could harm the children. Will the photo exploit the children for a dramatic story to sell the news? Will the publication of the image violate the rights of the children to privacy and stigmatize them? Are journalists telling people to pay attention to a problem, or are they feeding off someone's tragedy?

One problem with deciding which position is correct is the difficulty in predicting the long-term consequences of publishing the picture. Will the published photo actually prompt remedial action by officials or significantly increase public awareness of the problem of parental drug abuse? After an initial public response to the story, will the issue disappear once again from public view, without remedial action? Will the published photo really "stigmatize" the children for life? How do we know this to be true?

After examining the options, the best application of the minimizing harm principle is to use the photo but to alter the image to reduce the likelihood of harm to the children. In this case, some minimizing of harm is required because journalists have a duty not to harm innocent or vulnerable people like children. The argument that one can do some harm to the children to advance a larger good is not persuasive. Even if we wish to alleviate the problem of children of addicts, the rights and well-being of the children, as vulnerable people, must be considered. If anything can be done to reduce harm to the children, it should be done.

Moreover, methods of reducing harm are readily available. The story can avoid identifying the children and be vague on the location of the family. Newspapers and TV programs can blur the faces of the children. These are reasonable ethical restraints on the freedom to publish. The story and the image can still be published, while scrupulously protecting the children from being identified. Blurring the faces, for example, does not weaken the story unduly. Through such methods, the truth-telling function of the press can coexist with minimizing harm.

Media offense

Graphic images

Graphic images include images of bloody car accidents, the victims of disasters, and the bodies of dead soldiers. It is sometimes thought that graphic and gruesome images should never be published. These images, it is said, are sensational, unnecessary, and exploitive. While media exploit-ation and sensationalism occur, this fact does not support the general-ization that graphic and offensive images should never be used. Media history is replete with examples of graphic stories and images that needed to be published. During the Vietnam War, the shocking picture of a naked Vietnam child running down a small road after her village was bombed by US forces helped to change the public's perception of the conflict. Pictures of tortured detainees at the US-operated Abu Ghraib prison in Baghdad during the Iraq War alerted the world to inhumane actions. In June 2009, amid popular protests against Iran's flawed presidential election, a young Iranian woman, Neda Agha-Soltan, was fatally shot by an unknown gun-man. As she lay dying in a Tehran street, surrounded by relatives and friends, the last minutes of her life were recorded on video by a cell phone. Graphic images of her bloodied face and body were transmitted around the world via the Internet, making her a symbol of the Iranian democratic movement. The context of these images, and the importance of making them public, overrides complaints that their graphic nature may offend or shock.

When should graphic images be used to honor journalism's mandate to inform the public? Here, questions of minimizing harm intrude. Should the media warn readers about graphic content, or give them a choice as to the level of graphic detail they wish to subject themselves or their chil-dren? Graphic newspaper stories can begin with a warning. On web sites, viewers who "click" on a graphic story can be taken to an intermediary page that describes what they are about to see.

Case: Colonel Williams

Debate over graphic media reports and images are inescapable when mass murderers and disturbed individuals go to trial. The court listens to grue-some testimony and sees profoundly disturbing images. The media must judge what content to use.

In October 2010, Canadians were shocked by evidence at the trial of Col. David Russell Williams, the former base commander of CFB Trenton, Ontario. By day, Williams was a respected civic leader. By night, he was a serial criminal who preyed on children, often breaking into homes to gain access to them. Williams pleaded guilty to the murder of Jessica Lloyd and

Corporal Marie-France Comeau. He was sentenced to life for first-degree murder, two ten-year sentences for other sexual assaults, and 82 one-year sentences for burglary. Williams kept mementos from his many crimes. He left messages for his victims, some as young as nine years old. His pedophile tendencies induced him to steal the underwear of young girls and masturbate in the beds of his victims.

For four days, a Belleville, Ontario, court heard evidence. Major newspapers differed on what images to display on their front cover and online sites; TV news programs sought to warn viewers about the nature of the stories and explain why they were using graphic content. The Canadian Broadcasting Corporation (CBC) introduced graphic elements of the trial on its blogging of the trial with the following words: "WARNING GRAPHIC CONTENT."

The CBC's site explained why the broadcaster covered the difficult trial: "We cover it because we can be your eyes and ears in a courtroom, and we are committed to as open a justice system as possible," it stated. "We cover it because there is a strong public interest (and yes, maybe some of it is prurient) as well as a real need to understand how someone in a position of such authority, a senior member of the Canadian armed forces, could also commit these crimes."

On a morning radio show, John Cruickshank, publisher of the *Toronto Star*, said a decision to put on the front page a photo of Williams wearing stolen lingerie "left the newsroom divided." He said: "I think there probably is harm, but there is a greater good that arises as we get past that harm. This is a day you hate as a publisher." The publisher added: "We feel like we have to face up to the truth of our day, this is not the truth of every morning, but certainly is an extraordinary story about authority in Canada. It's a story we shouldn't turn our heads from, it's the reason we made the decision we did." When asked why the *Star* ran the "most explicit" front page of all newspapers, Cruickshank continued with his argument that not to run such images would be to avoid the truth and the reality of the case. "This is the most honest portrayal. This is a photograph of a character that is both enormously frightening and tremendously pathetic … What [the Star has] done is kept it very real."

Sylvia Stead, a senior editor for a rival Toronto paper, *The Globe and Mail*, took a different view. In an article called, "Why today's front page does not include a photo of Russell Williams in women's lingerie," Stead wrote that while the reports went into great detail, "we chose not to run the photographs of Williams in women's lingerie in part because the readers have no choice in what photographs they see on the front page. They can choose to read the articles and to stop when it might become difficult, but not so with photographs."

How does our minimizing principle apply to the debate between Cruickshank and Stead? The issue is not whether the image offended readers of the *Star*. Even if the image profoundly shocked some readers it did not constitute harm. The issue is the anxiety and mental pain that the front page story caused the families of victims of Williams. My view is that neither Cruickshank nor Stead violated media ethics, or the harm principle. Both actions – to publish or not to publish the Williams photo on the front page – are ethically permissible and justifiable options. Cruickshank can make a strong case that truth telling, not hiding the reality of the case, was part of his paper's journalistic duty, despite the pain it may have caused the families of Williams' victims. And Stead too is perfectly within her rights to seek to minimize harm and give readers a choice whether they want to see the picture or not. Both editorial decisions are ethically permissible.

My view of this case may surprise, since some people assume that reasoning in media ethics always results in black-and-white judgments: some course of action must be wrong and the other right. However, because principles can conflict and must be balanced, it happens with regularity that there is a range of ethically permissible actions. The Williams case shows, in stark terms, how difficult it is to make editorial decisions on graphic and offensive images.

Offense and global media

Let us consider another type of offensive story. A person or group sets out deliberately to use the media to insult another group, raising social tensions. Media coverage will cause profound offense and perhaps physical (and social) harm.

In July 2010, the minister of a small Florida church warned that his church members would burn copies of the Koran as the USA approached, nervously and disunited, the ninth anniversary of the 9/11 terrorist attack. Rev. Terry Jones and his Dove World Outreach Center announced that the burnings would proclaim the evil of Islam. By August, the pastor bathed in a global media spotlight. His unholy plan was top of the news around the world, sparking riots and prompting widespread criticism. On one day alone in late August, Jones' blatant media manipulation garnered front page coverage in over 50 US daily papers.

The questions asked repeatedly on media programs were: how did this little-known pastor get so much news coverage? Should the media have given him a global platform for his questionable views and potentially harmful actions? From the view of media ethics, the question is: what guidelines can help newsrooms respond responsibly to a Terry Jones and a soon-to-follow host of copycats?

Earlier, I said that reckless and provocative reports and images that do not advance deliberation about potentially explosive issues should be ethically condemned and challenged. This followed from my principle of unjustified profound offense. The principle applies to individuals, such as Rev. Jones, who use news media for their provocative aims.

In the Jones story, the question of responsible news selection involved two different time periods: in the summer, when the plan was first announced; and in late August, when the story had gone viral. In the early weeks, newsrooms should have ignored Jones' plan. There was no justification for selecting Jones' announcement as an important news story. At the very most, the announcement merited an initial item on the controversial pastor from Gainesville, Florida.

What should responsible editors do when the media system turns the story into an ugly global incident, with the news story starting to cause riots in many countries? Caught inside this media maelstrom, responsible editors cannot ignore the story. There are no easy answers. But media ethics does counsel that news organizations should minimize harm by reducing the amount of coverage, ignoring certain events and press statements, and refusing to publish certain images or publishing only selected images.

Editors also can consult the following principles:

Democracy needs intelligent news selection

A democracy whose media is distracted by sensational events is headed for trouble. A news media that does not – or will not – distinguish between trivial and essential news, or between genuine news makers and media manipulators, creates a society that is under-informed on the crucial issues that define its future. Journalists should ask to what degree their news selection is based on a sober assessment of what really is important – developments in the political, economic, legal, and social arenas of the body politic. When a Terry Jones gets too much air time, or when Paris Hilton's latest faux pas trends on Twitter – and the blogosphere is abuzz – this is exactly the time when journalists must push back in the opposite direction. They must question a news selection that feeds this media circus. Of course, media should cover pop culture and the merely novel; but the media's news selection should not be hostage to alleged news events or entertainment values.

Go hard on manipulators

News selection should be guided by who is seeking media attention and why. Jones guessed correctly that a book-burning would get attention. He loved appearing before the cameras and toying with reporters. Editors have every right to work against a manipulator's media strategy. It is not the job of journalists to provide unthinking coverage of events that are gratuitously manufactured to provoke and cause harm.

Swim against the flow by doing good journalism

Even if a story is too big to ignore, journalists and newsrooms are not helpless victims of a faceless "media world." They can do three things when confronted by a Terry Jones.

Practice proportionality and avoid the drama, reduce the quantity of coverage and reduce the prominence of the story. For example, in the lead up to September 11, the *Associated Press* announced that it would reduce the number of stories it would do on the Jones affair, and would not distribute images or audio that specifically showed Korans being burned.

Relentlessly provide context

Widen the story by avoiding a narrow focus on the event in question. For example, in the case of a Terry Jones, media should not follow his every

move or gather outside his church. Media need to explain who the pro-
vocateur is. In the case of Jones, this meant noting the size of his following. It meant noting Jones' previous attempts to get media attention and
questioning whether his views are affirmed by many Americans. On a
number of days, the *New York Times* reduced the impact of the Jones story
by folding the event into larger explanatory stories of how Americans were
approaching the 9/11 anniversary.

Be a catalyst for informed discussion

The ethical responsibility of media covering such stories includes deepening the story. In the case of Jones, media should include other voices, such
as moderate Muslim leaders and interfaith associations that were rallying
against Jones. Use this moment to bring intolerant views about Islam out
into the open for rigorous review. Rather than try to pretend that people
like Jones don't exist, use this shabby affair as an opportunity to spark
a more reasoned and intelligent discussion of religion. Meet intolerant,
uninformed speech with tolerant, informed speech.

   The Jones story shows that covering hateful or intolerant speech
requires a judicious editorial policy that makes truth-telling more important than updates on the latest statements by intolerant spokespersons.
Truth-telling includes verifying claims and adding context and other
voices. The justification for such restraining policies is based on the overall goal of journalism to promote informed coverage and deliberation, not
simply amplify any loud and angry voice. In this pluralistic world of global
media and instantaneous online commentary, media are fully justified in
following the principles of responsible news selection and of minimizing
harm when people set out to manipulate and provoke.

Danish cartoons and profound offense

Discussions of deliberately provocative stories would not be complete
without reference to the famous publication of cartoons of Mohammed by
a Danish newspaper, the *Jyllands-Posten*. On September 30, 2005, the paper
published twelve editorial cartoons, some of which depicted the Islamic
prophet. The newspaper announced that this publication was an attempt
to test the limits of free speech in Denmark. The cartoons were reprinted

in newspapers in more than 50 other countries. The visual depiction of Mohammed, at times seeming to depict him as a terrorist, was profoundly offensive to Muslims and sparked protests and violence.

Much has been written about the cartoons and whether they should have been published and republished. When it comes to publishing stories that so profoundly offend a religious group, is this where the freedom to publish ends? Was the publication of the cartoons consistent with the principles of responsible journalism, especially its restraining principles?

Publishing the cartoons was not consistent with media ethics. It was legally permissible but ethically wrong, or irresponsible. The publication amounted to unjustified profound offense. Legally, a liberal approach defends the legal rights of the newspaper to print the cartoons, and the legal right of Muslims to protest peacefully and to rebut the article in other publications. A free press and a robust public sphere needs the greatest legal freedom for the publication of views and images even if they are inaccurate, untruthful, and provocative. Ethically, however, things are different.

Earlier, I said that if media believe they should publish stories that may profoundly offend some persons or groups, they should make sure their stories are accurate and well researched. They should foster deliberation on legitimate, if sensitive, social issues. The Danish cartoons fail these criteria. The intent of the cartoons was to provoke Muslims. It was to test the limits of free speech in a manner almost certain to provoke protest and intolerant reactions. Some journalists have said the offended Muslims failed to see that the cartoons contained elements of social humor or satire. But it is unreasonable to expect that many Muslims would pick up on these nuances. Nor are these nuances relevant to the ethical analysis. What is relevant is that the publication of the cartoons represented the equivalent of someone sticking their finger in someone's eye to see if they recoil in pain and anger.

The cartoons were a reckless and clumsy attempt to stir up reaction. It downplayed (or ignored) the consequences of publication and it made no attempt to minimize harm. The cartoons did not attempt to promote deliberation on cultural differences and free speech. If the paper wanted to test views or start a dialogue, almost any other method would have been better than publishing offensive cartoons. It could have published a series of stories presenting a wide range of views, accompanied by informed analysis of Islam and its views on free speech. Instead, it resorted to images that would only increase fears and social tensions. Nothing justified the violent reaction to the cartoons; but neither is the publication of the cartoons an example of responsible journalism. Lastly, other news organizations were under no ethical obligation to reprint the cartoons. News organizations had a right to come to the legal defense of the Danish paper and to argue against censorship. But they were not compelled to republish ethically questionable material.

This chapter has explored media harm and offense. It has formulated three principles for avoiding and minimizing harm and offense, as guides for responsible media. The approach has sought to balance proactive principles that support a free and independent press with restraining principles that ask journalists not to harm others without justification, and to minimize harm even when they are justified in causing it. In the next chapter, we examine how these proactive and restraining principles should operate in the world of new media journalism.

Questions for discussion

1. Why do some philosophers think that not causing harm is a more important ethical principle than assisting others (or benevolence)? Do you agree? Why or why not?
2. What is your definition of harm? Do you agree that harm should be defined as a "setback to interests"?
3. Do you agree that what the chapter calls "trivial offense" is really trivial?
4. What is the difference between trivial and profound offense? Should media *ever* profoundly offend some person or some group? What rules should journalists follow when considering stories that may profoundly offend?
5. Would you ever publish graphic and gruesome images in a publication? How would you decide whether an image was too graphic? What would be the criteria for making this decision?
6. If you were covering the trial of Col. Williams, discussed in the chapter, what images and testimony would you publish? On what ethical grounds?

7. Do you agree with the publisher of the *Toronto Star* that the paper needed to publish an offensive picture of Col. Williams on its front page to inform readers about this case?
8. Would you publish the photo of the two children playing addicts? Why or why not? Would you attempt to minimize harm by altering the photo?
9. Do you think the publishing of the cartoons of Mohammed in the Danish newspaper was an example of irresponsible journalism, or an example of courageous testing of the limits of free speech?

6   The new media ethics

Over the past three chapters we have examined basic principles: truth, objectivity, and minimizing harm. These concepts are the pillars of mainstream media ethics.

Most of the principles and approaches were developed over the past century, originating in the construction of professional media ethics, as discussed in Chapter 2. Therefore, our discussion has revolved around a traditional approach to ethics developed originally for a news media of another era.

To what extent is this approach to ethics suitable for today's and tomorrow's news media? In this chapter we address this question by examining the reasons for concern about the applicability of traditional approaches, and by describing a new, emerging media ethics.[1] In Chapter 4, we reaffirmed truth and objectivity after we reconceived these concepts. In this chapter we go further and think more radically. We consider to what extent the entire structure of media ethics needs to be rethought and reinvented for the media of today, not of yesteryear.

Radical approaches are needed because a media revolution is transforming, fundamentally and irrevocably, the nature of journalism and its ethics. Our media ecology is a chaotic landscape evolving at a furious pace. Professional journalists share the journalistic sphere with tweeters, bloggers, citizen journalists, and social media users. Amid every revolution, new possibilities emerge while old practices are threatened. Today is no exception. The economics of professional journalism struggles as audiences migrate online. Shrinkage of newsrooms creates concern for the future of journalism. Yet these fears also prompt experiments in journalism, such as non-profit centers of investigative journalism.

---

[1] Some of the ideas in this chapter are from my "Ethics for the New Mainstream."

The changes challenge the foundations of media ethics. The challenge runs deeper than debates about one or another principle, such as objectivity. The challenge is greater than specific problems, such as how newsrooms can verify content from citizens. The revolution requires us to rethink assumptions. What can ethics *mean* for a profession that must provide instant news and analysis; where everyone with a modem is a publisher?

The media revolution has created a tension among values on two levels.

The first level is due to online journalism. The culture of traditional journalism, with its values of accuracy, pre-publication verification, balance, impartiality, and gate-keeping, rubs up against the culture of online journalism which emphasizes immediacy, transparency, partiality, non-professional journalists and post-publication correction. The second level is due to the emergence of a global journalism. If journalism has global impact, what are its global responsibilities?

The challenge for today's media ethics can be summarized by the question: whither ethics in a world of multi-media, global journalism?

Media ethics must do more than point out tensions. Theoretically, it must untangle the conflicts between values. It must decide which principles should be preserved or invented. Practically, it should provide new standards to guide online or offline journalism.

This chapter provides a framework for understanding the revolution in journalism. I use my theory of ethical revolutions to explain the current status of media ethics, and how, in all probability, it will develop.

I argue that we are moving towards an ethics for a new mainstream media; that is, an ethics for multiple media platforms. The old mainstream consisted of professionals working for large newspapers and broadcasters. The new mainstream is a hybrid of professional and amateur, working for both media outlets that integrate old and new forms of journalism.

I discuss the main principles and approaches of this new ethics, stressing how it should exhibit three features: (1) it should be an ecumenical ethics that is both an ethics of common principles and an ethics of difference – an ethics that sanctions different norms of practice for different forms of news media. (2) It should be an open, citizen-based ethics that brings the public directly into the process of articulating, monitoring, and practicing the norms of responsible media usage. (3) It should be global or cosmopolitan in attitude.

Chapter 7 will deal with (3), a global ethics.

Ethical revolutions

From conflict to integration

What is a revolution in journalism ethics?

A revolution, any dictionary will tell you, is a fundamental change or reversal of conditions. During political revolutions, a system of governance is replaced by another. In scientific revolutions, a conceptual system is superseded by another, e.g. Newtonian physics gives way to the relativistic physics of Einstein. In an ethical revolution, a system of norms replaces another. A revolution in journalism ethics, then, is a fundamental change in the prevailing ethical system. Principles are reinterpreted or they give way to new principles.

Value change does not occur *ex nihilo*. It is caused by changes in the socio-economic, technological, and political environment. For example, the 1960s social revolution with its stress on peace and equality – not to mention "sex, drugs, and rock and roll" – was prompted by a growing economy and education system, communication technology, the civil rights movement, and resistance to the Vietnam War. Revolutions create new opportunities, new attitudes, and new problems. Existing norms may fail to express the spirit of the times and seem irrelevant. This shift in values is captured by slogans, from the 1960s' "Make Love, Not War" to today's slogan for the YouTube web site, "Broadcast Yourself." Yet, the far-reaching implications of this shift may go unrecognized.

Analogously, revolutions in journalism ethics are caused by changes in the socio-economic, technological, and political environment which create new opportunities, new attitudes, and new problems. The far-reaching consequences of the shift are difficult to ascertain.

Revolutions are exceptional events. Therefore, we should distinguish between what Thomas Kuhn called, with respect to science, revolutionary and normal periods.[2] During normal periods, scientists share a paradigm of methods, assumptions, and theories. During revolutionary periods, the paradigm comes under attack and new conceptual schemes are put forward. A crisis occurs. Confusion reigns until a new paradigm is constructed and signals a new normal period.

---

[2] See Kuhn, *The Structure of Scientific Revolutions*.

Adapting Kuhn's views to journalism, we can say that, during normal periods, journalists share a common understanding of their aims, values, and methods. Ethical issues are discussed by reference to this paradigm. However, over time, the paradigm may come under criticism while new forms of journalism emerge. A crisis occurs. Journalism enters a revolutionary phase of conflicting values, methods, and practices. Eventually a new consensus is established around a new paradigm, a new normative system. Journalism ethics returns to a normal phase.

The normal–revolutionary scheme provides an abstract framework for understanding some forms of revolution. We can deepen our understanding of revolution in journalism ethics by noting two other features: one, in a revolution, the relationship between journalists and their public changes fundamentally. Two, the revolution typically passes through three stages: conflict, rapprochement, and integration. Let's consider each of these two points.

What is this relationship between journalist and public, and why is it important to journalism ethics? The relationship is the manner in which journalists communicate with, and serve, their public. The journalism–public relationship has three elements: (a) the journalists, (b) the public, and (c) how the two groups communicate, such as the technology used by journalists to deliver the news. For brevity's sake, let's call this relationship the "JCP" (journalists–communication methods–public).

In different eras, different forms of journalism create different relationships. The relationship of the seventeenth-century London editor and his readers is vastly different from the relationship of twentieth-century professional journalists and their mass audience. Embedded in the JCP is a set of expectations that constitute a social contract. The public recognizes the freedom of the press. In return, they expect journalists to perform certain information functions according to certain norms. Like any successful relationship, there must be trust and credibility on both sides.

Historically, journalism ethics grew out of the journalist's need to maintain a healthy JCP. Editors claimed to reliably report the truth or to be objective to maintain public confidence in their publications, to explain new practices, and to defend controversial decisions. Journalism ethics in any given era are the norms that define the journalist–public relationship. A revolution in journalism ethics occurs when technological and social changes alter journalism and the journalist–public relationship.

A revolution in journalism ethics tends to follow a three-step process of conflict, rapprochement, and integration.

During a period of conflict, social and technological trends prompt new forms of journalism. But not just any new forms will do. The new forms need to be so different as to alter substantially the JCP and create a crisis – a clash of values. The conflict destroys the ethical consensus of the previous normal period. Many journalists divide into two camps – the existing mainstream journalists versus the non-mainstream, new journalists.

Typically, a war of rhetoric ensues between the practitioners of the old and the new journalism. Traditionalists accuse the new journalism of being irresponsible or of not being journalism at all. The new journalists claim the traditional journalism is doomed. They claim to be the "real" journalists of a new, bold era. As we noted in Chapter 3, some of the new journalism radicals dismiss ethics in whole or in part (specific principles such as objectivity) as irrelevant because they identify ethics with the practices of mainstream news media. Ethics consists of norms meant for another form of journalism. The heady days of new forms of media encourage the idea that the development and practice of the new journalism is more important than adherence to old-fashioned ethical restraints. Meanwhile, citizens change their media habits. They become accustomed to the new media and use journalism in new ways. The JCP begins to change and the public itself debates the ethics of the old and the new media.

As the ideological battle runs its course, economic and other realities encourage a rapprochement between traditional and new media. Mainstream media do not disappear. They evolve, if slowly and awkwardly, by incorporating new forms of media and their editorial and publishing techniques.[3] The journalists, who now use both old and new media, begin to seek common ground. The conflict between old and new media abates, the hot rhetoric cools, the line between old and new media blurs.

Eventually, rapprochement leads towards integration across the media system. What emerges after a difficult transition is journalism that is a synthesis of old and new practices, guided by a new system of ethics that is a synthesis of old and new norms.

---

[3] The idea of news media adjusting and not just dying is a special case of the idea that forms of communication media co-evolve and co-exist, and new media emerge gradually out of old media. See Fidler, *Mediamorphosis*.

From partisan to objective journalists

Examples of ethical revolutions in journalism can be found across the 400-year history of modern journalism. In this section, I examine only one – the creation of a professional ethics for the mass commercial press of the late 1800s and early 1900s. I select this revolution because it created the ethics currently challenged by new media.

As we noted in Chapter 3, the creation of mass commercial newspapers at the end of the nineteenth century was a radical change in journalism, the prevailing JCP, and journalism ethics. Yet no sooner was the mass commercial newspaper, published by Pulitzer, Hearst and others, ascendant on both sides of the Atlantic, than doubts were raised about its ethics. The commercial press was accused of being sensational, irresponsible, and controlled by press barons and business interests. A rhetorical war ensued between the old elite journalism and the new "yellow" journalism.

By the turn of the twentieth century, conflict began to give way to rapprochement and integration. Journalists formed associations that created a new ethics that demanded accuracy, balance, and "just the facts." These demanding norms were thought necessary to reduce the blatant bias and lack of independence of journalists. The partisan libertarian approach to journalism was replaced by a professional model that stressed objectivity and impartiality. More and more newsrooms practiced the new objective journalism until it became the new mainstream. The professional ethics was a synthesis of old and new. Freedom of the press became part of an ethics that called for verification, independence, and minimizing harm.

The new journalism changed fundamentally the JCP. Journalists became powerful gatekeepers within large profit-seeking ventures. The public came to rely on newspapers as sources of information on most areas of society from the legislature to the sports arena. Reporters were asked to provide accurate news for a public that demanded less partisan journalism. The JCP became a one-to-many, hierarchical form of mass communication.

Where are we today?

Today's revolution

The idea of normal and revolutionary periods, the JCP, and the principle of integration are tools for understanding revolutions in journalism. These concepts tell us that we are entering a revolutionary phase when a consensus on the existing ethical paradigm starts to break down, and changes in technology and other factors radically change the relationship of journalists to their public.

What does this theory say about journalism today?

It tells us that we are indeed in the middle of an ethical revolution. In fact, we are in the middle of the fifth revolution in journalism ethics since modern journalism began in the seventeenth century. The rise of internet-based media is a revolutionary event because it substantially alters the prevailing professional model of the JCP. The journalistic element of this relationship is transformed to include, for the first time, ordinary citizens in great numbers. It becomes a sphere of professionals and non-professionals of varying ability, training, and motivation. The communication element has been revolutionized by interactive and global media. The public term of the relationship is altered almost beyond recognition. Citizens are no longer the passive, dependent consumers of professional media. Citizens have the technology to be active members of the JCP by creating content and using media tools to evaluate reports. Increasingly, citizens *are* the media.

Journalism, therefore, occupies an increasingly smaller portion of the public spheres which is being enlarged by a chaotic and expanding media universe. This media universe has led to a period of conflict, a clash of values between the professional and new media models.

The professional model values well-trained journalists who make sure their stories are accurate, verified, and well researched before publication. The story is the end product of an editorial process. Its authority depends mainly on the capabilities and character of the individual professional journalist. The ethical mantra is "filter, then publish," or "get it (news) first, but first get it right." In contrast, new media value the speedy posting of information by anyone, even if there is uncertainty about its source or accuracy. The slogan is: "publish, then filter." As a correction to inaccurate or bogus stories posted in haste, new media journalism recommends pre-publication warnings about the uncertain verity of material. New media ethics emphasizes the remedial function of post-publication assessments of stories by a "community of interest" – the people who regularly visit a web site or blog. The posted story is not the end of a process. It is the start of an online dialogue whereby everyone is free to critique the story and to enrich its sources, facts, and perspectives. Ideally, the authority of a new media story is not individual but communal. It must pass the scrutiny of online readers and experts around the world.

For the professional model, the role of the public is to be an audience – to receive the completed story. For the new media model, journalism should be a more co-operative project of citizens and journalists. The professional and new media models also differ on what sort of journalism democracy needs. The professional model thinks objective news reporting and well-informed analysis are essential for informed public decisions. The new media model favors a participatory model of democracy which is libertarian in spirit. A free and many-voiced marketplace of ideas, using the interactive medium of the Internet, is sufficient for democracy. What is crucial is the free expression and sharing of voices. New media communication is inclined towards opinion journalism and is suspicious of the ideal of objectivity. Rather than maintain an objective stance, new media journalists are transparent about their biases.

Signs of rapprochement

This clash of values has received extensive comment in the media. What has received less attention is the fact that a new type of journalism ethics is emerging from this conflict. Journalism ethics is entering a stage of rapprochement.

One sign of rapprochement is the sense that new media are no longer new. They are part of our daily lives. The line between new and old media blurs. Newspapers and major broadcasters are online and their web sites are popular. They have their own bloggers, citizen journalists, podcasts, web sites, Twitter and RSS feeds, Facebook pages, and interactive online forums. Increasingly, new media journalists write for traditional media. Successful bloggers attract large numbers of readers, resembling the influential newspaper columnists of a previous era. The distinction between big mainstream media and small, iconoclastic new media fades as the leaders of the new mainstream are large, corporate, online enterprises, such as Google. Citizen journalism sites become a permanent part of the media landscape. Partnerships between citizens and newsrooms are increasingly common. Citizens provide story ideas, video, eye-witness accounts and other information. Non-profit centers for investigative journalism are collaborative in nature. Their newsrooms combine the talents of many types of journalists.

A rapprochement in ethics is also underway. We are moving towards a new system of ethics, a mixed media ethics that defines responsible public journalism across media platforms. Recently, traditional news media such as the *Wall Street Journal, New York Times, BBC, The Associated Press* and *The Washington Post* have developed guidelines on how their journalists can responsibly use social media. Their guidelines encourage journalists to use social media, such as Facebook, but also to respect traditional values such as avoiding conflicts of interest. Bloggers and online journalists form associations and construct codes of ethics, engaging in the same ethics-creating exercise that occupied newspaper journalists a century ago.[4] The online codes are an interesting synthesis of old and new elements, reinterpreting – not rejecting – many of the major principles of professional journalism, such as truth-seeking and independence.

The motivations for rapprochement are the same as in previous revolutions. Traditional media need to adapt to survive, and to serve the changing media habits of the public. Everyone wants to figure out how to make money from the public's appetite for online content and love of interactivity. Also, journalists and citizens grow increasingly critical of the rumors and misinformation on the Internet. They seek to carve out a media sphere where journalists can work according to appropriate standards.

Finally, integration appears as a worthy goal because no one form of journalism has all the virtues while another form has all the vices. The virtue of the professional system is that, ideally, it supports reliable, professionally trained journalists dedicated to the public, thus maximizing accurate, unbiased news while reducing misinformation. The vice is that it places enormous influence in the hands of a privileged class of citizens (journalists) who work for powerful news organizations who may not care about ethics. The virtue of new media is that it places the freedom to publish in the hands of countless citizens. This reduces the power of mainstream journalists and media owners. The vice is that new media causes both misinformation and information overload. The power of journalism

---

[4] Increasingly, there are attempts to systematically discuss and codify the practices of online media, through the creation of associations such as the Media Bloggers Association (www.mediabloggers.org/), and the Online News Association (http://journalists.org/Default.asp). A well-known code by Jonathan Dube (www.cyberjournalist.net/news/000215.php) extends the principles of the Society of Professional Journalists to online journalism.

can be exercised by anyone with any ethics and any motivation. Good journalism and reliable information become lost in a sea of unreliable voices. Weakening the economics of mainstream journalism results in lay-offs for experienced journalists. Layoffs reduce journalism's ability to act as a watchdog on power.

For these reasons, the ethical task is to construct an ethics for the new mainstream which combines the virtues of both models.

Shape of a future ethics

Layered journalism

What will an integrated ethics look like?

It will be the ethics of the integrated newsroom, a newsroom that practices layered journalism. Layered journalism brings together different forms of journalism and different types of journalists to produce a multimedia offering of professionally styled news and analysis combined with citizen journalism and interactive chat.

The newsroom will be layered vertically and horizontally. Vertically, there will be many layers of editorial positions. There will be citizen journalists and bloggers in the newsroom, or closely associated with the newsroom. Many contributors will work from countries around the world. Some will write for free, some will be equivalent to paid freelancers, others will be regular commentators. In addition, there will be different types of editors. Some editors will work with these new journalists, while other editors will deal with unsolicited images and text sent by citizens via email, web sites, and Twitter. There will be editors or "community producers" charged with going out to neighborhoods to help citizens use media to produce their own stories.

Horizontally, the future newsroom will be layered in terms of the kinds of journalism it produces, from print and broadcast sections to online production centers.

To be sure, newsrooms in the past have had vertical and horizontal layers. Newspaper newsrooms have ranged vertically from the editor-in-chief at the top to the cub reporter on the bottom. Horizontally, large mainstream newsrooms have produced several types of journalism, both print and broadcast. However, future newsrooms will have additional and different layers. Some news sites will continue to be operated by a few people dedicated only to one format, such as blogging. But a substantial portion of the new mainstream will consist of these complex, layered organizations.

Layered journalism will confront two types of problems: vertical and horizontal. First, there will be "vertical" ethical questions about how the different layers of the newsroom, from professional editors to citizen free-lancers, should interact to produce responsible journalism. For example, by what standards will professional editors evaluate the contributions of citizen journalists? Second, there will be "horizontal" questions about the norms for the various newsroom sections.

Ecumenical ethics

The layered newsroom calls for an ecumenical approach to ethics. I bor-row "ecumenical" from its original Christian context, which is a desire to find unity among the sects of Christianity. Ecumenicalism does not seek to impose a unity that ignores (or is intolerant of) differences. It recognizes differences within a common framework of values.

By analogy, ecumenicalism in journalism is the search for a unifying set of values that are realized in different ways by varying forms of jour-nalism. Ecumenical ethics has two parts: (1) general aims and principles for all forms of journalism, and (2) specific standards and rules of practice for particular forms of journalism. Different forms of journalism have different practices and express different values. However, these distinct practices and specific rules must be consistent with the general aim and principles of (1).

What aims and principles might form the ethical basis of a new eth-ics? An ecumenical ethics must provide a unifying conception of the aims of democratic journalism. I believe the unifying aim is this: all partici-pants in the new journalism should promote a free and just democracy in which citizens flourish. A new ethics must explain journalism's role in a media-linked global world. It needs to update well-worn phrases such as "journalism in the public interest." It should explain how serving the public interest now includes facilitating online deliberation, empowering citizens to participate in media and in civic life, and building bridges of understanding among groups in pluralistic democracies.

The aim of democratic journalism implies several fundamental beliefs. One belief is that a healthy public sphere should be as free as possible, and populated by many forms of communication and a diversity of communicators. Different forms of journalism fulfil different public functions. Differences in practices and values are expected, given the different aims and methods of communication.

Ecumenical ethics affirms the continuing need for, and central role of, media ethics. Ethics provides the aims and principles that restrain and channel the freedom to publish. Ecumenicalism is liberal but not libertarian. It believes that a free marketplace of ideas is a necessary but not sufficient condition for good journalism. It is not enough for democracy to have "many voices" linked by a sophisticated media system. Democracy depends on the quality of information exchanged, the manner in which citizens speak to each other, the knowledge and skills of their journalists, and media "spaces" where reasonable citizens can deliberate.

Ecumenical ethics should articulate a number of principles that all integrated newsrooms embrace to promote the aforementioned aims. What might those principles be? Despite the current conflict of values, there is substantial common ground. As I discussed in Chapter 4, I believe that reconstruction in ethics begins with a reaffirmation of truth and objectivity in journalism, although our conceptions of truth and objectivity must be recast to apply to layered journalism. Mainstream and new media journalists both agree on the goal of truth and its two parts – truth-seeking and truth-telling. Online and traditional journalists may disagree on how journalists should seek truth. But few journalists would claim not to care about the truth.

The principle of objectivity is more contentious. Yet the principle should not be abandoned. Without a reaffirmation of truth and objectivity, journalism will lack the critical, independent, and non-partisan character that constitutes good public journalism. However, as Chapter 4 also argued, objectivity can only apply to mixed media if the traditional idea of news objectivity as a strictly neutral reporting of just the facts is replaced by a multi-dimensional, pragmatic objectivity. Journalists practice pragmatic objectivity when they adopt a critical stance towards their own beliefs, and evaluate their stories for empirical validity, coherence, and other virtues of good journalism.

These thoughts suggest that multi-dimensional objectivity is compatible with many forms of journalism, or at least more compatible than traditional objectivity. Objectivity as testing of interpretations is a flexible method that can apply in various ways and in various degrees to a wide range of journalism online and offline. But how does multi-dimensional objectivity fit with journalism as it is done in new media and its many platforms, from web sites to blogs? The key, again, is multi-dimensional objectivity's flexibility as a method which transcends the physical or technological form in which the journalism is published. What matters is not the platform but whether journalists wish to honor the values of pragmatic objectivity in whatever format he or she uses. There is nothing about a blog or a web-site article that prevents journalists from adopting an objective attitude and employing good empirical methods. Multi-dimensional objectivity can be an attractive conception for responsible online journalism. Practitioners of blogging, writing for web sites, and citizen journalism could employ at least some of the criteria of multi-dimensional objectivity to test their stories, aligning objectivity with their medium.

The claim of compatibility between objectivity and online journalism may surprise those who assume that objectivity is a principle limited to traditional forms of reporting. Part of the problem is the view that journalism objectivity must be as traditionally conceived – it must insist on strict neutrality and on the elimination of the "voice" and perspective of journalists. Such demands run counter to the more personal nature of communication on the Internet. However, if we redefine objectivity as multi-dimensional and pragmatic, we see that the objective stance and several of its major criteria express much of the spirit of online journalism. For example, take the objective stance as an attitude of approaching stories with a critical attitude, of being open to where the facts lead, and so on. Such attitudes support the online value of the Internet as a free "space" to question stories and events. Or take the criteria of coherence and self-consciousness. One of the dominant aspects of good online journalism is to use interactive dialogue and linkages to examine how claims or stories cohere with what other people around the world know about the topic. Also, online journalists often see themselves as being self-conscious and critical of the frames used by mainstream news media on major stories, and to offer alternative perspectives. These values are central to multi-dimensional objectivity. In addition, online journalism codes of ethics stress values that have links to truth. For example, the online emphasis on transparency about how stories are constructed and a frankness about one's biases can be seen as an attempt to be more truthful to the public about one's motivations. It can be seen as one of the virtues that influence either truth-seeking or truth-telling, or both.

The criteria that test for intersubjective objectivity are conceptually close to online journalism notions about how stories are to be tested by online communities. Multi-dimensional objectivity agrees with the idea, put forward by many who use the Internet, that the testing of ideas and stories is best achieved through interactive dialogue, not the inquiry of individuals. The Internet provides a tool for testing that includes many more people, and at much greatest ease, than was available to pre-internet newsrooms.

It is true that the idea of intersubjective objectivity in journalism has been understood differently. Traditional journalists talk about pre-publication testing and verification by teams of professional journalists within newsrooms. Online journalism raises the possibility of new forms of verification and correction – a post-publication testing by the many linked readers of a story. In this process, communities of online citizens collectively monitor postings for bias, manipulation of facts, bogus studies and bogus experts. Responsible journalists, online and offline, agree on the importance of a methodology that tests stories, although their methods may vary.

Beyond truth and objectivity, there are other areas of common ground to explore. The strong professional emphasis on editorial independence and the avoidance of conflicts of interest is not far from the ubiquitous stress on transparency among online writers. There is a good chance that rules for revealing and minimizing conflicts can be formulated that apply across media platforms. By integrating the values of professional independence and online transparency, journalists will advance another common value – media accountability.

These principles are not new. What is new is how they are to be understood and applied in the integrated newsroom. In the end, there may be deep differences over some principles, such as restraining one's reporting to minimize harm. However, this overlap in major principles is a good start for the construction of a new ethics.

Ethics of difference

Agreement on general aims and principles would not solve all problems. Integrated journalists would still face perplexing questions caused by different practices. Recall the vertical and horizontal issues of the layered newsroom. Even if all journalists subscribed to common principles such as truth-seeking, should they cover stories in a similar manner, according to the same protocols? Should online journalists be allowed to publish stories before print reporters because of the speed of the Internet? Should a newspaper allow anonymous commentators on its web site but refuse anonymity in its letters to the editor in the printed paper? When news reporters "tweet," can they be more opinionated than when they report for their paper?

These difficulties raise the following question: is it ethically permissible for sections of layered newsrooms to operate according to different guidelines because of the distinct nature of their media platforms?

The answer to this question is yes, as long as: (a) the protocols reflect the nature of the medium; (b) it is clear to the public what form of journalism is being practiced, including an understanding of its aim and its limits; and (c) the protocols do not violate the general aims and principles mentioned above. If conditions (a) to (c) are honored, then ecumenical ethics allows different rules for distinct areas of journalism.

Why do I qualify my answer by insisting on conditions (a) to (c)? I qualify the answer because the question is difficult and there are dangers. One doesn't want to say that any practice is valid just because the medium makes the practice possible. For example, I do not see how the reckless online posting of a false and damaging rumor could ever be ethically justified, even if the Internet makes possible the instantaneous circulation of rumors. As we develop ecumenical ethics, we will have to work carefully, going from case to case, until we reach a deeper understanding of how the new mainstream ethics should allow diversity within unity.

There are cases where conditions (a) to (c) are satisfied, and where old and new practices are integrated. Consider the vexed question of how newsrooms should use information supplied by citizens. It might appear that there can be no rapprochement between the practice of traditional journalism not to publish without verification and the practice of new media to post unverified video and text from little-known sources. Yet, rules for responsibly integrating these different practices can evolve. For example, mainstream news coverage of demonstrations in Iran after the June 2009 presidential election indicates how it is possible to develop protocols for using unverified information from citizens. In Iran, professional foreign journalists were forbidden to cover "unauthorized" demonstrations. Meanwhile, Iranian citizens used the new media of Twitter, YouTube, cell phones, and text messaging to circulate pictures and commentary worldwide.

Major broadcasters, such as the BBC and CNN, used the information carefully. News anchors repeatedly explained to the public the limitations on their own journalists and why they were using citizen-generated information. They warned viewers that they could not verify the veracity of many of the images, or the identity of the sources. Although bogus and erroneous information was circulated by these means, vital information was also made public. The Iran coverage shows that the ecumenical search for combining old and new forms of journalism is possible and developing.

On what principle is ecumenical tolerance towards differences in editorial rules based? It is what I call the principle of communicative intention:

> The norms of practice for any specific form of communication, including forms of journalism, is influenced by the nature and intent of the communication, as well as by what the public expects of this form of communication. So we should seek to shape the ethics of journalism to fit the communication form.

The validity of this principle was recognized, if implicitly, by traditional journalism ethics. Even at the height of news objectivity in the 1940s and 1950s, newspapers recognized the difference between reporting and column writing, between satirical journalism and news analysis, between investigative journalism and fashion reporting, and between feature writing and hard news reporting. Mainstream codes of ethics recognize these differences. For instance, the codes for broadcasters contain protocols for approaching certain types of stories, such as broadcasting live from hostage takings. These protocols are not found in newspaper codes of ethics.

Nothing is amiss as long as readers are alerted to different forms of journalism by labeling them "analysis" or "opinion" and the protocols do not violate basic principles, such as truth-telling. Similarly, we can argue that nothing is amiss if new media journalism follows different practices so long as the forms of journalism are clearly labeled, the public understands the communicative intent of the journalism, and the forms of journalism do not violate basic principles.

The ecumenical approach is inevitable, given the direction of journalism. It is unlikely that the vertical and horizontal questions of the layered newsroom will be resolved by insisting that the blogger, the tweeter, or the citizen journalist adhere completely to the more restrictive norms of practice that guide other forms of journalism, such as straight professional news reporting. Conversely, more traditional modes of journalism, such as verified reporting in quality papers, should not abandon the values that have long defined their medium. They should not simply opt for the more free wheeling practices of the Internet. The challenge is to maintain common values while showing how norms of practice can vary according to the medium.

So, it may turn out that there are areas where the values of pragmatic objectivity do not fit some of the practices of multi-platform journalism. For example, it may come to be seen that there is no way to reconcile multi-platform objectivity's stress on empirical verification and the speed of online communication. However, our discussion does suggest that, at the very least, there is no inherent opposition between multi-dimensional objectivity and new forms of journalism. In fact, there is a substantial overlap of values that ethicists can use to develop a new ethics of mixed media – standards that apply to offline and online journalism.

Toward an open ethics

The first half of this chapter has described the future of media ethics as the gradual construction of an integrated mixed media ethics that is both an ethics of commonality (or common principles) and an ethics of difference. The rest of this chapter explores the meaning of the second feature which a future media ethics should exhibit – an open approach to ethics.

The hypothesis is that developments in media are bringing about a transition from a closed professional ethics to an open mixed ethics where ethics is the concern of all citizens, whether they are professional journalists or non-professional media users. Part of this transition is being encouraged by the creation of a special group of online journalists – a global fifth estate. The fifth estate also functions as a global forum and interactive vehicle for media ethics, an agent of cross-border discourse on journalism practice in point of fact and also what practice *should* be. The evolution of a citizens-based public communication and a fifth estate has an important normative implication – it encourages discussion of the norms of journalism. It encourages a global conversation on what a global media ethics should be. This global discussion, by itself, is helping to make ethics discourse spill over the boundaries of professional media ethics.

In what follows, I explain the idea of an open media ethics and the idea of a fifth estate, and how the two concepts are related. I show how these phenomena are new and revolutionary in portent, going beyond the closed, professional ethics of a previous media era. I conclude by considering how the fifth estate operates and what this means for an open ethics.

Closed and open ethics

The first step is to be clear on how we use the terms "open" and "closed" ethics.[5] Then we can decide to what extent journalism is closed, and to what extent it is moving towards a more open ethics. Most of what follows applies to the evaluation of any group or professional ethics as closed or open, not just journalism.

To decide whether a practice of ethics by a group is closed or open, one needs to look at three features of its ethical discourse: (1) who are the *intended users* of the ethics, (2) who *participates* in ethical discourse and decisions, and (3) who determines and modifies the *content* of the ethics. For (2) and (3), it is not just who participates but also how they participate, and the quality and meaningfulness of that participation.

We need to distinguish between closed and open ethics with respect to what happens within a group and what happens between the group and

[5] The notion of open and closed ethics was first developed by Ward and Wasserman, in "Towards an Open Ethics."

other groups, or the public. For example, a group may be particularly open and democratic about making ethical decisions among its own members, yet place firm restrictions on the participation of non-members. In this chapter we are concerned with the second kind of closed and open ethics – the relationship of an ethics practice to non-members, and members of the public.

A closed ethics places significant limits on all three factors – users, participation, and content determination. An open ethics places fewer and less severe restrictions. A closed ethics may feature strong and active interaction among group members but it does not strongly encourage ethical discourse with non-members. An open ethics encourages interaction with non-members. Ideally, an open ethics seeks ever new ways to enhance participation, discussion, questioning, and interaction between the group and those outside the group.

Forms of ethical discourse can be placed on a continuum, ranging from extremely closed to extremely open. Extremely closed forms of ethics place severe limits on who uses and participates in ethics. An example is ethical discourse of a hierarchical religion where revered leaders issue ethical directives to followers, and do not encourage discussion with non-members. Let us look at each of three factors.

Intended users: a closed ethics is intended primarily for the ethical guidance of a group of practitioners. The evolution and current shape of the ethics reflects the history and evolution of the activity. Many norms and protocols have been developed to address specific and distinct problems of the practice. A closed ethics is distinguished in large part by the members of each group and their distinct set of concerns and problems.

Meaningful participation: intended users of a closed ethics, such as a professional group, attempt to control who participates in ongoing ethics discourse to a restricted class of users. Participation includes (a) criticizing the practice and behavior of group members, (b) discussing and debating the ethical aims and principles of the group, and (c) modifying or reforming the principles or "content" of the ethics.

Participation in the discourse of closed ethics is internal, or internally orientated.

Internal discourse keeps meaningful participation among intended users. "Meaningful" means that participants are not simply given a voice so they feel part of the ethical process, although their views are neglected. Meaningful participation means that their views are in fact taken seriously and these views have real and significant influence on the course of the discussion and the adoption of new ethical principles.

Professions and other groups have a number of ways to practice internal discourse. They can devote most of their resources and energy to discussing ethics in their professional or trade journals and magazines, at the group's workshops, meetings, and conferences, and on web sites and interactive media meant for group members.

Content determination and revision: a closed ethics is characterized by limits on who has significant influence on what results from discussion – the actual content of the ethics, in the form of rules, protocols, principles, as well as the creation of new content. An ethics is open or closed to the extent that participation allows members and non-members to play a part in redefining basic concepts, updating principles, and inventing new procedures.

Participation, therefore, has two moments: participation in discussion and participation in adoption. For example, a revised code of ethics for the Canadian Association of Journalists (CAJ) could involve a lengthy public consultation. Yet, in the end, whatever ideas emerge are adopted by vote among CAJ members only at an annual conference. A closed ethics places responsibility for making content changes primarily in the hands of its intended users. An ethical practice that allows participation in discussion and adoption is more open (or less closed) than an ethical practice that allows only one of these two moments.

As described, "closed ethics" and "open ethics" refer to models of ethical practice that operate across many groups, many professions, and many practices and endeavors. A relatively closed form of ethics applies to many professions and many types of applied ethics, from legal, business, and nursing ethics to accountancy ethics, bioethics, and media ethics. The ethics of the legal profession, for instance, is closed since it is primarily intended as a guide for lawyers and judges, and the ethical problems that emerge in the practice of law. The enforcement of ethical rules is carried out by fellow lawyers sitting on professional disciplinary councils.

At the same time, however, there are efforts to make a number of forms of applied ethics more open to public participation. As noted in Chapter 3, theorists have put forth models for ethical discussions on scientific issues that include the direct participation of the public.[6] Similarly in political ethics, advocates of open democratic discourse on issues have put forward such deliberative mechanisms as "citizen juries and assemblies."[7]

In summary, we can define closed ethics as a form of ethics practice and discourse that places substantial limits on intended users, non-member participation, and non-member influence on the content and revision of its principles. Central to deciding on the closed or open nature of an ethics practice is the political economy of the discourse: *who* has the power to control and shape the discourse both in terms of its manner of deliberation and in its outcomes? In closed ethics, there are marked differences between the power of group members and non-group citizens. In many cases, this asymmetry is intentional and thought to be legitimate. For many journalists, the idea that working journalists should have a greater say in the ethics of their practice than their readers seems obvious.

To this analysis, we add three important caveats: first, open ethics is a matter of degree, and judgments are relative, often imprecise. For example, if an ethics practice is open with regard to participation in discussion but weak on participation in content adoption, is it more or less open relative to an ethics practice that is strong on participation in adoption but not on participation in discussion? How do we measure the degree of openness of complex practices? Often we can only reach a rough, comparative judgment. To make matters worse, sometimes there are forces pulling in opposite directions. In journalism, for example, there may be trends that seek to strengthen its independence from external forces, such as strengthening its economic basis and its professional associations; and there may be pressures on newsrooms to be more open and transparent

---

[6] Burgess, "What Difference Does Public Consultation Make to Ethics?"

[7] The idea of citizen assemblies has been used in Canada, the Netherlands, and other countries to explore questions about politics, forms of government, etc. For example, the province of British Columbia created a citizen assembly to consider new election systems, such as systems based on proportional representation. On assemblies, see www.auburn. edu/academic/liberal_arts/poli_sci/journal_public_deliberation/citizensassembly/ pandemic.htm.

to the public. Moreover, we can disagree on where along the continuum we should place an ethics practice; and we can differ on whether a practice is moving towards either greater closeness or openness, and why.

Second, the ethics practice of a group can be categorized as closed yet still have external links to other groups and to the public. A closed ethics may allow a degree of public consultation, criticism, and input into the practice. Forms of journalism that, for example, have public editors, press councils, and online spaces where the public can scrutinize editorial decisions. Along the continuum of closed and open ethics, most forms of practice are hybrids of closed and open features. To say that journalism ethics is closed is compatible with recognizing that the profession has linkages with the public. It would be surprising if journalism had no such linkages given that it is a profession that publishes for a public. To say that journalism ethics has been closed, traditionally, is not to say it has been hermetically sealed from external relations to the world.

Third, to call an ethics closed or open is not to automatically criticize or praise it. Reasonable normative disagreement is possible on whether a closed ethics is always undesirable and an open ethics is always desirable. There is room for debate on what degree of openness is appropriate for the ethics in question. It is possible to disagree on the appropriate mechanisms of openness.

Why closed?

Using the discussion above, we understand why media ethics can be described as closed.

Historically, as shown in Chapter 3, the birth of modern media ethics coincided with the birth of a powerful mainstream newspaper press that dominated news and media advertising. The origin of professional media ethics favored a closed ethics. The doctrine of journalistic autonomy and objectivity established a normative barrier between journalist and external influences, whether the influences were corporations, social groups, or the public at large. The intended users of media ethics were a clearly defined group: professional journalists at major newspapers and eventually major broadcasters. Modern media ethics, therefore, developed as a closed ethics. It was a set of guidelines for journalists; the determination of the content of that ethics, and its application to practice, was primarily the concern and responsibility of journalists. Media ethics was part of the self-regulation of the press.

Media ethics remained closed for most of the twentieth century. Much of the ethics discourse has been and continues to be "in-house," occurring at conferences staged by such groups as the Society of Professional Journalists and the World Association of Newspapers, or in magazines such as the *Columbia Journalism Review* and academic journals such as *Journal of Mass Media Ethics*. The marketing of ethics textbooks has been directed at journalists, journalists' associations, and journalism instructors. Ethical discussion occurs in practical workshops for journalists hosted by journalism think tanks and media institutes or on journalism web sites. The creation, revision, and adoption of new codes tends to be the construction of editors and editorial committees within newsrooms.

The maintenance of an internal form of participation is not only the result of history, or a desire of professionals to exchange views. It is also the result of a "closed" attitude among journalists who believe there is not much to be gained from engaging the public on ethical issues. These journalists complain that, when ethical issues are discussed at public meetings or on the Internet, the discussion becomes dominated by ranters and ideologues. Some journalists worry that inviting the public into the discussion might reduce their autonomy to make editorial decisions. Others believe that ordinary citizens lack sufficient newsroom experience to discuss journalism decisions in an informed manner.

In 2009, for example, the ethics committee of the Society of Professional Journalists condemned the Washington State News Council (WNC) in Seattle for holding a "virtual" public meeting on its web site to discuss a complaint against a Seattle broadcaster who had aired questionable stories on alleged electoral irregularities. The state news council received a complaint from Secretary of State Sam Reed against KIRO 7 Eyewitness News, a CBS affiliate. Reed complained that two stories (aired October 15 and November 3, 2008) about voting irregularities were "incorrect" and "sensationalized." KIRO did not reply to the WNC's invitation to respond to the complaint. Eventually, Reed decided not to seek a public WNC hearing. With the complaint process stalled, the council took an unprecedented step. It held a "virtual public hearing" on the complaint. The WNC invited citizens to view the stories, read the complaint, then vote and comment as a Citizens Online News Council. Of about 100 people who voted online, only a few defended KIRO while most supported Reed's position. In its press release, the SPJ accused the press council of "gimmickry" in asking the public to vote. The release suggested that journalism decisions are too complex for the public. The release said: "The experiment (public online meetings) should be abandoned, the Ethics Committee believes. Discussions of journalism ethics are often complex and nuanced."

The closed nature of media ethics, however, is not extreme. News media have always asked for, and do receive, public input on stories. Under threat of government regulation and a wish to avoid law suits, some news organizations in the second half of the twentieth century established ombudsmen and press councils. Some newsrooms, attempting to reconnect with the public, experimented with civic journalism, which included citizen advisory councils, town hall meetings, and guest editorials by citizen groups. At times, news organizations will partner with a concerned group to make a presentation before a federal regulator or legislative committee, or lobby in public against a proposed law that affects media operations. Within newsrooms, editors have attempted to enhance media credibility by articulating their standards and explaining their journalism – how stories were developed, what sources were used, and the reasons for controversial editorial decisions.

Yet the extent to which these mechanisms have shifted the ethics from closed to open is limited. Public participation is often limited to lodging a complaint of inaccuracy against a specific news story and to seek a correction. Press councils use a "product complaint" model. News councils and ombudsmen are usually industry-funded agents who arbitrate complaints about stories *after* publication. The role of the public is that of a disappointed consumer. Citizens complain to a press council if the news product, a story, like a cheap pair of shoes, does not live up to expectations.

Often, media ethics is a response to a specific scandal, such as a reporter fabricating sources or taking kickbacks from corporations. In recent years, major mainstream newsrooms from the *New York Times* to CBS News and the BBC have conducted investigations into dubious behavior or erroneous stories by its journalists. The investigators recommended new ethical protocols and guidelines. Yet the process was internal and guided by senior editors. The committee informed the public about their findings and recommendations after they had done their work. The public was not intrinsically involved in these internal discussions. The news organizations retained firm control of the process.

Interestingly, much of the pungent criticism of news media today comes from a political economy perspective which assumes that media and media ethics is a closed practice. News media are an enclosed and powerful institution. The biggest (or only) media ethics issue is who owns the media and how they use that power to maintain the status quo in society. This approach derives from Marx who, in a famous passage in *The German Ideology*, said that those who own the means of material production also control the means of "mental production" as a tool of the ruling class. Left-wing writers such as Noam Chomsky see themselves as critics external to an autonomous, powerful, and closed media system closely aligned with large corporations and conservative politicians. Media performs a propaganda role for the ruling classes of Western societies.[8] Citizens concerned with democratic media are a virtuous "we" that stands over and against "them," journalists in powerful newsrooms. Mainstream media are conceptualized as the "other." In such a context, media ethics as a co-operative or participatory dialogue between news media and the public is not possible or is naive, or worse, it indicates support for a corrupt media system. Fierce criticism and ideological confrontation with the media powers is the only realistic strategy.

Other forms of criticism from the political economy perspective, such as the writings of the American media scholar, Robert McChesney, is less negative and more "active" in putting before citizens a number of ways in which they can improve or save their media such as by joining democratic media movements, by intervening in hearings by media regulators, and by supporting alternate, non-mainstream media.[9] The hope is that public scrutiny and media activism will create a media revolution that challenges and reduces mainstream media power.

New media and open ethics

From the standpoint of open ethics, the most important trend is the development of a citizen-based journalism, combined with a fifth estate. It is

[8] See Chomsky, *Necessary Illusions*.
[9] McChesney, for example, has led a "free media" movement. In a recent book he and a co-author explained how the government should save journalism through a range of policies and subsidies. McChesney and Nichols, *The Death and Life of American Journalism*.

reshaping media ethics and it has the potential to create a global ethics discourse that is inclusive and participatory.

Citizen uses of media, where the citizen is both consumer and producer of media, are changing the media sphere as a whole. New media, small and large, from cell phones to personal blogs, increasingly occupy more of society's "available communication space than before" and lead to such concepts as "mediascape" and "media ecology."[10] These changes in the media ecology are translating into changes to media ethics in terms of intended users, the level and nature of participation, and the content. Put simply, the changes are altering the way media ethics gets done.

With respect to intended users, the fact that citizens around the world are now acting, at least some of the time, as journalists, or are performing journalism-like functions, means the intended users of ethics broadens to all users of media insofar as their tweets, blog comments, and social media sites impact on others. In one sense, public participation is the process of asking the public what they expect of their media. What do they expect, ethically, of today's news media? What norms of practice do they want bloggers to honor? What forms of editing should be used online? Do they want traditional media to remain committed to the values of gate-keeping and pre-publication verification? But it goes beyond this sense because the public, as themselves producers of media content, need to construct an ethics for their own blogs and web sites. If citizens act as providers of information, then ethics is needed to guide *their* use of media. No longer is ethics just about the behavior of "them," journalists inside newsrooms. Ethics is a concern for all of "us" – all of us who circulate speculation, rumors, facts, photos, information, and views through a global grid of communications.

The aim of media ethics is no longer adequately conceptualized as extending professional ethics so that it welcomes input from non-professionals. The aim of media ethics becomes a discourse about the media practice of a huge and ill-defined collection of citizens and many forms of journalism and communication.

---

[10] Christians, *et al.*, *Normative Theories of the Media*, 241.

New media communication also alters notions of meaningful participation and content control in media ethics. In a global media world, citizens do not need an invitation, or permission, to discuss media ethics, to critique journalism practice, or to suggest revisions and new norms. Discussing media normatively is a natural part of producing media. Ethical questions arise irresistibly when media activity is weaved into almost every aspect of one's life. Citizen-based ethics discourse is not an "add on" to discussions at professional meetings or inside newsrooms. It is the activity of citizens reflecting, participating and shaping ethical discourse through global, interactive online discussions.

Moreover, the culture of new media favors transparency and interactivity. This culture expects the editorial process of mainstream and non-mainstream media to be open to scrutiny and public debate on contentious issues. Traditional media, in recent years, have attempted to catch up to this transparent, interactive communication online by asking (continually) for readers' and viewers' reactions to stories, and by incorporating the technology of blogging, texting, Twitter and Facebook into their work and on their web sites. The new ethics discourse cannot be dismissed by professionals as a debate among "ranters." Much of the ethics discourse online and offline involves rich exchanges among professionals and non-professionals. The movement, then, is toward a more open media ethics in terms of discussion.

The fifth estate

For this new media ethics, one group of communicators is of particular importance: a revitalized fifth-estate media that presents itself as an alternative or supplement to the mainstream press – the fourth estate. The press was first called a fourth estate in the late 1700s.[11] Historically, the fifth estate was any group that influenced the public sphere or the governance of a nation but was not part of the four estates – the clergy, nobility, commoners, and the professional mainstream press. Among the groups that have been called a fifth estate are trade unions, political pundits, and organized crime.

---

[11] Ward, *The Invention of Journalism Ethics*, 306.

Fifth-estate media have made the transition from print-based counter culture to cyber culture. The fifth estate began in the 1960s with left-wing oppositional papers, followed by "independent" media (or "Indy media") in recent years. For example, in 1965 the *Fifth Estate* newspaper began publishing in Detroit as part of the underground press, a left-wing bi-weekly on politics and the arts. The fifth estate also exists in public broadcasting. The Canadian Broadcasting Corporation has a news magazine called "The Fifth Estate," so called to indicate that the program goes beyond daily news to original, investigative journalism.

Today, fifth-estate media have been revitalized and turned into a global network by the use of online communicators who monitor mainstream media and offer alternative coverage of issues and alternative forms of journalism. The fifth estate includes bloggers, tweeters, and web site writers. Stephen D. Cooper called bloggers a fifth estate insofar as they report on stories ignored by mainstream media and they critique mainstream media practices.[12] Christians, *et al.* apply the term "fifth estate" to a group of "extramedia activities" of research, monitoring, reflection, and means of accountability that "subject the media themselves to scrutiny."[13]

However, the fifth-estate media can be understood not as "extramedia" but as part of the media landscape and the discourse about ethics. The fifth estate is characterized by several foci. One focus has already been mentioned: criticism of the mainstream press. However, the fifth estate has additional foci such as engaging in a global conversation on media and its ethics. This global online conversation extends the concern of media ethics beyond questions of accuracy and bias to broader socio-economic questions about the influence of the Western media system on non-Western cultures, the role of economics and political power on media ethics, the representation of minorities and the developing world, how media approach global issues, and the possibility of a global media ethics. These issues will be taken up in the next chapter.

Another focus is using new media to discover new ways of doing journalism, such as online non-profit centers of investigative journalism, or the publication of alternate perspectives on online web sites. The fifth estate also includes the use of media, such as cell phones and web sites,

---

[12] Cooper, *Watching the Watchdog.*
[13] Christians, *et al., Normative Theories of the Media*, 241.

by social movements and NGOs. It includes new uses of old media, such as the use of tabloids for political mobilization in developing countries such as South Africa.

Duncan refers to the emergence of a "fifth estate" in terms of alternative media networks created by social movements in order to remind the traditional, commercial media of their societal responsibilities.[14] For Duncan, new social movements worldwide are busy reclaiming the traditional media. Increasingly, non-commercial media are on the agenda of social movements internationally. Free-speech radio and television stations are being established as spaces for non-commercial journalism, and a new layer of emerging grassroots media is springing up. Social movements are increasingly producing their own media to further their causes. Because of the global reach afforded to these alternative voices by means of new technologies, the process through which alternative grassroots media like Indymedia have come into being has been referred to as an example of "globalization from below."[15]

Engaging in these forms of journalism influences media ethics discourse and has the potential to change fundamentally the approach to, and the content of, media ethics. The new experiments in media raise ethical questions, and suggest new aims for journalism, as well as different norms and protocols. These movements and developments are examples of trends that point toward a global, diverse, and open discourse on ethics reaching far beyond the narrow confines of professional newsrooms.

The notion of a fifth estate, therefore, is not simply a technological or ideological category. It does not refer simply to journalists who use new media (e.g. blogosphere) nor does it refer only to alternate left-wing media. The fifth estate refers to those citizens and journalists interested in developing new forms of journalism and in reconstructing media ethics for an era of global and interactive media.

These changes cause us to reconsider the idea of journalistic authority and how journalism can restore public trust in news media. Under a closed ethics, credibility and trust was thought to be a matter of finding mechanisms for external voices to provide input into the news process. But the global media revolution has reduced this approach to only one part of a

[14] Duncan, "Another Journalism is Possible."
[15] Frenzel and Sullivan, "Globalization from Below?"

new process called open ethics. New forms of journalism authority require a closer relationship between news media and citizens. Considering the future of newspapers, Alan Rusbridger, editor of *The Guardian*, recently argued for a shift in journalism's professional foundation from one of "authority" to one of "involvement":

> Here the tension is between a world in which journalists considered themselves – and were perhaps considered by others – special figures of authority. We had the information and the access; you didn't. You trusted us (to) filter news and information and to prioritise it – and to pass it on accurately, fairly, readably and quickly. That state of affairs is now in tension with a world in which many (but not all) readers want to have the ability to make their own judgments; express their own priorities; create their own content; articulate their own views; learn from peers as much as from traditional sources of authority. Journalists may remain one source of authority, but people may also be less interested to receive journalism in an inert context – i.e. which can't be responded to, challenged, or knitted in with other sources.[16]

The authority of journalists as professional interpreters of the world is waning. Instead they are becoming collaborators, facilitators, and curators of a vast gallery of information through which they themselves and their audience have to find their way.

Fifth-estate and ethics discourse

What role do new media technologies play in facilitating alternative spaces for ethical engagement and critique? This section of the chapter identifies three forms of engagement: the classic "us" versus "them" criticism of media ethics; a collaboration of mainstream and non-mainstream media to support ethical values; and peer-to-peer exchanges. Since examples from previous chapters were drawn from North American media, the following examples are drawn from Britain, Europe, and Africa.

Us and them

Earlier in this chapter, we noted how some forms of media criticism, such as the writings of Chomsky, take an external approach that pits the public

[16] Rusbridger, "Does journalism exist?"

against big media. Today, even though the dividing line between professional journalists and the public is blurred, members of the public still
draw a clear line between themselves and the media when they are disturbed by unethical behavior by the mainstream news media.

Increasingly, new media platforms are used to extend such ethical
protests beyond local or national media where the unethical behavior
occurred. In these instances, the web and especially social networking
sites like Twitter or Facebook may be used to conduct viral campaigns that
call individual journalists to account, critique mainstream media outlets,
or expose errors of fact or bias in reporting. Online media, with its many-
to-many communication, encourages a global media activism against the
misuse of media power.[17] These activities have led to the coinage of terms
such as "network armies," "netwars," and "smart mobs."[18]

Online activism includes protests against violations of media ethics
codes. In these cases, protests may call for boycotts of licensing fees, lobby
for institutional change, or mobilize marches.[19] Online media may be used
to call for regulatory agencies to act against media institutions that act
unethically. In these cases, a clear distinction is drawn between the media
and the public. Criticism describes the public and the media as two parties in a social contract where one party, the media, has reneged on their
agreement by violating ethical principles. Criticism underlines the distance between "us," the public, and "them," the elitist media.

An example of this form of engagement was the overwhelming reaction against a homophobic newspaper column by Jan Moir that appeared
in the *Daily Mail* newspaper in Britain. Campaigns against Moir on Twitter
and Facebook pitted the "us" of the public versus "them" in the media.
The public engagement served not so much to undermine the notion of
journalistic professionalism but to appeal to professional ethical values
and professional structures such as the UK Press Complaints Commission
(PCC). The aim of the complaints was not to supplant professionalism with
something else, but rather to challenge the mainstream media to function
better, from an ethical perspective.

---

[17] Kellner, "Globalization, Technopolitics and Revolution," 184.

[18] Bennett, "New Media Power: The Internet and Global Activism."

[19] An example of this phenomenon can be found among the activities of South
Africa's protest organizations, the Television Industry Emergency Coalition and
Save Our SABC, who use Facebook to campaign for reform against corruption and
mismanagement at the South African public broadcaster.

Jan Moir's article on the death of the Boyzone singer Stephen Gately was originally titled "Nothing 'natural'." It was later changed online to "A strange, lonely and troubling death." The column prompted a record number of complaints to the PCC – 22,000 in a single weekend, more than it had received in the previous five years. The deluge was largely the result of an online campaign that urged people to protest what was seen as a virulent homophobic article in which Moir concluded that the death of the gay singer "strikes another blow to the happy-ever-after myth of civil partnerships." On the paper's online site, the comments section below the story was flooded with angry reactions. Jan Moir's name "trended" on Twitter (an indication of frequent use of a tagged word). Also on Twitter, a spoof account was created in her name that allowed Twitter users to express outrage against the column.

Protest became activism when the Facebook page created to call for a retraction of the column, www.facebook.com/group.php?gid=151083562155, published contact details of the brands advertising in the *Daily Mail* alongside Moir's article. It urged people to contact these commercial organizations and complain. The Facebook site also provided sample text for citizens who wished to complain to the editor of the *Daily Mail*, Paul Dacre. Although the criticism was mostly directed against the person of Jan Moir, the attack was often extended to include the media in general, who were portrayed as unaccountable, sensationalist, and intent on making profits at all costs. The participants in the campaign did not constitute a unitary "public." Although Moir called the criticism an "orchestrated campaign," the collaborative effort could better be described as "viral," in the sense of being passed on from individual to individual within a conducive environment.

The campaign against Moir's article brought renewed attention to the Press Complaints Commission. It also highlighted flaws in the self-regulatory system such as the PCC's controversial stipulation that only parties directly affected by the column in question could lay a complaint. The PCC would not consider complaints of discrimination by someone not directly related to Gately. Campaigners pointed out that the PCC was too close to the media industry it regulates. They noted the irony that Paul Dacre, editor of the *Daily Mail*, chaired the PCC's ethics code committee, and concluded that complaining to the PCC was therefore pointless.

One result of the campaign was that the PCC in February 2010 set up its own Twitter account. Media critic Charlie Beckett pointed out (on Twitter) that this move by the PCC was a result of the Jan Moir campaign on Twitter. However, it remains to be seen whether the PCC will use social media as a public relations platform rather than an opportunity for sincere and recipro- cal engagement with the public. Its first tweet suggested that it will be using Twitter as a one-directional communication tool rather than a platform for debate: "The PCC is on Twitter! We'll be using it to keep you up to date with news on our cases, events and more. Follow us and see what we're up to."

These "us" versus "them" online campaigns by the public can be regarded as positive or negative trends. Positively, they may encourage eth- ical behavior by newsrooms, despite commercial pressures to act unethic- ally – if only out of fear for the commercial losses those public reprisals may bring. Negatively, the online media environment, with its demand for increased "hits," may foster even greater commercial competition among media outlets, leading to a further erosion of ethical standards. The Internet may be used to justify the reduction of regulation, subjecting journalism to the imperatives of corporate self-interest.

Collaborative engagement

The Trafigura story covered by *The Guardian* newspaper in 2009 was an example of how ethical discourse can be advanced in a multi-media world by a collaboration of mainstream and citizen journalism. The ethical norms of truth-telling and respect for human dignity were advanced by a global conversation among journalists and their audiences.

In 2006, Trafigura, a multinational oil company, was accused of dumping truckloads of chemical waste illegally in Abidjan, Ivory Coast. Thousands of people reported illnesses ranging from skin lesions to diarrhea and breathing problems. Trafigura secured a "super-injunction" preventing the media from reported on the class action by 30,000 Africans and even barring the media from reporting on a question asked on the matter in Parliament. Within 12 hours of the editor of *The Guardian* tweeting about the injunction, it became the most popular trending topic in Europe. The parliamentary question was unearthed, published online by bloggers, and disseminated on Twitter. Within hours the efforts of what Rusbridger calls the "mass collaboration of strangers" forced Trafigura to drop the ban.[20]

---

[20] Rusbridger, "Does journalism exist?"

This was a case of the public working *with* the mainstream media and the public acting *as* media to uphold the values of freedom of speech, truth-telling and the restoration of human dignity for the African victims of the toxic-waste dumping. By taking up the cause on behalf of *The Guardian*, bloggers and citizen journalists sided with the media against those that threatened to silence it. Citizens around the world associated themselves with the values that *The Guardian* was trying to uphold.

Peer-to-peer ethics

In the online media environment, the uni-directional relationship of professional journalists to audiences is no longer primary. Communication takes place along a rhizomatic network featuring exchanges between professional journalists and responsive audiences, between citizen journalists and their professional counterparts, and among the citizen journalists themselves. Ethical self-regulation takes place through a complex peer-to-peer discourse.

Peer-to-peer discourse can take the form of comments on blog posts, responses to Twitter feeds, or exchanges that take place parallel to citizen journalism posts, for instance on sites like *The Guardian*'s "Comment is Free" space (www.guardian.co.uk/commentisfree). In comments on opinion pieces, citizen journalists are held accountable for misrepresentations, falsehoods, or inaccuracies by fellow commentators or visitors to the site.

Increasingly, these peer-to-peer exchanges take place on a global level, such as the political debates on global news sites like France 24's Observer's website (http://observers.france24.com). The site publishes eye-witness reports and analyses from professional and citizen journalists from around the world. Similar discussions occur at Global Voices Online (http://globalvoicesonline.org). Sometimes the issue may be as simple as the correction of facts. For instance, in one story an incorrect date for the forced demolition of houses in China was corrected at the behest of commentators.[21] At other times the facts under dispute are only the entry point into much deeper political differences which, when debated in the comment forum, create an alternative public sphere. For instance, a report

[21] Yee, "China: Forced Demolition."

on the percentage of black shareholding in a South African cell phone company led to a debate about affirmative action and "Black Economic Empowerment."[22]

Conditions for ethical dialogue

What the new media have is a *potential* to open up media ethics to global, inclusive discussion, beyond the control of professionals. There is always a gap between what can be and what will be. The fact that the new journalism, and its fifth estate, is interactive and global does not entail that such dialogue will be fair and inclusive, or that it will lead to sound principles for a global and "open" media ethics. Paradoxical as it may sound, many conditions need to be satisfied and many obstacles cleared for a genuine ethical open discourse on a global scale can be achieved. Chapter 7 will address what an open global media ethics should be. For now, we can note several important considerations.

First, we should not assume that global media stories and media discussions are always a good thing. They may aggravate tensions among groups as a result of cross-cultural encounters and power differentials, which are now amplified globally.[23] The global communication facilitated by the Internet may confront us with the realization that there might be "deep – perhaps irresoluble – conflicts between diverse sets of basic values, norms, practices, beliefs, etc." of people and societies around the globe.[24] On the other hand, global discussions may increase respect for cultural differences and encourage a less ethnocentric view of the world. The internet-mediated intercultural contact may bring the recognition that our own norms and values are not unique or universal.

Second, misunderstandings can occur even in attempts to construct an ethical debate around the notions of cultural representation and ethnic difference. An example of this is an episode between South African and American users of Twitter. When a (black) South African user posted a humorous tweet under the tag #thingsdarkiessay, this led to a trending topic because the theme was quickly picked up by other tweeters.

---

[22] Friedman and Macklenin, "White supremacy rears its ugly head over 'racist Vodafone.'"

[23] Ess, *Digital Media Ethics*, 107.   [24] *Ibid.*, 109.

However, when these tweets were read in the United States, the terminology caused offense. It led to an angry response by US tweeters to what was perceived as a discussion originating among racist white South Africans. This misunderstanding came about as a result of different semantic connotations to the word "darkie," which in America is considered a derogatory, racist term. In South Africa the term has been appropriated by the formerly oppressed and given positive content.[25] This example illustrates that even well-meaning attempts to defend ethical principles in online peer-to-peer networks can go astray and succumb to cultural slippages.

Third, we should remember that ethical speech and discourse can hide a non-ethical agenda, such as to advance a particular interest. Ethics discourse can be, manipulative, self-interested, dogmatic, or non-deliberative. The discourse may support an unjust status quo. In particular, we must be on guard against an illusion of equal participation by many voices in media across borders. For instance, in the Trafigura example, the voices missing from the campaign for press freedom were the African victims. They were spoken for, but not heard. A truly open ethics would seek to include the voices of all stakeholders, everyone with an interest in the outcome of the ethical discussion.

Fourth, ethics discourse should not reduce media ethics to a non-deliberative populism that simply asks the public to vote on ethical issues. Ethics should not devolve into shifting opinion polls. The suggestion is that if we want to know what standards journalists should follow, or how they should apply those standards, journalists should be guided by public opinion surveys. If we want to know whether journalists should investigate the private lives and business activities of politicians, let us ask the public. If we want to know how patriotic the news media should be in covering a war, let us survey the public. If we want to know how graphic television images should be, let us consult vague "community standards." Public opinion surveys on the role of journalism in a democracy are insufficient for media ethics because such surveys may reflect a relatively uninformed public view, or a majority "feeling" that flies in the face of basic journalistic principles, or the basic social

---

[25] For an account of the incident, see Langa, "Yesterday, a short-lived war broke out."

roles of news media – such as offering critical but unpopular coverage of war. Public opinions about journalism need to be tested by facts and logic, not simply accepted. They have to be balanced against existing principles of journalism. We need to structure public dialogue online and offline so that it is representative, reflective, and based on the core principles of good journalism. The new public forums and mechanisms should be carefully structured so as to be accessible and deliberative. Just as I argued for deliberative democracy as the goal of journalism, so I argue here that we need to strive to make open ethics discourse both principled and deliberative. What open ethics needs, in addition to many voices and deliberation, is a philosophical framework within which discussion can take place – a philosophical view of the purpose and ethical standards of good journalism.

Conclusion

This chapter has taken seriously the idea that the problems of media ethics require a bolder and more radical reconception of its principles, plus new open processes for ethics discourse. It also took seriously the idea that we have to consider the nature of ethical revolutions and what this means for today's revolution.

The chapter predicted that media ethics is moving slowly towards a mixed ethics as it passes along the three stages of conflict, rapprochement, and integration. This integration is necessary if there is to be sufficient ethical guidance for journalism done on so many media platforms. The chapter argued that an integrated ethics should be ecumenical and open. These reflections provide signposts to the future. It is difficult to foresee in detail the shape of a future media ethics. The construction of a future media ethics is a work in progress. Nevertheless, one far-reaching fact remains: media ethics is changing and shifting in the direction of open, mixed ethics. We have entered into a new era of media ethics.

The next chapter examines the global aspect of today's mixed media and argues that media ethics must become global. In addition to being ecumenical, open, and deliberative, the new mixed media ethics should also be based on a cosmopolitan ethics. This global conception requires a further radical reworking of media ethics.

Questions for discussion

1. What does "mixed media ethics" mean? Why is this concept important today?
2. Define the idea of a "new mainstream"? Why does this new mainstream require a new form of media ethics?
3. If there are many new forms of journalism, online and offline, name an ethical principle that all journalists should support. Can you name a second or third principle?
4. Should bloggers and other citizens journalists follow the same rules for publishing stories that apply to journalists for newspapers and major TV broadcasters? Why or why not?
5. Should a newsroom that employs print and broadcast journalists, as well as bloggers and citizen journalists, require that all of these journalists follow the same editorial rules?
6. If we think that online media demands speed and immediacy does this justify the publication of rumor, lies, or unverified information?
7. What is the "new" fifth estate that is a part of our global online world? Identify some examples of the "fifth estate" in your country's media. Has the fifth estate published any significant reports or stories in recent years?
8. What is the difference between a closed and an open ethics? Discuss examples of closed ethics in professions other than journalism and news media. Can you identify any examples of open ethics in society today?

7   Global media ethics

A media ethics of the future needs to be ecumenical, open, and global. This chapter explores the third feature, a global ethics for news media. It argues that media ethics needs to take a global approach to responsible journalism. Its aims, principles, and practices have to be altered to reflect the global nature of media. The emergence of multi-media communication is not unrelated to the rise of global news media. The same technology that allows media to be interactive across multiple platforms – satellites, digital computers, the Internet – allows media to be global in scope. The three features cited above are inseparable in reality. However, for purposes of analysis, we focus in this chapter on the theoretical and practical impact on ethics of the globalization of media.

The discussion begins by explaining why media ethics needs to "go global" and what is meant by global media ethics. Then, I argue that the best philosophical basis for a global ethics, in general and in media, is cosmopolitanism. I show how cosmopolitanism reinterprets the media's aims and principles in terms of promoting a global human good. Cosmopolitanism would change how global events are covered and would alter how journalists think about patriotism. The chapter concludes by discussing how ethicists, citizens, and journalists can build a global media ethics, theoretically and practically.

Going global

Why go global?

Historically, journalism ethics has been parochial with its standards applying to particular groups. Journalism ethics was developed for a journalism of limited reach. The evolution of journalism ethics gradually enlarged the class of people that journalism was supposed to serve, from political parties to the general public. Yet, even today, the news media's claim that it serves the public has its limits. It is usually assumed that the public includes readers of local newspapers, audiences of regional TV broadcasts, and at most, the citizens of a country. The four hundred codes of journalism ethics in the world today are for local, regional, or national media. Too little is said about whether journalists have a responsibility to citizens beyond their town or country. Media ethics, it seems, stops at the border.

In a global world, how valid is the idea of ethics within borders? Why not take the next step and define the media's public as citizens within and without one's country? Responsibilities would be owed to readers and viewers scattered across the world. Standards would be redefined to promote a news media for citizens across borders. However, the question can be turned back. Why should we consider taking this audacious step? Isn't ethics complicated enough without adding global concerns?

There are several reasons to go global. One reason is that news media and the practice of journalism are increasingly global. The facts are familiar: media corporations are increasingly global enterprises. New technology gives news organizations the ability to gather information from around the world. News reports, via satellite and the Internet, reach people around the world and influence the actions of governments, militaries, humanitarian agencies, and warring ethnic groups. The reach of the Al-Jazeera and CNN networks, for example, extends beyond the Arab world and the US public. These developments have consequences for the ethics of journalism.

However, the need for a global ethics is due not only to technological innovation and new ownership patterns; it is due to changes in the world that journalism inhabits. Of primary importance is the fact that this media-connected world brings together a plurality of different religions, traditions, ethnic groups, values, and organizations with varying political agendas. Our world is not a cozy McLuhan village; our world is connected electronically like never before, yet this grid of connections coexists with a collision of cultures. Publishing materials deemed offensive by certain groups, as happened with the publication of the cartoons of Mohammed, can result in violence that ripples across borders. In such a climate, the role of the news media must be re-examined. What are the ethical responsibilities of media in a radically plural world, no longer divided politically into two Cold War camps?

A globally minded media is of great value because a biased and parochial media can wreak havoc in a tightly linked global world. Unless reported properly, North American readers may fail to understand the causes of violence in the Middle East or of a drought in Africa. Jingoistic reports can portray the inhabitants of other regions of the world as a threat. Reports may incite ethnic groups to attack each other. In times of insecurity, a narrow-minded, patriotic news media can amplify the views of leaders who stampede populations into war or promote the removal of civil rights for minorities. A global ethics is a bulwark against undue influence of parochial values and social pressures on journalists. We need a cosmopolitan media that reports issues in a way that reflects this global plurality of views and helps groups understand each other better. We need a more global attitude in journalism for the same general reason we need it in ethics in general: to make sure we don't withdraw into an insular ethnocentrism as a response to the confusing, pluralistic world around us. A global attitude refuses to allow us to hunker down into "a narrow and minimalist ethics that refuses to confront the major issues."[1]

Finally, we need globally responsible media to help citizens understand the daunting global problems of poverty, environmental degradation, technological inequalities, and political instability. These problems require concerted global action and the construction of new global institutions. Moreover, without global principles, it is not possible to criticize media practices in other countries, including draconian restrictions on the press.

Therefore, the answer to "why go global?" is this: with global reach comes global responsibilities. Media ethics will not be credible if it avoids engagement with these new complexities. But engagement will not be easy. Progress in a global ethics of any kind is not assured. To the contrary, there are many forces against a global approach, including ancient attachments to tribe and race, as well as modern attachments to extreme nationalism. The concerns of journalism are often narrow. Sometimes, the only goal is to publish another day of news in a way that pleases the preferences and prejudices of a limited audience. For many newsrooms, economic survival is more important than discussions of global ethics. Media scholars may suspect that talk about global ethics is code for the imposition of Western media values on other cultures. To avoid these misunderstandings, an

---

[1] Christians, "Ethical Theory in a Global Setting," 5.

exposition of global media ethics needs to start slowly, by explicating the relevant senses of "globalization," "global," and "global ethics."

What type of theory?

Many scholars investigate globalization as a trend in economics, trade, and culture. They investigate globalization as a *process* by which money markets, business, culture, technology, communication, and governing structures have become global. It is now a cliché to point out that what happens in the financial markets of Europe affects financial markets elsewhere. At least three senses of "global" appear in discussions of globalization. One sense deals with the location of an activity. A global activity or process is global if it occurs in different locations around the world, such as the game of soccer, or the process of environmental degradation. Another sense of global refers to the reach or impact of an activity or institution. The Vatican is a global institution not only because the Roman Catholic Church is located around the world but also because the Vatican's decisions impact political affairs, social values, and actions far beyond its borders. Similarly, Hollywood films influence popular culture around the world. A third sense of global is that of interconnectedness or mutual dependency – whether that dependency is wanted or not. Financial markets are global not only in terms of location and reach but also in terms of interconnectedness. China's decision on how much greenhouse gases it will produce next year affects the environment of countries on other continents. Global issues are difficult to address because of interconnectedness; they require co-operation by many countries.

All three senses are used to describe news media as global. Journalism is global in location, since it is practiced in almost every culture. But journalism as global in location is not new and doesn't adequately explain the way "global media" is used today. After all, cultures have been practicing journalism for centuries. "Global" as reach and interconnectedness is closer in meaning to current uses of global media. As noted above, one reason to go global is that multinational media organizations have global reach. They can gather information speedily from around the world and disseminate news stories to a global public via the Internet and other technology. This global reach means global impact on international events. The development of satellite-based news in the 1980s and internet-based journalism in the late 1990s has given media a global reach and impact that far surpasses the telegraph-based communication system of the nineteenth century. Global reach also leads to global interconnectedness. Media is globally interconnected in many ways. It is interconnected in that many newsrooms in different parts of the world need to co-operate to produce the content of a multinational media organization. Also, it is interconnected as a communication system of many rival newsrooms. Newsrooms in one part of the world respond to the reports carried by newsrooms in other parts of the world. Media also makes cultures interconnected. As noted above, media link cities, groups, and nations together in a 24-hour communication and feedback loop of global proportions.

Media as global in location, reach, and interconnectedness is studied empirically by many scholars, as part of a larger process of global communication.[2] Some theorists, such as the Spanish sociologist Manuel Castells, study how global communication has created a global public sphere with new players, new communication tools, and new ways to have political influence.[3] Some scholars study the development of media producers in the Global South, such as Bollywood films, as an alternative to dominant Western producers – a process called the production of "contra" flows of information.[4] Another line of study examines the power of global, 24-hour news channels to influence world reaction to major events – a process called The "CNN effect."[5]

These studies provide valuable data for global media ethics. But they are not doing global media ethics. They are empirical studies about the process of globalization and its impact on the public sphere and politics. They study the facts of globalization and seek theoretical explanations of these facts. They are not normative theories although they may make normative assumptions or place certain trends, e.g. concentration of media ownership, in an unfavorable light. The focus of these studies is not an explicit theory about what media should do, or how they should change their behavior, given the facts of globalization. The aim of these empirical studies is not to produce new principles for codes of ethics.

---

[2] On global communication, see McPhail, *Global Communication*. On global forms of journalism, see Seib, *The Global Journalist*, and de Beer and Merrill, *Global Journalism*.
[3] See Castells, *The Information Age*.
[4] Thussu, "Mapping Global Media Flows and Contra-Flow."
[5] Livingston, "Clarifying the CNN Effect."

A global media ethics, however, *is* focused on these normative questions. It is a type of theory that wants to know, given global developments, how media ethics should change. Global media ethics is interested in the ethical implications of the fact of global journalism. It asks: how should ethics change if it is to take account of the global reach and interconnectedness of news media? A global media ethics would contain three major areas of study: (1) new ethical foundations: a reinterpretation of our basic understanding of what journalism is (and should be) as part of the global public sphere. Here the question is: what ethical theory can ground a global approach to media?; (2) new principles and standards: the construction of norms as evaluative guides for the practice of global journalism; (3) new practice: the application of these ideas to the coverage of international events and global issues.

Therefore, global media ethics is called global for several reasons: (1) the global nature of what it studies: it aspires to be an ethics for a practice that is global in location, reach, and interconnectedness; (2) the global nature of its intended audience: a global ethics should, as we will argue below, seek to serve a global public – ultimately, all of humanity; (3) the global nature of its aims and purposes: serving a global public means promoting the good of citizens everywhere, of helping people flourish and enjoy just societies around the globe; (4) global principles to ground codes of ethics. A global ethics works to establish aims and general principles that responsible journalists across borders can agree to and honor in their own way, in their own media cultures.

Ethical foundations

Cosmopolitanism as global ethic

In Chapters 1 and 2, I explained how media ethics is ultimately based on principles outside its own normative sphere. The development of a global media ethics is another occasion when we have to look outside of media ethics for ideas and principles. Deep theories about universal principles are not to be found in media ethics. We have to look to philosophy, philosophical ethics, world religions, declarations of human rights, and other normative traditions. Once we have developed a global ethics from such sources, we can apply the ideas to media and examine the implications for practice.

What theory should we use to provide a foundation for the construction of a global media ethics? A good place to start is cosmopolitanism.

Cosmopolitanism does not mean being sophisticated in the ways of the world; it is an ancient ethical theory. Cosmopolitan ethics asserts the equal value and dignity of all people, as members of a common humanity. Cosmopolitanism emphasizes universal principles of human rights, freedom, and justice. Brock and Brighouse write: "Each human being has equal moral worth and that equal moral worth generates certain moral responsibilities that have universal scope."[6] The nationality, ethnicity, religion, class, race, or gender of a person (or group) is morally irrelevant to whether an individual is a member of humanity and comes under the protection of cosmopolitan principles.

The roots of the modern cosmopolitan attitude go back to the Stoics of antiquity, the laws of the Roman Empire, and the idea of a universal humanity in Christian humanism. Cosmopolitanism began with the idea that people outside my tribe or city – foreigners – were human like me. Therefore, I owe them certain decencies, such as hospitality or some privileges of citizenship. In philosophy, Kantian thought grounds a good deal of modern cosmopolitanism. Kant's categorical imperative enjoins us to universalize our maxims and to treat others as moral equals, as members of a "kingdom of ends." Kant's political writings envisage a world that seeks perpetual peace through a federation of free states governed by international law and respect for humanity. Outside philosophy, cosmopolitan attitudes have influenced the International Committee of the Red Cross, the human rights movement, international law, and the establishment of the United Nations. In recent years, Nussbaum has recommended cosmopolitanism as an antidote to parochialism in ethics.[7]

Cosmopolitanism is a thesis about ethical identity and responsibility. Cosmopolitans regard themselves as defined primarily by the common needs and aspirations that they share with other humans. This cosmopolitan identity is more important to their sense of self and ethical identity than facts about their place of birth, social class, or nationality. In terms of responsibility, cosmopolitanism "highlights the obligations we have to those whom we do not know, and with whom we are not intimate, but whose lives touch ours sufficiently that what we do can affect them."[8]

---

[6] Brock and Brighouse, *The Political Philosophy of Cosmopolitanism*, 4.
[7] See Nussbaum, "Patriotism and Cosmopolitanism."
[8] Brock and Brighouse, *The Political Philosophy of Cosmopolitanism*, 3.

Cosmopolitanism has received increasing attention because of the debate over the role of the nation-state in a global world and the responsibilities of developed countries to the appalling poverty and illness on this planet. Cosmopolitanism rules out assigning ultimate ethical value to collective entities such as states or nations. It rules out positions that accord no value to some types of people or establish a moral hierarchy where some people count for more than others.

Cosmopolitanism is often misunderstood. The trouble arises over the imperative to make our primary ethical allegiance to a borderless, moral community of humans. Cosmopolitanism has been dismissed as an ethic that only a philosopher could love – some abstract principles about universal humanity. To the contrary, cosmopolitanism wears a human face. It is the ability to perceive our common humanity in the many situations of life. It is respect for humanity's rational and moral capacities wherever and however they are manifest. It is in our concrete dealings with others that we recognize humanity's vulnerabilities, and capacities, as well as its potential for suffering.

The cosmopolitan attitude does not deny or devalue cultural diversity or legitimate partialities. The cosmopolitan thinker is under no illusion that people will stop loving their family and country. The cosmopolitan attitude does not deny that particular cultures and traditions are valuable. Instead, the cosmopolitan attitude is concerned with the *priority* and *limits* of our attachments. To say that our primary allegiance is to humanity is to say that more partial concerns have a prima facie right to be recognized but may be trumped by broader concerns. The claim of humanity acknowledges the stoic view that we live simultaneously in two communities: the local community of our birth and a community of common human aspirations. It insists only that, in negotiating our way between these two communities, we should not allow local attachments to override fundamental human rights and duties. When there is no conflict with cosmopolitan principles, life can be lived according to partial principles.

While cosmopolitanism is clear in its general orientation, there are difficult questions about what it requires. Today, many people would agree, philosophically, with the idea of human equality. After all, such sentiments are found in the USA's Declaration of Independence and other basic political documents. But cosmopolitanism, taken seriously, has difficult implications. It poses this tough question: if you accept the principle of an equal and common humanity, how does that fit with the fact that your family and country mean more to you? Peter Singer has written that the way out of our modern pursuit of self-interest is to embrace the idea of an ethical life with its openness to others. This ethical life rejects an indifference "to the vast amount of unnecessary suffering that exists in the world today."[9] Yet here lies the rub: how much do we owe to strangers and at what cost to near and dear? Does equal moral worth entail that every human should have an equal share of the world's land? Are comfortable North Americans ethically bound to contribute to foreign aid to the point of damaging their ability to provide for their children's university education?[10]

Despite uncertainties, there is a growing consensus among cosmopolitans that people everywhere should be able to meet their basic needs and develop their capacities to some tolerable extent. Today, the issue that engages cosmopolitanists and their critics is not whether we have special relationships with friends, family, and our country. The issue is to what extent citizens in one country owe assistance to citizens in other nations. One answer is weak cosmopolitanism: there are *some* extranational obligations. Another is strong cosmopolitanism: our obligations are very strong and global. Our fellow nationals have no special claim on us, and we have no right to use nationality to determine our obligations or to guide discretionary behavior. The challenge is to construct an ethically legitimate and detailed position between weak and strong cosmopolitanism.[11]

The human good

Cosmopolitanism is an extremely general idea. It tells us to affirm humanity; to express our love of humanity. This is our supreme value. But how does this well-meaning admonition help us to understand how we should

---

[9] Singer, *How Are We to Live?* ix.
[10] Fishkin, in his *The Limits of Obligation*, discusses how positive, general obligations of "ordinary morality" become paradoxical when extended to large numbers of people in other countries.
[11] Held, in "Principles of Cosmopolitan Order," 18, argues for a "layered cosmopolitanism" that provides a framework of principles that allows for argument and negotiation of "particular spheres of value" in which national and regional affiliations are weighed.

act in the world? Affirming humanity can take many forms. What do we affirm and how?

We start with the idea that to express a love of humanity is to create, maintain, or advance the good life for all humans. Or, expressed differently, it means to advance the most important goods of life. Which goods are they? They are the goods that are necessary for human life to exist and hopefully to flourish. They are primary goods in the sense that these are the goods that allow us to pursue non-primary goods. All of us, with some reflection, can think of some primary goods – physical security, shelter, food and drink, education, health, sufficient wealth, freedom to pursue one's plans, living under the rule of law, and so on. Cosmopolitanism, to be more concrete, needs a notion of the human good. It needs to specify the types of primary goods that a global ethics should promote, so that humans may flourish.

In *Global Journalism Ethics*, I presented a theory of the human good as consisting of four types of primary goods. I then argued that a global journalism needed to promote the goods on all four levels.[12] Here is a summary of the main ideas. Global ethics should be based on human flourishing. Flourishing means the exercise of one's intellectual, emotional, and other capacities to a high degree in a supportive social context. Ideally, flourishing is the fullest expression of human development under favorable conditions.[13] In reality, humans flourish in varying degrees. Few people are fully flourishing. Life often goes badly; many live in desperate conditions where flourishing is a remote ideal. Nevertheless, the ideal of flourishing is important for evaluating social and political systems.

However, it is not enough to say that a global ethics should promote flourishing. A full statement requires that we say that a global ethics should promote ethical flourishing. Why *ethical* flourishing, and not just flourishing? Because flourishing can be unethical and unjust; for example, I flourish at your expense. Ethics insists that humans do more than develop their

---

[12] Ward, *Global Journalism Ethics*, Chapter 3.

[13] Aristotle was one of the first philosophers to apply this biological perspective to the analysis of the good life. In modern ethical theory, the concept of flourishing received special attention from G. E. M. Anscombe in "Modern Moral Philosophy," 43–44. The concept has subsequently been used in political theory. It appears in Nussbaum's *Frontiers of Justice*, Sen's *Development as Freedom*, 70–77, and Kraut's *What Is Good and Why*.

capacities. Any capacity, virtue, emotion, or talent – from the capacity for rational thought to the virtue of loyalty – can be misused or employed for dubious purposes. We do not want people to develop their capacities for cruelty, blind hatred, and war-mongering. Surely these capacities should not be part of an ethical notion of flourishing. We need to develop capacities in ways that support our ethics, our sense of the ethically good life. When we exercise our capacities to think, emote, and pursue our goods in an ethical manner, we don't just flourish; we flourish ethically. When we ethically flourish, we enjoy such goods as trust, friendship, and right relations with others. Civility and civic virtue define our social interactions. When humans seek to be who they *should* be, they flourish ethically, as well as physically and socially.

In *Global Journalism Ethics*, I explained ethical flourishing as the development of four levels of primary goods – individual, social, political, and ethical goods. To achieve the goods of each level is to achieve a corresponding form of human dignity: individual, social, political, and ethical dignity. By individual goods, I mean the goods that come from the development of each individual's capacities. This level includes the physical goods that allow physical dignity. All persons need food, shelter, and security to live a normal length of life in health. This level also contains the rational and moral goods that allow physical capacity to flower into distinct human traits. A person enjoys the rational and moral goods when she develops her capacities to observe and think as a critical individual, and to carry out a rational plan of life. Such a person is able to form emotional attachments, and to use their imagination to produce (or enjoy) creative and intellectual works. Also, the person is able to be a moral agent. She is able to empathize with others and to form a sense of justice. She is able to deliberate about the good of others.

The social goods arise when we use our rational and moral capacities to participate in society. Human reality is "social" not just because, instrumentally, humans need society to develop language and culture. Humans come to value participating in common projects as a good-in-itself. Among the social goods are the freedom to enter into and benefit from economic association, the goods of love and friendship; the need for mutual recognition and respect. In this manner, we achieve a social dignity.

By political goods, I mean the goods that accrue to us as citizens living in a just political association. These goods include basic liberties, such as freedom of speech and freedom to pursue one's goods, combined with the opportunity and resources to exercise these freedoms. Citizens are able to participate in political life, to hold office, and to influence decisions. The primary means to these public goods are constitutional protections, the rule of law, barriers against undue coercion, and means for the peaceful resolution of disputes. A citizen who enjoys these goods has a political dignity, through self-government. I believe that the best form of political association, the best realization of political goods, is a flourishing and just democracy.

By ethical goods, I mean the goods that come from living among persons and institutions of ethical character, who attempt to follow ethical principles and promote ethical aims. To enjoy a full measure of the human good we need to live not only in a society of rational people – that is, people motivated to pursue their own interests. A society motivated *only* by purely rational agents would be a terrifying "private" (or extremely individualistic) society. To flourish, we also need to live among people who are disposed to be what Rawls calls morally "reasonable."[14] Reasonable citizens are motivated to consider the interests of others and the greater public good. Ethical flourishing means more than restraining our actions within laws. It indicates something positive: constructing societies where citizens come to appreciate the positive goods of justice and living in right relations. Of course, many people are not motivated to adopt the ethical stance. Nevertheless, under certain conditions, humans can appreciate interacting ethically as a good-in-itself.

These are the four levels of the human good. The goods of each level should be integrated and developed simultaneously. I do not pick out one good (or one level) as sufficient to define the human good, such as pleasure, or utility. The human good is a composite of basic goods, none of which are reducible or eliminable. The satisfaction of one type of good allows another to exist. To be sure, we need to secure the physical goods before we can move on to other goods, but that doesn't make the other levels less important. In many countries, unstable political structures – that is, the lack of political goods – interfere with attempts to provide physical and social goods to citizens.

The idea of ethical flourishing, through the advancement of the four levels of the human good, is an important conceptual foundation for

[14] Rawls, *Political Liberalism*, 48–54.

cosmopolitanism and for global ethics. The aim of global ethics is defined as affirming humanity by aiming at global ethical flourishing. The aim is not the promotion of flourishing in Canada or China. The goal is the promotion of the four levels for all of humanity, across all borders. The individual, social, political, and ethical dignity that we seek for citizens in our society, we seek for humanity at large. Ethical flourishing expresses the central principle of cosmopolitanism – the equal value and dignity of all, as members of a common humanity. Cosmopolitanism interpreted as ethical flourishing is an attractive basis for global ethics and, as we will see, for a global media ethics.

Application to journalism

In the previous section, we left the domain of media ethics to look at much broader ethical theories. We found two theories that together provide a plausible basis for global ethics: cosmopolitanism and a four-fold theory of the human good.

In the rest of this section, we show how these two theories can be used to turn media ethics into a global media ethics, by redefining the allegiances, aims, and principles of a globally responsible journalism. The fundamental changes entail changes to practice. If journalists were to adopt cosmopolitanism and ethical flourishing as primary concepts, it would begin a chain of reinterpretations of primary concepts and revisions of codes of ethics. The changes would reverberate across the entire field of media ethics.

Identity and aims

If journalists adopted the cosmopolitanism approach, they would alter their self-identity and their notion of who they serve. Cosmopolitanism requires journalists to honor the following three imperatives:

> *Act as global agents:* journalists should see themselves as agents of a global public sphere. The goal of their collective actions is a well-informed, diverse, and tolerant global "info-sphere" that challenges the distortions of tyrants, the abuse of human rights, and the manipulation of information by special interests.
>
> *Serve the citizens of the world:* the global journalist's primary loyalty is to the information needs of world citizens. Journalists should refuse to

define themselves as attached primarily to factions, regions, or even countries. Serving the public means serving more than one's local readership or audience, or even the public of one's country.

Promote non-parochial understandings: the global journalist frames issues broadly and uses a diversity of sources and perspectives to promote a nuanced understanding of issues from an international perspective. Journalism should work against a narrow ethnocentrism or patriotism.

Cosmopolitanism changes journalists' self-conception from that of a citizen of one country to that of a global citizen serving humanity. Cosmopolitanism means journalists place greater emphasis on their responsibilities to people beyond their borders. But it means more than that. One can recognize responsibilities to foreigners in need but not be a cosmopolitan. Cosmopolitanism makes the serving of humanity the *primary* allegiance of journalists. Journalists owe credible journalism to all potential readers of a global public sphere. Loyalty to humanity trumps other loyalties, where they conflict.

This change in identity and aim is further specified by adding the aim of promoting the four levels of primary goods. Journalists, as global citizens, seek individual, social, political, and ethical dignity for humanity at large. One important implication of adopting the four levels is that the political goal of journalism changes. To be sure, the political goods tell journalists to use their powers of investigation and communication for the development of a just and participatory political association at home. But the political goods, globalized, expand the aim from the promotion of a just liberal democracy at home to an attempt to establish well-ordered global society, a global community marked both by the development of democracy abroad and the development of global democratic institutions.[15]

Promoting the four levels

Global ethical flourishing may be attractive as a philosophical idea. But, practically speaking, how can global journalism promote something as

---

[15] For an exposition of a "cosmopolitan democracy," see Held, *Democracy and the Global Order*, 267–286, and "The Changing Contours of Political Community."

abstract as levels of primary goods? We need to specify how media can promote each level.

Journalism can promote the individual goods by monitoring basic levels of physical and rational dignity in their own country and around the world. Journalism can promote individual goods in at least three ways:

(1) *Provide information on (and an analysis of) world events and trends.*
    Journalism should be occupied with providing timely, accurate,
    and contextual information on political, social, and economic
    developments, from reports on new legislation and political
    instability to news of global trends in business and environment. This
    information is the basis for the deliberation of autonomous citizens in
    any nation.
(2) *Monitor basic levels of physical, individual, and social dignity.* Physical
    dignity: journalism has a duty to help citizens be aware of the
    ability of their society and other societies to provide for citizens a
    decent level of physical goods such as food, shelter, health, wealth,
    a reasonable length of life, and physical security through effective
    laws (and regulatory agencies) to protect the vulnerable. Journalism
    has a duty to provide the same scrutiny of the ability of citizens
    in the development of their rational and moral capacities. This
    duty requires journalistic inquiry into the educational system's
    effectiveness in developing rational and imaginative citizens, the
    capacity of the social fabric to develop citizens' emotional capacity
    through supportive communities, and the capacity of the public
    sphere to develop citizens' rational capacities through opportunities
    for philosophical, scientific, and cultural engagement.

    Journalism has a duty to bring forward for debate the fairness of
    existing physical, social, and educational opportunities within coun-
    tries and also globally. By using a variety of metrics and by making
    cross-cultural comparisons, journalism can contribute to progress in
    these areas.
(3) *Investigate inequality.* Journalism has a duty to conduct in-depth
    investigative stories on people and groups who have been denied
    physical, rational, and moral dignity, and by supporting global
    institutions that seek redress of these inequalities. Global journalism
    should reveal whether gender, ethnicity, and other differences
    account for inequalities. By exploring below the surface of society

and our global economic systems, journalism promotes citizens'
awareness of how egalitarian their society is, and the impact of
policies on human development and dignity.

Journalism can promote the social goods by taking up its duty to report
on, analyze, and critique the ways in which citizens interact and create
associations so as to enjoy the goods of social co-operation. Journalism
should promote social goods in at least five ways:

(1) *Report critically on economic associations.* Journalism has a duty to report
on and analyze how societies allow citizens to participate and benefit
from its various forms of economic association, including fair economic
competition. It needs to monitor society's use of economic power and
its effect on egalitarian democracy and the principles of justice.

(2) *Assess the quality of social life.* Journalism should report on the types of
social life, social and technological trends, and social possibilities
available for citizens. It should inquire into whether such trends
nurture caring relationships, meaningful collective activity, and
flourishing communities.

(3) *Assist social bridging.* In a pluralistic world, journalism has a duty to
act as a bridge between diverse classes, ethnic groups, religions,
and cultures within and among countries. Journalism has a two-
fold task to make visible, for consideration and critique, both the
commonalities and the differences among citizens, and to encourage
tolerant but frank cross-cultural discussion of issues.

(4) *Assist media literacy and the evaluation of media.* Journalism has a duty
to inquire into the impact of journalism, media, and communication
technology on the global public sphere and on their society; and how
new communication technology and new forms of journalism can be
used to advance ethical flourishing and the social goods.

(5) *Use global comparisons.* Journalism has a duty to evaluate the level of
human and social goods among countries and to investigate
different approaches to major social problems. In this way,
journalism is a force for progressive ideas and "experiments
in living."

Journalism can promote the political and ethical goods by helping to
nurture morally reasonable citizens willing to discuss essential issues

objectively and fairly, and to nurture a society where the pursuit of the rational side of life is restrained within firm and effective principles of justice. Journalism can promote political goods in at least four ways:

(1) *Critique the basic structure.* Journalism of the public good has a duty to inquire into and to encourage deliberation upon fundamental justice from a global perspective. Journalism should report on the basic institutional structures of societies and how well the principles of justice and international law are embodied by institutions, political processes, and legal systems.

(2) *Monitor the basic liberties.* Journalism has a duty to promote and defend basic liberties around the world and to ask to what extent citizens are able to enjoy the full value of basic liberties, such as freedom of speech, freedom of association, freedom from discrimination, and other constitutional protections. Are citizens able to exercise these freedoms for the purpose of self-development and to enjoy the goods on the other three levels?

(3) *Encourage participation.* Journalism needs to monitor (and help to make possible) citizens' participation in public life and their ability to have a meaningful influence on debate about government decisions. Journalism should engage in various forms of "civic" journalism that enhance public involvement in basic social issues and discourage public cynicism about civic engagement.[16]

(4) *Report on diversity and representation.* Journalism has a duty to insist on, and to help make possible, a diverse public forum within and across borders, with adequate representation of non-dominant groups. Journalism must be self-conscious about how groups can use language to manipulate, stereotype, and persuade citizens unethically. Through the media, powerful groups can dominate the public sphere.

Journalism contributes to the ethical goods, by helping to produce citizens with the ethical capacity and disposition to make ethical flourishing (including the public good) their primary aim. The role of journalism is to encourage citizens to seek goods beyond the goods of rationality or

[16] See Glasser, *The Idea of Public Journalism.*

enlightened self-interest, or even loyalty to one's ethnic or religious group. Journalism can promote the ethical goods as follows:

(1) *Take the public good perspective.* When covering major public issues or major public events, such as elections, media should focus on how the public good is served or not served by proposals, promises, and actions. They should examine critically any claims by public officials, large private corporations, and any other agency to be acting solely for the public good.

(2) *Highlight those who enhance the public good.* Cover individuals and groups who have enhanced the ethical goods of society, through courageous and public-minded actions.

(3) *Support the exercise of public reason through deliberative media.* As discussed in previous chapters, how citizens speak to each other is almost as important as what they say. At the core of the global media system should be deliberative spaces where reasonable citizens can robustly but respectfully exchange views and evaluate proposals. Moreover, a substantial number of journalists need to recommit to the ideals of truth and objectivity described in Chapter 4.

In summary, journalism has a two-fold task in developing these levels. One is to promote the free and creative self-realization of liberal citizens in the spirit of Mill. Journalism should promote liberal, autonomous persons fulfilling their capacities. Journalism should oppose social structures that would unduly limit creative plans of life. At the same time, journalism has a simultaneous commitment to liberal ideas of equality and justice. It should support not only creative, energetic individuals, but also a reasonable citizenry and reasonable discussion in pursuit of just social arrangements.

Journalism, from an ethical perspective, is not only about freedoms and rights; that is, helping people to seek their goods. Nor is it just about supporting communal solidarity, justice, or "harmonious" structures. It is about constantly seeking to *combine* the rational and reasonable, the pursuit of the goods and the just structures that allow and restrain such a pursuit. Journalism is neither about free speech nor any particular freedom or basic right; it is concerned with a family of rights and values, which include equality and justice. Journalism ethics is neither solely libertarian nor communitarian; it is both. It seeks to support the good in the right and the right in the good. It should help societies deal with the precarious and difficult task of finding ways to balance these ethical ideals. In this view, justice is a sort of freedom, or it is a condition of freedom. This dual task defines the contemporary meaning of "a free and responsible press."

Changing concepts and practices

These new global aims cannot be embraced without creating a sea change in media ethics' concepts and practice. All the things we have endorsed in the preceding chapters, from a dedication to truth and objectivity to the promotion of deliberative democracy, need to be reinterpreted as global commitments. These values need to find their meaning within a global ethics framework.

To get a sense of the change needed, consider the idea of journalism's social contract – the public's expectation that the news media will provide accurate and essential information in return for guarantees of press freedom. In a global public sphere, if cosmopolitan journalism has a social contract, it is not with a particular public or society; instead, it seems to be something much more diffuse – a multi-society contract. The cosmopolitan journalist is a transnational public communicator who seeks the trust and credence of a global audience. Also, the ideal of objectivity in news coverage takes on an international sense. Traditionally, news objectivity asks journalists to avoid bias toward groups within one's own country. Global objectivity would discourage allowing bias toward one's country as a whole to distort reports on international issues. The ideas of accuracy and balance become enlarged to include reports with international sources and cross-cultural perspectives. Global media ethics asks journalists to be more conscious of how they frame major stories, how they set the international news agenda, and how they can spark violence in tense societies.

Adopting a cosmopolitan media ethics also requires a major change in the area of patriotism and serving the public. What happens when the journalist's commitment to informing their country conflicts with informing the world as global citizens? What happens when patriotism asks them to set aside their global ethics?

Such conflicts are possible because cosmopolitanism holds that transnational principles of human rights and social justice take precedence over personal interests and national interests, when they conflict. This emphasis on what is ethically prior provides some direction to journalists caught in the ethical maze of international events. When my country embarks on an unjust war against another country, I, as a journalist (or citizen), should say so. If I am a Canadian journalist and I learn that Canada is engaged in trading practices that condemn citizens of an African country to continuing, abject poverty, I should not hesitate to report the injustice. It is not a violation of any reasonable form of patriotism or citizenship to hold one's country to high standards.

A cosmopolitan media would alter how journalists approach covering international events such as a conference on climate change or talks on a new global trade agreement. A parochial journalism ethics would not object to journalists serving the public of their nations by reporting a climate change conference mainly from the perspective of their co-patriots. Parochial journalists would tend to ask: what is in it for their country? What strategies will serve the national interests of their fellow citizens? As for global trade, parochial journalists would focus on how changes to a global trade agreement could open up markets for their country's farmers or oil producers. A cosmopolitan attitude would oppose such narrow, nationalistic reporting. It would require that journalists approach such events from the perspective of the global public good. What is the global problem concerning climate change and how should all countries co-operate to reach a fair and effective agreement? Cosmopolitan journalists from the West would report the legitimate complaints that developing nations have against the environmental policy of Western countries. Cosmopolitan journalists would question a global trade proposal made by their country if it advances their national interests while further impoverishing developing nations. Global media ethics directs journalists to make issues of global justice a major part of their reporting and analysis.

The cosmopolitan attitude limits parochial attachments in journalism, such as patriotism, by drawing a ring of broader ethical principles around them. When there is no conflict with cosmopolitan principles, journalists can report in ways that support local and national communities. They can practice their craft parochially.

Finally, a global media ethics rethinks the role of patriotism. In a global world, patriotism should play a decreasing role in ethical reasoning about media issues. At best, nation-based forms of patriotism remain ethically permissible if they do not conflict with the demands of a global ethical flourishing. Global media ethics requires that journalists commit themselves only to a moderate patriotism, subjecting the easily inflamed emotion of love of country to rational and ethical restraint.[17] A moderate patriotism means that one has a special affection for one's country and that one is willing to help it flourish and pursue its goals. But this special affection, based either on a love of the culture or respect for its laws, does not make one's country superior to other countries. A loyalty to one's country does not justify an aggressive national posture on the world stage whereby one's country pursues its goals at the expense of other countries. Where patriotism is extreme, and it asks journalists to ignore global justice and violations of human rights, such patriotic claims are to be denied.

Moderate patriotism, therefore, rejects all forms of extreme nationalism and patriotism based on race or superiority of culture. It rejects xenophobic portrayals of other cultures. A globally minded media should not participate in demonizing other groups, especially in times of tension. The duty of journalism in times of looming conflict or war is not to follow a patriotism of blind allegiance or muted criticism of the actions of one's country. In such times, journalists serve their countries – that is, they are patriotic – by continuing to provide independent news and analysis. This dogged determination of journalists to continue to bring a critical attitude toward their country's actions, despite the strong patriotic feelings of their fellow citizens, is an example of what the Spanish philosopher Jose Ortega Y Gasset called "criticism as patriotism."[18]

Global media ethics does not entail that news organizations should ignore local issues or regional audiences. It does not mean that every story requires a cosmopolitan attitude. However, there are situations, such as military intervention in a foreign country, climate change, and the establishment of a fair world trading system, where we need to assess actions from a perspective of global justice and reasonableness. What is at issue is a gradual widening of basic editorial attitudes and standards – a widening

---

[17] Ward, "A Theory of Patriotism for Journalism."
[18] Ortega Y Gasset, *Meditations on Quixote*, 105.

of journalists' vision of their responsibilities. It asks them to consider their society's actions, policies, and values from a larger perspective.

Building global media ethics

In this concluding section, we descend from the theoretical level of ideas to the practical level of how media practitioners and ethicists might develop global media ethics.

Global ethics as a movement

Throughout this chapter, we have discussed global ethics in the hypothetical tense with phrases such as "if journalists were to adopt cosmopolitanism." We talked about redefining media ethics for the future. Talk of "what might be" cannot be avoided because a complete and adequate global media ethics does not exist. At present it remains a movement, a set of ideas, a proposal. However, to recognize the urgency of developing global ethics is only the start. To agree that news media have global responsibilities does not mean that we have a clear and defensible list of global duties for journalists around the world.

When it comes to news media and its ethics, predicting the future is as difficult as it is in any other area of society. However, it is possible to name several things that have to be accomplished for global ethics to become a dominant part of media ethics.

Theoretically, the task is to develop a comprehensive ethical framework that invents new principles, redefines existing concepts, and responds adequately to objections. Several layers of ideas will have to be constructed. One layer will be a philosophical section that contains the most general aims and principles, such as affirming humanity and ethical flourishing. Another section will explain how the philosophical level applies to media conduct, such as showing how the four levels of the good entail journalistic duties. A third level would be even more concrete and practical, consisting of two parts. One part would provide a global code of media ethics similar to the SPJ's code, but reinterpreting the standards from a global perspective. The code, of course, would be consistent with and follow from the other two levels. Another part would explain how a globally minded media should cover global issues and international events. Perhaps this part could use case studies to bring out the differences between coverage from a parochial perspective and coverage from a global perspective.

The tough theoretical work is producing content for global media ethics. That is, formulating clear aims and principles by using philosophy, ethics, and any other conceptual tool. Equally important, and equally difficult, will be finding a process by which such content can be formulated and accepted by large numbers of journalists and ethicists. In this pluralistic world, a "top-down" approach simply won't work. Attempts by a philosopher of journalism, a government agency, or a media institution to impose a set of principles, or to declare that they have found a set of global principles that others should support, will only be met with skepticism by the denizens of different media cultures. The process of building global media ethics must start at a grassroots level and, through open dialogue across cultures, work towards a recognition of overlapping principles and values. The dialogue must be inclusive and global. These discussions must bring together global principles and local differences in media cultures in a respectful and rich encounter.

Grassroots dialogue does not mean that philosophers and other thinkers cannot bring their best ideas to the table for international debate. The only thing they should not do is claim *ex cathedra* that their ideas are evidently the best, prior to dialogue. It is important that ethicists put forward ideas, such as ethical flourishing, as a *proposal*, asking others to consider thinking about the issues in this manner. We are at a historic stage in the evolution of global media ethics where different conceptions are possible. Therefore scholars should put forward ideas in an experimental and non-dogmatic spirit. Undoubtedly, some ideas will fail; some approaches will turn out to be unproductive. In such a climate, the age-old philosophical posture of speaking from certain knowledge or special insight is inappropriate and unhelpful. My expectation is that, if and when a global media ethics takes definitive shape, it will be a hybrid of good ideas contributed by co-operating ethicists and journalists over many years.

On the positive side, a movement towards identifying global principles and engaging in global conversations is already underway, and it is growing in strength. Centers and web sites for global media and global media ethics are being established, and there is a growing movement of scholars, journals, and books on global media ethics.[19] Ethicists have begun a search for the fundamental principles of a global media ethics.

Groups of media ethicists, and persons concerned about global media, have started meeting in different locations around the world to develop global media principles.[20] In addition, groups have created international statements on access to information and news media principles, such as the Windhoek Declaration on Promoting an Independent and Pluralistic African Press in 1991. When African journalists drew up the declaration, they invoked the Universal Declaration of Human Rights to promote press freedom on their continent.

De-Westernizing the discipline

Building a global media ethics also requires a change in the discipline of media ethics – how we study and teach media ethics around the world. A narrow approach to teaching media ethics can reinforce parochial attitudes. In academia and schools of media, it is possible to create an awareness of global media ethics. Many schools of media are already introducing global elements into their curriculum, and UNESCO (and other agencies) have sponsored global conferences for media educators and the production of global journalism curricula.

These educational initiatives should adopt the goal of de-Westernizing media ethics. De-Westernizing media ethics does not mean making media ethics anti-Western. Rather it means enriching the study with non-Western approaches and ideals. Non-Western media practices and theories should be more central to Western discussions of journalism ethics. De-Westernization also means using cross-cultural comparisons when discussing the principles of media ethics, and giving due weight to African, Indian, and Eastern ethical systems.

---

[19] See Black and Barney, "Search for a Global Media Ethic," and Ward and Wasserman, *Media Ethics Beyond Borders*. Two recent textbooks devote articles to the global context of journalism studies and media ethics: Wahl-Jorgensen and Hanitzsch, *The Handbook of Journalism Studies*, and Wilkins and Christians, *The Handbook of Mass Media Ethics*.

[20] For example, I belong to a group of media scholars who have begun meeting every two years in places such as South Africa and Dubai to present papers on global media ethics. These meetings have resulted in attracting the interest of other scholars and in creating foundational publications. A round table in South Africa in 2007 led to the publication of Ward and Wasserman, *Media Ethics Beyond Borders*.

Another implication of de-Westernization is that media ethics should place more emphasis on a nuanced representation of other peoples. Misrepresentation can spark wars, demean other cultures, and support unjust social structures. Paying attention to issues of representation means questioning the everyday news practices that routinely exclude less powerful voices. This means defining "news" to include issues of social justice and their historical context, not just daily events and facts. It means seeking a greater diversity of sources in stories, and telling such stories from the perspective of non-dominant groups. Our understanding of the media's imperative to "seek truth and report" is thereby transformed. Reporting is not viewed as stenography of facts but rather as an informed interpretation of events in a larger cultural context.

To practice global media ethics, journalism and media students need a deeper cultural knowledge and a deeper appreciation of how language can distort "the other." Media education should supplement the traditional emphasis on reporting skills and fact-gathering with a more ethnographic approach that stresses cultural and international knowledge. The ultimate goal is educating a new generation of journalists and media practitioners who are more ready than preceding generations to be global citizens and cosmopolitan public communicators.

In summary, we need to enlarge the conceptual base of media ethics. There is an entire range of thinking in academia today – feminist, postmodern, communitarian, and post-colonial – that changes the basic discourse of media ethics and needs to be incorporated into ethical theory, textbooks, and teaching. Including these perspectives widens media ethics' conception of its main issues. The key debates extend beyond the need to teach accuracy to journalism students. The key issues extend beyond the traditional debate between libertarian and social responsibility theory. The debate now includes such issues as the relationship of ethics and power, media representation and dominant cultures, the social construction of identities, differences in ways of knowing and valuing, and the relationship of the local and global.

Realistic expectations

At the beginning of this chapter we warned that building global media ethics would not be easy. The economic imperatives of news media may resist the new global duties of media. Given the diversity of forms of media, it is reasonable to wonder to what extent dialogue, even if open and inclusive, can lead to agreement on global principles. A cursory survey of the many codes of journalism ethics would find agreement on such values as reporting the truth. Yet, a survey would also find differences. Some media cultures emphasize more strongly than others such values as the promotion of social solidarity, not offending religious beliefs, and not weakening public support for the military. Even where media systems agree on a value, such as freedom of the press or social responsibility, they may interpret and apply such principles in different ways. It would be unrealistic to expect that all journalists will, in the near future, meet to endorse one set of principles, or one code of global media ethics.

Therefore, we end this chapter, and this book, with reflections on what we might reasonably expect from efforts to develop a global media ethics, at least in the short- to medium-term. First we need to frankly admit that the project of global media ethics may fail. It may remain a utopian ideal. The divide between what news media the world needs – a globally minded and responsible news media – and the media it too often gets – parochial and nationalistic – may be unbridgeable. But it is crucial that advocates of global media ethics do not come to the conclusion that a global ethics is impossible before making every effort to overcome obstacles. Second, we need to see the process of coming to an agreement as a gradual, imperfect process. Conceiving of the goal as unanimous agreement among all journalists and media ethicists on one universal ethic is too ambitious a goal. But it is not too ambitious to build piece by piece, principle by principle, one journalism association after another. The construction can be seen as a slowly evolving process by which responsible media, scholars, and members of the public come to agree on certain global principles, while agreeing to disagree on other matters. What realistically can be hoped for, in the short term, is that increasing numbers of journalists and scholars become interested in global ethics. Perhaps they will join the existing movement of global media scholars and join their discussions. Reform begins by raising awareness, questioning existing practice, and putting forward ideas for debate.

For those who remain skeptical about the prospects for global media ethics, I can only ask them to remember the power of new ideas and of pioneering movements over long periods of time. As philosophers, we plant ideas like seeds in the hope of germination in the future.

Questions for discussion

1. In what sense have the codes of media ethics been "parochial"? How does parochialism conflict with recent trends in media?
2. Define cosmopolitanism as an ethical theory. What are its distinguishing features? How would media ethics change if cosmopolitanism was applied to media ethics?
3. Is cosmopolitanism at odds with patriotism for one's country? Can a journalist be both a patriot and a cosmopolitan?
4. What does it mean for the media to take as its aim the promotion of humanity? How would that change current media coverage and media practices?
5. If journalists are global citizens, how would they report on wars, especially where their own country is part of the conflict?
6. Are there any media organizations that practice a global media ethics? Which organizations come closest to practicing global media ethics?
7. What real-world obstacles stand in the way of developing a global media ethics? Do you think that the influence of economics and nationalism, plus trends in technology, will support or hinder the construction of a global media ethics?
8. Should media attempt to construct a global media ethics or not? Why, or why not, should ethics "go global"?

Bibliography

Adams, Robert M. *Finite and Infinite Goods*. Oxford University Press, 1999.

Altman, Andrew. "Freedom of Speech and Religion." In Hugh LaFollette (ed.) *The Oxford Handbook of Practical Ethics*. Oxford University Press, 2003, 358–386.

"The Right to Get Turned on: Pornography, Autonomy, Equality." In Hugh LaFollette (ed.) *Ethics in Practice*, 3rd edn. Malden, MA: Blackwell Publishing, 2007, 387–397.

Alston, William. *A Realist Conception of Truth*. London, UK: Cornell University Press, 1996.

Anscombe, G. E. M. "Modern Moral Philosophy." In Roger Crisp and Michael Slote (eds.) *Virtue Ethics*. Oxford University Press, 1997, 26–44.

Apodaca, Clair. "The Whole World Could Be Watching: Human Rights and the Media." *Journal of Human Rights*, 6:2 (2007): 147–164.

Applebaum, Arthur I. *Ethics for Adversaries: The Morality of Roles in Public and Professional Life*. Princeton University Press, 1999.

Aristotle. *The Ethics of Aristotle: The Nicomachean Ethics*. Trans. J. A. K. Thomson. London, UK: Penguin, 1976.

"Metaphysics." In R. McKeon (ed.) *The Basic Works of Aristotle*. New York, NY: Random House, 2001, 681–926.

"On Interpretation." In Richard McKeon (ed.) *The Basic Works of Aristotle*. New York, NY: Modern Library, 2001.

Arthur, John. "Sticks and Stones." In Hugh LaFollette (ed.) *Ethics in Practice*, 3rd edn. Malden, MA: Blackwell Publishing, 2007, 398–410.

Audi, Robert. *The Structure of Justification*. Cambridge University Press, 1993.

The Good in the Right: A Theory of Intuition and Intrinsic Value. Princeton University Press, 2004.

Practical Reasoning and Ethical Decision. London, UK: Routledge, 2006.

Moral Value and Human Diversity. Oxford University Press, 2007.

Austin, John L. *How to Do Things with Words*. Cambridge, MA: Harvard University Press, 1962.

Ayer, Alfred J. *Language, Truth and Logic*. New York, NY: Dover, 1952.

Baldasty, Gerald. *The Commercialization of the News in the Nineteenth Century.* Madison, WI: University of Wisconsin, 1992.

Barber, Katherine (ed.) *The Canadian Oxford Dictionary.* Don Mills, ON: Oxford University Press, 2001.

Barnes, Barry, and David Bloor. "Relativism, Rationalism and the Sociology of Knowledge." In Martin Hollis and Steven Luke (eds.) *Rationality and Relativism.* Oxford, UK: Blackwell, 1982, 21–47.

Baron, Marcia. "Kantian Ethics." In *Three Methods of Ethics*, Marcia Baron, Philip Pettit and Michael Slote. Malden, MA: Blackwell Publishing, 1997.

Baron, Marcia, Philip Pettit and Michael Slote. *Three Methods of Ethics.* Malden, MA: Blackwell Publishing, 1997.

Baughman, James L. *Henry R. Luce and the Rise of the American News Media.* Boston, MA: Twayne Publishers, 1987.

Bell, Martin. "The Truth is Our Currency." *The Harvard International Journal of Press/Politics* 3(1) (1998): 102–109.

Bennett, W. Lance. "New Media Power: The Internet and Global Activism." In Nick Couldry and James Curran (eds.) *Contesting Media Power.* London, UK: Rowman and Littlefield, 2003, 17–37.

Berlin, Isaiah. "Two Concepts of Liberty." In *Four Essays on Liberty.* Oxford University Press, 1969.

Bessette, Joseph. "Deliberative Democracy: The Majority Principle in Republican Government." In R. A. Goldwin and W. A. Schambra (eds.) *How Democratic is the Constitution?* Washington, DC: American Enterprise Institute, 1980.

Black, Jay. "Foreword." *Journal of Mass Media Ethics*, 21(2&3) (2006): 99–101.

Black, Jay, and Ralph Barney (eds.) "Search for a Global Media Ethic" [Special issue]. *Journal of Mass Media Ethics*, 17(4) (2002).

Black, Jay, Bob Steele and Ralph Barney. *Doing Ethics in Journalism: A Handbook with Case Studies.* Boston, MA: Allyn and Bacon, 1999.

Blackburn, Simon. "Relativism." In Hugh LaFollette (ed.) *The Blackwell Guide to Ethical Theory.* Malden, MA: Blackwell Publishing, 2000, 39–51.

Being Good: A Short Introduction to Ethics. Oxford University Press, 2002.

Truth: A Guide. Oxford University Press, 2005.

Bonjour, Laurence. *The Structure of Empirical Knowledge.* Cambridge, MA: Harvard University Press, 1985.

Bowman, Shayne, and Chris Willis. *We Media: How Audiences Are Shaping the Future of News and Information.* Reston, VA: American Press Institute, 2003.

Brink, David O. *Moral Realism and the Foundations of Ethics.* Cambridge University Press, 1989.

Brison, Susan J. " 'The Price We Pay'? Pornography and Harm." In Hugh LaFollette (ed.) *Ethics in Practice*, 3rd edn. Malden, MA: Blackwell Publishing, 2007, 377–386.

Brock, Gillian, and Harry Brighouse (eds.) *The Political Philosophy of Cosmopolitanism*. Cambridge University Press, 2005.

Brook, S. Jan Moir: more than 22,000 complain to PCC over Stephen Gately piece. *The Guardian*. October 19, 2009. www.guardian.co.uk/media/2009/oct/19/jan-moir-complain-stephen-gately. Accessed on January 29, 2010.

Brucker, Herbert. *Freedom of Information*. New York, NY: Macmillan Co., 1949.

Burgess, Michael. "What Difference Does Public Consultation Make to Ethics?" Electronic working paper series, W. Maurice Young Centre for Applied Ethics, University of British Columbia, www.ethics.ubc.ca, 2003.

Burke, Peter. *A Social History of Knowledge*. Cambridge, UK: Polity, 2000.

Butler, Christopher. *Postmodernism: A Very Short Introduction*. Oxford University Press, 2002.

Campbell, W. Joseph. *Yellow Journalism: Puncturing the Myths, Defining the Legacies*. Westport, CT: Praeger, 2001.

Castells, Manuel. *The Information Age* (3 Vols.) London, UK: Blackwell Publishing, 1997.

Chomsky, Noam. *Necessary Illusions: Thought Control in Democratic Societies*. Cambridge, MA: South End Press, 1989.

Christians, Clifford G. "Ethical Theory in a Global Setting." In Thomas Cooper, *et al.* (eds.) *Communication Ethics and Global Change*. White Plains, NY: Longman, 1989, 3–19.

   "Preface." In Richard Keeble (ed.) *Communication Ethics Today*. Leicester, UK: Troubador Publishing Ltd., 2005.

   "The Case for Communitarian Ethics." In M. Land and B. Hornaday (eds.) *Contemporary Media Ethics*. Spokane, WA: Marquette Books, 2006, 57–69.

Christians, Clifford, John Ferre and Mark Fackler. *Good News: Social Ethics and the Press*. New York, NY: Oxford University Press, 1993.

Christians, Clifford, and Karle Nordenstreng. "Social Responsibility Worldwide." *Journal of Mass Media Ethics*, 19(1) (2004): 3–28.

Christians, Clifford, and John Merrill (eds.) *Ethical Communication: Moral Stances in Human Dialogue*. Columbia, MO: University of Missouri Press, 2009.

Christians, Clifford, Theodore Glasser, Denis McQuail, Kaarle Nordenstreng and Robert A. White. *Normative Theories of the Media*. Urbana, IL: University of Illinois Press, 2009.

Cohen, Joshua. "Freedom of Expression." In David Heyd (ed.) *Toleration*. Princeton University Press, 1996, 173–225.

Connor, Steven. *Postmodernist Culture*. Oxford, UK: Blackwell, 1989.

Cooper, Stephen D. *Watching the Watchdog: Bloggers as the Fifth Estate*. Spokane, WA: Marquette Books, 2006.

Cornford, Francis. *The Republic of Plato*. New York, NY: Oxford University Press, 1968.

Crisp, Roger. "Deontological Ethics." In Ted Honderick (ed.) *The Oxford Guide to Philosophy*. Oxford University Press, 2005, 200–201.

Cronin, Mary, and James McPherson. "Reaching for Professionalism and Respectability: The Development of Ethics Codes in the 1920s." A paper presented at the annual conference of the American Journalism Historians Association, October, 1992 at Lawrence, KS.

Cunningham, Brent. "Rethinking Objectivity." *Columbia Journalism Review*, Issue 4 (2003): 24–32.

Darwall, Stephen. *Contractarianism/Contractualism*. Malden, MA: Blackwell Publishers, 2003.

Philosophical Ethics. Boulder, CO: Westview Press, 1998.

"How Should Ethics Relate to Philosophy?" In Terry Horgan and Mark Timmons (eds.) *Media Ethics after Moore*. Oxford, UK: Clarendon Press, 2006, 17–37.

De Beer, Arnold, and John Merrill (eds.) *Global Journalism: Topical Issues and Media Systems*. Boston, MA: Allyn & Bacon, 2004.

Denzin, Norman, and Yvonna Lincoln (eds.) *Handbook of Qualitative Research*, 2nd edn. Thousand Oaks, CA: Sage Publications, 2000.

Dewey, John. *Reconstruction in Philosophy*. Mineola, NY: Dover Publications, 2004.

Democracy and Education. New York, NY: The Free Press, 1944.

Dreier, James (ed.) *Contemporary Debates in Moral Theory*. Malden, MA: Blackwell Publishing, 2006.

Duncan, John. "Another Journalism is Possible: Critical Challenges for the Media in South Africa." Centre for Civil Society, Harold Wolpe Lecture, 2003.

Durkheim, Emile. *Moral Education: A Study in the Theory and Application of the Sociology of Education*. Trans. Everett K. Wilson and Herman Schnurer, ed. Everett K. Wilson. New York, NY: Free Press of Glencoe, 1951.

Dworkin, Ronald. *Law's Empire*. Cambridge, MA: Harvard University Press, 1986.

Freedom's Law. Cambridge, MA: Harvard University Press, 1996.

Sovereign Virtue: The Theory and Practice of Equality. Cambridge, MA: Harvard University Press, 2000.

Elliott, Deni (ed.) *Responsible Journalism*. Beverly Hills, CA: Sage Publications, 1986.

Ess, Charles. *Digital Media Ethics*. Cambridge, UK: Polity Press, 2009.

Feinberg, Joel. *Harm to Others*. Oxford University Press, 1984.

   Offense to Others. New York, NY: Oxford University Press, 1985.

Fidler, Roger. *Mediamorphosis: Understanding New Media*. Thousand Oaks, CA: Pine Forge Press, 1997.

Fishkin, James. *The Limits of Obligation*. New Haven, NJ: Yale University Press, 1982.

   Democracy and Deliberation: New Directions for Democratic Reform. New Haven, CT: Yale University Press, 1991.

Foot, Philippa. "The Problem of Abortion and the Doctrine of the Double Effect," in *Virtues and Vices*. Oxford, Basil Blackwell, 1978.

Frankfurt, Harry G. "On Bullshit." In *The Importance of What We Care About: Philosophical Essays*, 117–133. Cambridge University Press, 1988.

   The Reasons of Love. Princeton University Press, 2004.

   On Truth. New York, NY: Alfred A. Knopf, 2006.

   Taking Ourselves Seriously and Getting It Right. Palo Alto, CA: Stanford University Press, 2006.

Frenzel, Fabian, and Sian Sullivan. "Globalization from Below? ICTs and Democratic Development in the Project 'Indymedia Africa.'" In Fred Mudhai, Wisdom J. Tettey and Fackson Banda (eds.) *African Media and the Digital Public Sphere*. New York, NY: Palgrave Macmillan, 2009, 165–182.

Frey, Robert G. "Act-Utilitarianism." In Hugh LaFollette (ed.) *The Blackwell Guide to Ethical Theory*. Malden, MA: Blackwell Publishers, 2000, 165–182.

Friedman, Steven, and Victor Macklenin. "White supremacy rears its ugly head over 'racist Vodafone'". France 24 Observers, 2009. http://observers.france24.com/en/content/20091124-white-supremacy-rears-its-ugly-head-over-racist-vodafone-bee-vodacom?page=1. Accessed February 10, 2010.

Friend, Cecilia, and Jane Singer. *Online Journalism Ethics: Traditions and Transitions*. Armonk, NY: M. E. Sharpe, 2007.

Gadamer, Hans-Georg. *Truth and Method*. 2nd rev. edn. London, UK: Continuum Publishing, 2004.

Gert, Bernard. *The Moral Rules*. New York, NY: Harper and Row, 1973.

   Reason and Morality. University of Chicago Press, 1978.

   Morality: Its Nature and Justification. Oxford University Press, 1998.

   Common Morality. Oxford University Press, 2004.

Gibbard, Allan. *Wise Choices, Apt Feelings: A Theory of Normative Judgment*. Cambridge, MA: Harvard University Press, 1990.

Gillmor, Dan. *We the Media: Grassroots Journalism for the People, by the People*. Sebastopol, CA: O'Reilly Media: 2004.

Glasser, Theodore L. *The Idea of Public Journalism*. New York, NY: Guilford, 1999.

Greenawalt, Kent. *Fighting Words*. Princeton University Press, 1995.

Grey, Thomas. "Civil Rights versus Civil Liberties." *Social Philosophy and Policy*, 8: 81–107.

Haack, Susan. *Evidence and Inquiry: Towards Reconstruction in Epistemology*, Oxford, UK: Blackwell, 1997.

   Manifesto of a Passionate Moderate: Unfashionable Essays. University of Chicago Press, 1998.

Habermas, Jurgen. *Theory of Communicative Action*, trans. Thomas McCarthy. Boston, MA: Beacon Press, 1984.

   The Inclusion of the Other. Ed. Ciaran Cronin and Pablo De Greiff. Cambridge, MA: MIT Press, 1998.

Hackett, Robert A., and Yuechi Zhao. *Sustaining Democracy? Journalism and the Politics of Objectivity*. Toronto, ON: Garamond Press, 1998.

Hacking, Ian. *The Social Construction of What?* Cambridge, MA: Harvard University Press, 1999.

Hamelink, Cees. "The Ethics of the Internet: Can We Cope with Lies and Deceit on the Net?" In Katherine Sarikakis and Daya Thussu (eds.) *Ideologies of the Internet*. Creskill, NY: Hampton Press, 2006, 15–129.

Hare, R. M. *The Language of Morals*. New York, NY: Oxford University Press, 1952.

   Moral Thinking. Oxford, UK: Clarendon Press, 1981.

   Objective Prescriptions and Other Essays. Oxford, UK: Clarendon Press, 1999.

   "Descriptivism and the Error Theory." In *Objective Prescriptions and Other Essays*. Oxford, UK: Clarendon Press, 1999, 65–86.

Harman, Gilbert. "What is Moral Relativism?" In A. I. Goldman and J. Kim (eds.) *Values and Morals*. Dordrecht and Boston, MA: D. Reidel, 1978.

   "Convention." In Stephen Darwall (ed.) *Contractarianism/Contractualism*. Malden, MA: Blackwell Publishers, 2003, 138–148.

Harman, Gilbert, and J. Thomson, *Moral Relativism and Moral Objectivity*. Oxford, UK: Blackwell, 1996.

Hauser, Marc. *Moral Minds: How Nature Designed Our Universal Sense of Right and Wrong*. New York, NY: HarperCollins, 2006.

Hawkesworth, Mary E. "From Objectivity to Objectification." In Allan Megill (ed.) *Rethinking Objectivity*. London, UK: Duke University Press, 1994, 151–177.

Held, David. *Democracy and the Global Order: From the Modern State to Cosmopolitan Governance*. Cambridge, UK: Polity Press, 1995.

   "The Changing Contours of Political Community: Rethinking Democracy in the Context of Globalization." In Barry Holden (ed.) *Global Democracy: Key Debates*. London, UK: Routledge, 2000, 17–31.

"Principles of Cosmopolitan Order." In Gillian Brock and Harry Brighouse (eds.) *The Political Philosophy of Cosmopolitanism.* Cambridge University Press, 2005, 10–27.

Models of Democracy. 3rd edn. Cambridge, UK: Polity Press, 2008.

Herodotus. *The Histories.* Trans. Robin Waterfield. Oxford University Press, 1998.

Hobbes, Thomas. *Leviathan.* London, UK: Penguin Books, 1985.

Hohenberg, John. *Free Press, Free People: The Best Cause.* New York, NY: Free Press, 1971.

Hooker, Brad. "Rule Consequentialism." In Hugh LaFollette (eds.) *The Blackwell Guide to Ethical Theory.* Malden, MA: Blackwell, Publishers, 2000, 183–204.

"Consequentialism." In Ted Honderick (ed.) *The Oxford Guide to Philosophy.* Oxford University Press, 2005, 162–165.

Hursthouse, Rosalind. "Virtue Theory and Abortion." *Philosophy and Public Affairs,* 20 (1991): 223–246.

Husak, Douglas N. "Legal Paternalism." In Hugh LaFollette (ed.) *The Oxford Handbook of Practical Ethics.* Oxford University Press, 2003, 387–412.

Ignatieff, Michael. *The Lesser Evil: Political Ethics in an Age of Terror.* Princeton University Press, 2004.

Kant, Immanuel. *The Critique of Practical Reason.* Trans. L. W. Beck. New York, NY: Bobs-Merrill, 1956.

"On the Common Saying." In Hans Reiss (ed.) *Kant: Political Writings.* 2nd enlarged edn. Cambridge University Press, 1991, 54–60.

The Metaphysics of Morals. Trans. Mary Gregor. Cambridge University Press, 1996.

Groundwork of the Metaphysics of Morals. Ed. Mary Gregor. Cambridge University Press, 1997.

Katz, Jon. "No News is Good News." *Hotwired.* www.hotwired.com. Accessed October 9, 1996.

Kellner, Douglas. "Globalization, Technopolitics and Revolution." In John Foran (ed.) *The Future of Revolutions.* London, UK: Zed Books, 2002, 180–194.

Koehn, Daryl. *Rethinking Feminist Ethics: Care, Trust and Empathy.* London, UK: Routledge, 1998.

Kovach, Bill, and Tom Rosenstiel. *The Elements of Journalism.* New York, NY: Crown Publishers, 2001.

Kraut, Richard. *What is Good and Why: The Ethics of Well-Being.* Cambridge, MA: Harvard University Press, 2007.

Kuhn, Thomas S. *The Structure of Scientific Revolutions.* Chicago, IL: University of Chicago Press, 1962.

Kunne, Wolfgang. *Conceptions of Truth*. Oxford, UK: Clarendon Press, 2005.

Kupperman, Joel J. *Value… and What Follows*. Oxford University Press, 1999.

LaFollette, Hugh (ed.) *The Blackwell Guide to Ethical Theory*. Malden, MA: Blackwell Publishing, 2000.

(ed.) *Ethics in Practice*, 3rd edn. Malden, MA: Blackwell Publishing, 2007.

"Free speech." In *Ethics in Practice*, 3rd edn. Malden, MA: Blackwell Publishing, 2007, 371–376.

Land, Mitchell, and Bill W. Hornaday (eds.) *Contemporary Media Ethics: A Practical Guide for Students, Scholars and Professionals*. Spokane, WA: Marquette Books, 2006.

Langa, Khayad. "Yesterday, a short-lived war broke out between the US and SA." *Mail & Guardian Thought Leader*. November 5, 2009. www.thoughtleader.co.za/khayadlanga/2009/11/05/yesterday-a-short-lived-war-broke-out-between-america-and-south-africa. Accessed February 10, 2010.

Lippmann, Walter. *Public Opinion*. New York, NY: Macmillan, 1922.

Livingston, Stephen. "Clarifying the CNN Effect." Cambridge, UK: Shorenstein Center on Press and Politics, 1997.

Longino, Helen. *Science as Social Knowledge*. Princeton University Press, 1990.

Lukes, Steven. *Moral Relativism*. New York, NY: Picador, 2008.

Lynch, Michael. *Truth in Context: An Essay on Pluralism and Objectivity*. Cambridge, MA: MIT Press, 1998.

MacIntyre, Alasdair. "Epistemological Crisis, Dramatic Narrative, and the Philosophy of Science." In *The Tasks of Philosophy*, Vol. I of *Selected Essays*. Cambridge University Press, 2006, 3–23.

Mackie, John L. *Ethics: Inventing Right and Wrong*. New York, NY: Penguin, 1977.

Macpherson, C. B. *The Life and Times of Liberal Democracy*. Oxford University Press, 1977.

Marmor, Andrei (ed.) *Law and Interpretation: Essays in Legal Philosophy*. Oxford, UK: Clarendon Press, 1995.

May, Larry. *The Morality of Groups: Collective Responsibility, Group-Based Harm, and Corporate Rights*. University of Notre Dame Press, 1987.

McChesney, Robert. "The Media System Goes Global." In Daya K. Thussu (ed.) *International Communication: A Reader*. Malden, MA: Blackwell Publishers, 2000, 188–220.

McChesney, Robert W., and John Nichols. *The Death and Life of American Journalism: The Media Revolution that will Begin the World Again*. Philadelphia, PA: Nation Books, 2010.

McMahan, Jeff. "Moral Intuition." In Hugh LaFollette (ed.) *The Blackwell Guide to Ethical Theory*. Malden, MA: Blackwell Publishing, 2000, 92–110.

McPhail, Thomas L. *Global Communication: Theories, Stakeholders, and Trends*. Malden, MA: Blackwell Publishing, 2006.

Megill, Allan. *Rethinking Objectivity*. London, UK: Duke University Press, 1994.

Meiklejohn, Alexander. *Free Speech and Its Relation to Self-Government*. Port Washington, NY: Kennikat Press, 1948.

Mill, John Stuart. *On Liberty and the Subjection of Women*. Ed. Alan Ryan. London, UK: Penguin Books, 2006.

"Utilitarianism." In Henry R. West (ed.) *The Blackwell Guide to Mill's Utilitarianism*. Malden, MA: Blackwell Publishing, 2006.

Mindich, David T. Z. *Just the Facts: How "Objectivity" Came to Define American Journalism*. New York University Press, 1998.

Miraldi, Robert. *Muckraking and Objectivity*. New York, NY: Greenwood Press, 1990.

Moore, George E. *Principia Ethica*. Mineola, NY: Dover, 2004.

Moser, Paul K. *Knowledge and Evidence*. Cambridge University Press, 1989.

Mott, Frank Luther. *American Journalism: A History, 1690–1960*. 3rd edn. New York, NY: Macmillan, 1962.

Nietzsche, Friedrich. *The Twilight of the Idols* and *The AntiChrist*. Trans. R. J. Hollingdale. Harmondsworth, UK: Penguin, 1968.

Nussbaum, Martha C. "Patriotism and Cosmopolitanism." In Joshua Cohen (ed.) *For Love of Country: Debating the Limits of Patriotism: Martha C. Nussbaum with Respondents*. Boston, MA: Beacon Press, 1996, 3–17.

Frontiers of Justice. Cambridge, MA: Belknap Press, 2006.

Offe, Claus, and Ulrich Preuss. "Democratic Institutions and Moral Resources." In David Held (ed.) *Political Theory Today*. Cambridge, UK: Polity Press, 1991.

Ortega Y Gasset, Jose. *Meditations on Quixote*. Trans. Evelyn Rugg and Diego Marin. Urbana, IL: University of Illinois Press, 2000.

Overholser, Geneva. *On Behalf of Journalism: A Manifesto for Change*. Annenberg Public Policy Center. Philadelphia, PA: University of Pennsylvania, 2006.

Pateman, Carole. *Participation and Democratic Theory*. Cambridge University Press, 1970.

Patterson, Philip, and Lee Wilkins. *Media Ethics: Issues and Cases*. 4th edn. New York, NY: McGraw-Hill, 2002.

Peterson, Theodore. "The Social Responsibility Theory of the Press." In Fred Siebert, Theodore Peterson and Wilbur Schramm (eds.) *Four Theories of the Press*. Urbana, IL: University of Illinois Press, 1956.

Pettit, Philip (ed.) *Consequentialism*. Aldershot, UK: Dartmouth Publishing, 1993.

Plato, *The Republic*. 2nd edn. Trans. Desmond Lee. London, UK: Penguin Classics, 2007.

Postema, Gerald J. "Bentham's Utilitarianism." In Henry R. West (ed.) *The Blackwell Guide to Mill's Utilitarianism*. Oxford, UK: Blackwell Publishing, 2006, 26–44.

Pratte, Paul Alfred. *Gods within the Machine: A History of the American Society of Newspaper Editors, 1923–1993*. Westport: CT: Praeger, 1995.

Putnam, Hilary. *Words and Life*. Cambridge, MA: Harvard University Press, 1994.

   Pragmatism. Oxford, UK: Blackwell Publishers, 1996.

Quine, Willard Van Orman. *Word and Object*. Cambridge, MA: MIT Press, 1960.

Rachels, Stuart. *The Elements of Moral Philosophy*. 5th edn. New York, NY: McGraw-Hill, 2007.

Railton, Peter. "Moral Factualism." In James Dreier (ed.) *Contemporary Debates in Moral Theory*. Malden, MA: Blackwell Publishing, 2006, 201–219.

Rawls, John. *A Theory of Justice* (12th impression). Oxford University Press, 1992. (Original work published 1972.)

   Political Liberalism. New York, NY: Columbia University Press, 1993.

Reeves, Richard. *John Stuart Mill: Victorian Firebrand*. London, UK: Atlantic Books, 2007.

Rescher, Nicholas. *Coherence Theory of Truth*. Oxford University Press, 1973.

Rorty, Richard. *Philosophy and the Mirror of Nature*. Princeton University Press, 1979.

Rorty, Richard, and Pascal Engel. *What's the Use of Truth?* New York, NY: Columbia University Press, 2005.

Rosen, Jay. *Getting the Connections Right: Public Journalism and the Troubles in the Press*. New York, NY: Twentieth Century Fund Press, 1996.

Ross, Charles G. *The Writing of News: A Handbook*. New York, NY: Henry Holt, 1911.

Ross. W. D. *The Right and the Good*. Oxford University Press, 1930.

Rusbridger, Alan. 2010. "The Hugh Cudlipp Lecture: Does journalism exist?" *The Guardian*, January 25, 2010. www.guardian.co.uk/media/2010/jan/25/cudlipp-lecture-alan-rusbridger. Accessed on January 29, 2010.

Russell, Bertrand. *The Problems of Philosophy*. New York, NY: Henry Holt and Company, 1912.

Scanlon, Thomas M. *What We Owe to Each Other*. Cambridge, MA: Harvard University Press, 1998.

Schauer, Frederick. "The Phenomenology of Speech and Harm." *Ethics*, 103: 635–653.

Searle, John L. *Speech Acts: An Essay in the Philosophy of Language*. Cambridge, MA: Cambridge University Press, 1969.

Seib, Philip. *The Global Journalist: News and Conscience in a World of Conflict*. Lanham, MD: Rowman and Littlefield, 2002.

Sen, Amartya. *Development as Freedom*. New York, NY: Alfred A. Knopf, 1999.

Seters, Paul van (ed.) *Communitarianism in Law and Society*. Lanham, MD: Rowman and Littlefield Publishers, 2006.

Shafer-Landau, Russ. *Moral Realism: A Defence*. Oxford, UK: Clarendon Press, 2003.

Shepherd, Tamara. "Twittering in the OECD's 'Participatory Web'": Microblogging and New Media Policy." *Global Media Journal – Canadian Edition*, 2(1) (2009): 149–165.

Shriffin, Steven. *Dissent, Injustice, and the Meanings of America*. Princeton University Press, 1999.

Sidgwick, Henry. *The Methods of Ethics*, 7th edn. Indianapolis, IN: Hackett Publishing, 1991.

Siebert, Fred, Theodore Peterson and Wilbur Schramm. *Four Theories of the Press*. Urbana, IL: University of Illinois Press, 1956.

Singer, Marcus. *Generalization in Ethics*. New York, NY: Knopf, 1961.

Singer, Peter. "Sidgwick and Reflective Equilibrium." *The Monist*, 58 (1974): 490–517.

 How Are We To Live? Ethics in an Age of Self-Interest. New York, NY: Prometheus Books, 1995.

Skorupski, John. "The Place of Utilitarianism in Mill's Philosophy," in Henry R. West (ed.) *The Blackwell Guide to Mill's Utilitarianism*. Malden, MA: Blackwell Publishing, 2007, 45–59.

Slote, Michael. "Satisficing Consequentialism." In Philip Pettit (ed.) *Consequentialism*. Aldershot, UK: Dartmouth Publishing, 1993, 351–375.

 "Virtue Ethics" in Marcia Baron, Philip Pettit and Michael Slote (eds.) *Three Methods of Ethics*. Malden, MA: Blackwell Publishing, 1998, 175–238.

Smith, Adam. *The Theory of Moral Sentiments*. Amherst, NY: Prometheus Books, 2000.

Smith, Michael. *The Moral Problem*. Oxford, UK: Blackwell, 1994.

 "Moral Realism." In Hugh LaFollette (ed.) *The Blackwell Guide to Ethical Theory*. Malden, MA: Blackwell Publishing, 2000, 15–37.

Steiner, Linda, and Chad Okrusch. "Care as a Virtue for Journalists." *Journal of Mass Media Ethics*, 21(2 & 3) (2006): 102–122.

Stevenson, Charles L. *Ethics and Language*. New Haven, CT: Yale University Press, 1944.

Sunstein, Cass. *Democracy and the Problem of Free Speech*. New York, NY: Free Press, 1993.

Thagard, Paul. *Conceptual Revolutions*. Princeton University Press, 1992.

Thussu, Daya K. "Mapping Global Media Flows and Contra-Flow." In Daya K. Thussu (ed.) *International Communication: A Reader*. Malden, MA: Blackwell Publishing, 2000, 221–238.

Tsukamoto, S. "Social Responsibility Theory and the Study Of Journalism Ethics in Japan." *Journal of Mass Media Ethics*, 21(1) (2006): 54–68.

Tuchman, Gaye. *Making the News: A Study in the Construction of Reality*. New York, NY: Free Press, 1978.

Wahl-Jorgensen, Karin, and Thomas Hanitzsch (eds.) *The Handbook of Journalism Studies*. New York, NY: Routledge, 2009.

Waldron, Jeremy, "Mill on Liberty and on the Contagious Diseases Acts," In Nadia Urbinati and Alex Zakaras (eds.) *J. S. Mill's Political Thought: A Bicentennial Reassessment*. Cambridge University Press, 2007, 11–42.

Walzer, Michael. "Deliberation, and What Else?" In Stephen Macedo (ed.) *Essays on Democracy and Disagreement*. Oxford University Press, 1999.

Ward, Stephen J. A. "Objective Public Journalism for Global Media." In Thomas Hanitzsch, Martin Loffelholz and Ronny Mustamu (eds.) *Agents of Peace: Public Communication and Conflict Resolution in an Asian Setting*. Jakarta: Friedrich Ebert Stiftung, 2004, 25–49.

"Philosophical Foundations for Global Journalism Ethics." *Journal of Mass Media Ethics*, 20(1) (2005): 3–21.

The Invention of Journalism Ethics: The Path to Objectivity and Beyond. Montreal, QC.: McGill-Queen's University Press, 2005.

"Truth and Objectivity." In Lee Wilkins and Clifford G. Christians (eds.) *The Handbook of Mass Media Ethics*. New York, NY: Routledge, 2009, 71–83.

Global Journalism Ethics. Montreal, QC: McGill-Queen's University Press, 2010.

"Ethics for the New Mainstream." In Paul Benedetti, Tim Currie and Kim Kierans (eds.) *The New Journalist: Roles, Skills, and Critical Thinking*. Toronto, ON.: Emond Montgomery Publications, 2010, 313–326.

"Inventing Objectivity." In Christopher Meyers (ed.) *A Philosophical Approach to Journalism Ethics*. New York, NY: Oxford University Press, 2010, 137–152.

"A Theory of Patriotism for Journalism." In Stephen J. A. Ward and Herman Wasserman (eds.) *Media Ethics Beyond Borders: A Global Perspective*. New York, NY: Routledge, 2010, 42–58.

"Multi-Dimensional Objectivity for Global Journalism." In Robert S. Fortner and Mark Fackler (eds.) *A Handbook of Global Communication Ethics*. Malden, MA: Blackwell Publications, forthcoming.

Ward, Stephen J. A., and Herman Wasserman. "Towards an Open Ethics: Implications of New Media Platforms for Global Ethics Discourse." *Journal of Mass Media Ethics*, 25(4) (2010): 275–292.

Ward, Stephen J. A., and Herman Wasserman (eds.) *Media Ethics Beyond Borders: A Global Perspective*. New York, NY: Routledge, 2010, 42–58.

West, Henry R. *The Blackwell Guide to Mill's Utilitarianism*. Malden, MA: Blackwell Publishing, 2007.

Wilkins, Lee, and Clifford G. Christians (eds.) *The Handbook of Mass Media Ethics*. New York, NY: Routledge, 2009.

Wilkins, Lee, and Renita Coleman. *The Moral Media. How Journalists Reason about Ethics*. Mahwah, NJ: Lawrence Erlbaum Associates, 2005.

Williams, Bernard. *Truth and Truthfulness: An Essay in Genealogy*. Princeton University Press, 2002.

Wong, David. "Moral Relativism." In Edward Graig (ed.) *Routledge Encyclopedia of Philosophy*. New York, NY: Routledge, 1998.

Yee, Andy. "China: Forced Demolition." *Global Voices Online*. December 8, 2009. http://globalvoicesonline.org/2009/12/08/china-forced-demolition. Accessed on February 10, 2010.

Index

accountability: images and, 194, 195; journalistic, 76; and online journalism, 220; pragmatic objectivity and, 157; as restraining principle, 66, 77; SPJ code and, 73; and truth, 156
Adams, Claude, 158
advocational journalism, 64, 65, 67, 122
American Society of News Editors (ASNE), 122
applied ethics, 18–19, 33, 35
Aristotle, 47, 125
Arthur, John, 174
Assange, Julian, 88, 191
Audi, Robert, 49
authoritarianism, 61, 67, 93, 94, 120, 165

Bagehot, Walter, 97
Barney, Ralph, 77
Baron, Marcia, 42
Beckett, Charlie, 238
Bentham, Jeremy, 39, 163
Berlin, Isaiah, 91
Black, Jay, 67, 77
blackouts, news, 189
bloggers, 60, 207, 231–234, 240
Border, Daniel, 121
Bowman, Shayne, 107
Brave New World (Huxley), 41
Brighouse, Harry, 251
Brock, Gillian, 251
Brucker, Herbert, 122
Buckley, Samuel, 94

Canadian Association of Journalists (CAJ), 190, 226
Canadian Broadcasting Corporation (CBC), 78, 199
care, ethics of, 66, 67, 68
Carlyle, Thomas, 99
Castells, Manuel, 249
categorical imperative, 28, 44, 251
Chomsky, Noam, 231, 236
Christians, Clifford, 66, 234
citizen journalism, 2, 60, 89, 207, 213, 214, 231
civic journalism, 65, 230
codes of ethics: and difference, 222; global, 246, 266; harm minimization in, 188; online activism and, 237; and online journalism, 215; principles of journalism and, 72, 100, 212; truth/objectivity in, 122, *see also* Society of Professional Journalists (SPJ) code of ethics
coherence theory, 123, 146, 219
commonsense realism, 126, 127
communicative intention, principle of, 222
communitarianism, 66, 68, 102
Comte, Auguste, 178
conflicts of interest, 69, 220
consequentialism, 35–36; act-, 36; framework ethics and, 35; non-consequentialism and, 41, 42, 43; rule-, 37; satisficing-, 38; utilitarianism and, 39; utopian thinking and, 41
contractualism, 29, 34, 63, 94, 263

Cooper, Stephen D., 234
cosmopolitanism, 247, 250–257, 263, 265
Cruickshank, John, 199
cultural/group tensions: freedom to
    publish and, 111; global media and, 241
cultural relativism, 30, 32

Dacre, Paul, 238
Delane, John, 97
deliberative democracy, 108, 109,
    110, 113
deliberative journalism, 111–112, 115
democracy: about, 105; free press and,
    88, 103, 107; as goal of journalism,
    105; liberalism and, 103; media ethics
    and, 102; objective reporting and,
    131; professional/traditional vs new
    journalism and, 214
democratic journalism/press, 104;
    deliberative democracy and, 109;
    and ecumenical ethics, 217; free
    press and, 90; informative function,
    114; interpretive function, 114;
    investigative function, 114; liberal
    press and, 98; media ethics and,
    105; objectivity and, 71; and public
    discussion, 112
deontological theories, 41, 42, 44, 46
descriptivism, 22, 23, 24, 27, 31
Dewey, John, 102, 105
difference, ethics of, 221
disinterest, see impartiality
Doing Ethics in Journalism
    (Black;Steele;Barney), 77
Duncan, John, 235
Durkheim, Emile, 49
Dworkin, Ronald, 48

ecumenical ethics, 217, 218
empirical premises, 69, 70
epistemological objectivity, 30, 128, 131,
    137, 138
ethical language, 22, 24
ethical premises, 69, 70
ethical relativism, 31
ethical revolutions, 209

ethical statements, justification
    of, 25
ethics: about, 1; defined, 9; of difference,
    221; doing of, 9; as fair agreement,
    29, 34; identifiable concerns of,
    13; impartial stance of, 14; as
    individualistic and social, 8; laws
    compared to, 15; layered journalism
    and, 221; as lived experience, 10;
    meaning of, 8; media ethics compared
    to, 53, 56; morality vs, 8, 13; and non-
    ethical agenda, 242; norms vs, 11–12, 15;
    open vs closed, 224, 227; purpose of, 34;
    reflection within/upon, 10; as reflective
    engagement, 1; scope of, 9; seriousness
    of, 13–14, see also media ethics
Evidence and Inquiry (Haack), 148
expressivism, 24

Facebook, 214, 215, 233, 237, 238
fairness, 156, 157
Feinberg, Joel, 166, 175, 179
fifth estate, 60, 224, 231, 233, 241
Fishkin, James, 109
flourishing: ethical, 254–257, 261;
    human, 254
Foot, Philippa, 41
Fourth Estate, 60, 121, 233
framework ethics, 20, 35, 68
Frankfurt, Harry G., 136, 138
Franklin, Benjamin, 95
free press: authoritarianism and, 61;
    and citizen journalists, 89; classical
    liberalism and, 62; and cultural
    tensions, 111; deliberative democracy
    and, 109; and democracy, 88, 103,
    107; and democratic press, 90; as goal
    of journalism, 105; history of, 92;
    liberalism and, 97; and media ethics,
    89, 101; media responsibility and, 55;
    objectivity and, 132; as primary value,
    88; and responsibility, 90, 101, 103; and
    trivial vs profound offense principles,
    182, 183; value of, 90
Frey, Robert G., 36
Fung, Melissa, 78, 189, 190

Gert, Bernard, 162
Gillmor, Dan, 107
global ethics: ethical flourishing and,
    254, 257; pluralism and, 246, 267
global media, 208; and global problems,
    247; and group tensions, 241; multi-
    dimensional objectivity and, 158;
    primary goods, 254
global media ethics: and
    cosmopolitanism, 251, 263, 265;
    defined, 250; development of, 266;
    features of, 250; and parochialism, 247;
    and patriotism, 264
globalization, 248; of journalism, 2, 3,
    246; of media ethics, 246; of news
    media, 246
goods, 254; ethical, 256, 261; individual,
    255, 260; journalism and, 258; political,
    255, 258, 261; social, 255, 260–261
Gordon, Thomas, 94
Green, Thomas, 102

Haack, Susan, 148
Habermas, Jurgen, 29
Hamilton, Alexander, 95
Hare, R. M., 25
harm minimization, 75, 185, 187; global
    offense and, 201; images and, 195; and
    justified harm, 184; and publication
    of secrets, 191, 192; as restraining
    principle, 66, 77; in SPJ code, 73; truth
    and, 189
harm-to-others principle, 167, 181,
    182, 185
harm(s), 161; avoidance, 162, 164, 187;
    definitions of, 163, 173; group, 187;
    images and, 194; justifiable vs non-
    justifiable, 175; and liberty-restricting
    principles, 164; and media ethics,
    165; media practice, 186; monetary,
    186; morality and, 163; physical, 186;
    psychological, 187; to reputation,
    186–187; and restraining principles,
    164; social, 187
Herodotus, 30
Hobbes, Thomas, 34

holism, 27, 76–79
Hume, David, 62, 95
Hutchins Commission into Freedom of
    the Press, 64
Huxley, Aldous, 41

images, 194–197
impartiality: freedom to publish and, 91;
    objectivity and, 114, 120; and truth,
    119
independence, 75; and conflict of
    interest, 69; and liberal press, 77;
    online journalism and, 220; of press,
    62; SPJ code and, 73
inquiry, 144; and justification, 148, 149;
    methods of, 148; truth and, 136,
    see also pragmatic inquiry
Internet: access, 110; domination, 110;
    libertarianism and, 104, 107; and
    participatory democracy, 107;
    restraining principles and, 88–89; as
    revolutionary, 213
interpretationism/interpretations, 65, 67,
    145, 150, 151; coherence and, 146,
    149, 151; holism and, 149; and liberal
    press, 64; objectivity and, 153, 155;
    truth and, 151, 152
intuitionism, 27
investigative journalism, 114, 122, 157,
    158, 207, 214

Jackson, Mason, 98
Jefferson, Thomas, 95

Kant, Immanuel, 28, 31, 44, 251
KIRO Eyewitness News, 229
Kuhn, Thomas, 132, 209

layered journalism, 216, 221, 223
liberal press, 60, 77, 97, 98
liberalism, 62, 67, 102; classical, 62; and
    democracy, 103; and free press, 97
libertarianism, 62, 103; disillusionment
    and, 99, 100; ethics and, 101; and
    harm-to-others principle, 167; and

Internet, 104, 107; liberal press theory and, 97; new journalism and, 214

liberty-restricting principles, 165, 166; and harm, 164, 181; liberal principles of, 166; non-liberal principles of, 169; and offense principles, 180, 181; and practice of media, 182, 184

Lippmann, Walter, 131

Locke, John, 94, 97

Longino, Helen, 153

Luce, Henry, 65, 132

Lukes, Steven, 13, 162

Macpherson, C. B., 106

Mailer, Norman, 132

marketplace of ideas, 99, 101–102, 105, 214, 218

Marx, Karl, 231

mass commercial press, 98, 99, 111, 212, 228

McChesney, Robert, 231

McLuhan, Marshall, 111, 246

media: criticism of, 231, 236; ecology, 2, 207, 232; meaning of, 3–6

media ethics: aims of journalism and, 70–71; collaborative engagement in, 239; and conflicts between values, 208; de-Westernization of, 268; defined, 6, 53, 54; and democracy, 102; democratic journalism and, 105; disillusionment and, 99; and ecumenical ethics, 218; ethics compared to, 53, 56; freedom and, 89, 101; global responsibilities of, 247; globalization of, 246; harm and, 165; history of, 59; issues of, 58; and libertarianism, 101; and liberty-restricting principles, 182; mass commercial press and, 212, 228; media ecology and, 2; media revolution and, 3, 208; at micro vs macro level, 58; model for cases/issues, 79–80; for multi-media platforms, 208; new journalism and, 211; new media and, 214, 232, 241; as non-deliberative populism, 242; objectivity and, 134; open vs closed, 223, 228, 230, 231, 235,

243; origin of, 53; participation in, 225, 232; peer-to-peer discourse, 240; pluralistic society and, 102; practice of, 53; professional vs citizen journalists and, 3; public participation in, 229, 230; and reflective engagement, 1; and responsibility, 102; revolutions in, 2, 209, 213; and social justice, 102–103; truth/objectivity and, 137, 142; us vs them criticism, 237, 239

media revolution, 207, 213

meta-ethics, see philosophical ethics

metaphysics, 26

Metaphysics (Aristotle), 125

Mill, John Stuart, 39; and classical liberal press, 62; and harm, 161, 164, 170, 171, 173–177; and liberal theory, 97; and liberty, 181, 185; *On Liberty*, 62, 90, 170, 171; *Utilitarianism*, 178; and utility, 39

Milton, John, 62, 97

Mist, Nathaniel, 121

Moir, Jan, 237

monism, 28

Moore, G. E., 27

moral realism, 23

morality: ethics vs, 8, 13; and harm, 163

multi-media journalism: ethics, 208, 215; freedom/responsibility balance and, 102–103; as layered journalism, 216; objectivism and, 60; pragmatic objectivity and, 223

naturalism, 23, 26

new media: and media ethics, 214, 232, 241; and objectivity, 214, 218; and transparency, 233

new media journalism: ethics of, 214; and media ethics, 211; and objectivity, 218; and participatory democracy, 214; professional/traditional vs, 213, 214; traditional vs, 211; and truth, 218

Nietzsche, Friedrich, 136

non-consequentialism, 35, 40, 41, 43

non-descriptivism, 22, 24, 25

non-maleficence, 162

non-naturalism, 23
normative ethics, 20
norms: ethics vs, 11–12, 15; and traditional objectivity, 130
Nussbaum, Martha C., 251

objective journalism, 60
objective stance, 154, 155, 157
objectivism, 63; objectivity, 30, 63, 67; coherence and, 155, 157; complaints against, 132; decline of, 131–132; and democratic journalism, 71; empirical validity and, 154; facts and, 130; feminism and, 133; global, 263; importance of, 138; intersubjective, 155, 220; and media ethics, 134, 142; multi-dimensional, 156, 158, 220; new media and, 214, 218; online journalism and, 219; postmodernism and, 132; relativism and, 32, 33; roots in journalism, 121; skepticism about, 133; SPJ code and, 73; in testing interpretations, 153; theory of, 140, 142; traditional, 127, 140, 151–153, 156–158; truth and, 118, 119, 137, 138, *see also* epistemological objectivity; ontological objectivity; pragmatic objectivity
offense principle(s), 167, 179, 181; free press and, 182, 183; liberty-restricting principles and, 180; and practice of media, 182; social, 200; trivial vs profound, 179, 180, 182, 183, 185, 200, 201, 204
ombudsmen, 230
On Liberty (Mill), 62, 90, 170, 171
online journalism, 207, 208; codes of ethics, 215; and coherence, 219; global activism of, 237; and objectivity, 219; and self-consciousness, 219; and story testing, 220; and transparency, 220
ontological objectivity, 30, 128, 137, 138
Ortega y Gasset, Jose, 265

Paine, Thomas, 62, 95, 97
parochialism, 247, 251, 264

participatory democracy, 106; Internet and, 107; new journalism and, 214
Pateman, Carole, 106
paternalism, 167, 169, 171
patriotism, 247, 263, 264
Peabody, Charles, 99
Peirce, C. S., 136
Peterson, Theodore, 132
philosophical ethics, 18, 19, 21–22, 33
Plato, 30, 34, 47, 126
pluralism, 49, 102, 113, 246, 247, 267
pragmatic inquiry, 143–144, 146, 150, 151
pragmatic objectivity, 114, 143–144, 152, 153, 156, 157, 219, 223
pragmatic truth, 143–144, 146, 151, 156
pragmatism, 144
prescriptivism, 24
Press Complaints Commission (PCC), 237, 238
press councils, 230
pro-active principles, 72, 73, 77, 205
public participation: in applied ethics, 226; deliberative democracy and, 110; in media ethics, 225, 229, 230, 232; political, 92
public reason, 113

rationality, 26
Rawls, John, 29, 43, 45, 49, 91, 113, 256
realism, 124, 137
Reed, Sam, 229
relativism, 30, 31, 33
religion, 26, 32, 93
Renaudot, Theophraste, 121
Republic (Plato), 34
responsibility, 54; cosmopolitanism and, 251; and freedom to publish, 90
restraining principles, 72, 73, 77, 89, 99, 164, 205
revolutions, 209
Richelieu, Cardinal, 121
Right and the Good, The (Ross), 162
Roederer, Pierre-Louis, 121
Rorty, Richard, 133
Ross, Charles D., 122
Ross, W. D., 27, 41, 162, 178

Rusbridger, Alan, 236, 239

satirical journalism, 157
Scanlon, Thomas, 13, 29
scientific realism, 126, 127
Scott, C. P., 97
secrets, publishing, 190, 192; self-consciousness: objectivity and, 155, 157; online journalism and, 219
Sidgwick, Henry, 27
Singer, Peter, 253
Skorupski, John, 172
Slote, Michael, 46
social liberalism, 102
social media, 207, 214, 215, 237
social responsibility theory, 60, 63, 64, 67, 102
Society of Professional Journalists (SPJ) code of ethics, 73, 101, 122; and harm minimization, 188; and holism, 77, 78, 79; and images, 195
Stead, Sylvia, 199
Steele, Bob, 77
Stevenson, Charles, 25

Trafigura, 239–240, 242
transcendentalism, 126
transparency, 69, 156, 157, 220, 233
Trenchard, John, 94
truth: common sense realism and, 126; components of principle of, 118; correspondence theory and, 125; decline of, 131–132; disinterest and, 119; facts and, 130; and harm minimization, 189, 191; images and, 194, 195; importance of, 134, 138; and inquiry, 136; and media ethics, 142; moral virtues and, 119; new media journalism and, 218; objectivity and, 118, 119, 137, 138; pragmatic pursuit of, 147, 149, 152; roots in journalism, 121; scientific realism and, 126; seeking, 73, 77; subjective, 137; theory of, 140, 142; transcendentalism and, 126
Twitter, 107, 110, 116, 202, 214, 216, 222, 233, 238, 239, 240, 241

utilitarianism, 20, 28, 39; act-, 37, 40; rule-, 38, 40
Utilitarianism (Mill), 178
utility, 39, 40
utopianism, 41, 61, 67

values: changes in, 209; conflicts between, 70, 79, 164, 208, 211, 213; plurality of, 11
virtue theories/ethics, 35, 46

Walley, Henry, 121
Walzer, Michael, 108, 110
Washington State News Council (WNC), 229
We Media (Bowman;Willis), 107
We the Media (Gillmor), 107
WikiLeaks, 88, 191–193
Wilkes, John, 96
Williams, David Russell, 198
Willis, Chris, 107
Windhoek Declaration on Promoting an Independent and Pluralistic African Press, 268
Wolfe, Tom, 132
Wong, David, 31
Writing of News, The (Ross), 122

Zenger, John Peter, 95